INFORMATION STRATEGIES

New Pathways to Corporate Power

GERALD M. GOLDHABER, Ph. D.
State University of New York at Buffalo

HARRY S. DENNIS, III, Ph. D.
The Executive Committee

GARY M. RICHETTO, Ph.D.
The Williams Companies

OSMO A. WIIO, Ph. D.
University of Helsinki

PRENTICE-HALL, INC., ENGLEWOOD CLIFFS, NEW JERSEY 07632

Library of Congress Cataloging in Publication Data

Main entry under title:

Information strategies.

Bibliography.
1.–Communication in management. I.—Goldhaber,
Gerald M.
HD30.3.I53   658.4'5   79-756
ISBN 0-13-464651-7

Editorial/production supervision: Serena Hoffman and Jeanne Hoeting
Jacket design: Jorge Hernandez
Manufacturing buyer: Harry P. Baisley

Printed in the United States of America

10 9 8 7 6 5 4 3 2 1

Prentice-Hall International, Inc., *London*
Prentice-Hall of Australia Pty. Limited, *Sydney*
Prentice-Hall of Canada, Ltd., *Toronto*
Prentice-Hall of India Private Limited, *New Delhi*
Prentice-Hall of Japan, Inc., *Tokyo*
Prentice-Hall of Southeast Asia Pte. Ltd., *Singapore*
Whitehall Books Limited, *Wellington, New Zealand*

Contents

PART TWO
Information and Communication
in Managerial Work

APPENDIX
From Theory to Practice

Preface

All of us know from our experience that communication does not always succeed. It may be a surprise to most of us, however, that unsuccessful communication seems to be the rule and not the exception. Some studies about advertising, radio, and television suggest that in optimal conditions communication efficiency is 25–50 percent, often as low as 1–5 percent—*which approaches statistical randomness*.

What surprises us is that managers usually act on the assumption that communication efficiency is 100 percent or close to it: "You should know this; we sent a memo about the matter two years ago!"

Information Strategies: New Pathways to Corporate Power is a book for managers, supervisors, and leaders in any organization. It is a book about how to communicate to achieve optimal power in an organization—not the kind of power obtained with rank or title, but the information power achieved by developing and using the organization's intelligence system to its fullest potential. *Information Strategies: New Pathways to Corporate Power* describes both the major ingredients of one's intelligence system and how to effectively monitor and develop it.

Part One provides an overview of our theory of information power. We describe the key external and internal contingencies affecting an organization's information system. This is consistent with our view that there is no one best way to communicate. It all depends upon the contingencies affecting an organization at the time.

We develop a theory of information power that states that organizations can achieve such power through both monitoring and reacting to the variables and contingencies that constitute their organization's intelligence system. We suggest that there are four possible conditions of organization intelligence in which an organization may find itself, based upon both the rate of change in contingencies affecting it and the ability of its communication system to cope with such changes:

1. Is the organization in a state of *proactive relaxation*, in which the environment is relatively stable and the communication system very effective? Is it experiencing a "honeymoon period" in which it may be lulled into complacency? As with most marriages, wait until the honeymoon ends!

2. Is the organization in a state of *proactive coping*, in which the environment is highly uncertain? Conditions within and outside the organization are changing rapidly and the effects of the changes are felt directly on the organization and its

communication system. However, the organization is equipped with a highly effective communication system and can cope with these changes, just as a good marriage is equipped to handle the instability of living.

3. Is the organization in a state of *reactive hibernation*, in which the environment is stable, but the communication system is ill suited to cope with any sudden and dramatic changes? Similar to a time bomb slowly ticking away, organizations in hibernation are about to explode the moment the environment changes.

4. Finally, is the organization in a state of *reactive stress*, in which the environment becomes highly unstable and the communication system is unable to cope? The fun begins. The consultants are called in, usually to share the blame because it is too late. The explosion has occurred and collapse is inevitable.

In Part Two, we present the major personal, relational, and organizational communication variables that constitute an organization's information system.

In Part Three, we offer a variety of tools and methods that can help you monitor and assess the communication system in your organization. Measurement approaches are organized around the personal, relational, and organizational variables discussed in Part II. Next, we present very detailed information about one highly successful evaluation approach—the Organizational Communication Development measurement system. The OCD system has been used successfully in the United States and Europe and is now presented for the first time in a book, along with instructions and norms for implementing and explaining it.

Part Three also illustrates how organizational intelligence systems can be developed. We present a unique feedback model which allows you to interpret the results of your evaluation and predict in which state of organizational intelligence your organization finds itself. Finally, we offer examples of how other organizations have successfully developed their intelligence systems to maximize their information power and ultimately their organizational effectiveness.

We conclude our book with an appendix that describes the revolutionary Scandinavian work experiments. We show how Volvo's Kalmar plant in Sweden was able to adapt to the changes in contingencies affecting the industry, to apply organizational intelligence, and to use information power to become more effective as automobile manufacturers.

As with any book, we owe much to the many people whose work and lives have influenced our own. To our wives—Marylynn, Cynthia, Suzanne, and Leena—who tolerated and understood our needs as writers; to our editor Brian Walker, whose patience contributed to our peace of mind; to our reviewers, whose helpful comments and insights kept us in line with both contemporary theory and realistic practice; to Sharon G. Rosenthal, Carol Steck, and Pat Rackl, whose precise typing, editing, and proofreading enabled us to produce a truly polished manuscript, we are sincerely grateful. To Bob Nourse, Jim Handy, and all the company presidents affiliated with the Executive Committee, our thanks for tolerating the many questions we asked about your views concerning organizational intelligence.

Finally, as authors separated by thousands of miles and the Atlantic Ocean, we have learned much about the effect of organizational space upon ultimate effectiveness.

G.M.G.
H.S.D.III
G.M.R.
O.A.W.

Dedication

We can think of no man who better represented the principles of information power than Robert Kibler—our editor, our close friend and our inspiration for this book.

OTHERS WOULD TALK
Bob would listen

OTHERS WOULD SHOUT
Bob would reason

OTHERS WOULD BE CLOSED
Bob would be open

OTHERS WOULD OFFER INFERENCE
Bob would offer evidence

OTHERS WOULD BE INSENSITIVE
Bob would be compassionate

OTHERS WOULD IGNORE
Bob would praise

AND WHERE OTHERS GAINED COMPLIANCE
Bob gained commitment.

With respect for his ideas and love for his person,
We dedicate this book to Bob Kibler.

About the Authors

Gerald M. Goldhaber is Associate Professor of Communication at the State University of New York at Buffalo and Director of the International Communication Association's Communication Audit project. He has published 8 books in the field of communication, including the best-selling *Communication Probes* (SRA, 1974, 2nd ed., 1977), read by over 200,000 college students and *Organizational Communication* (W.C. Brown, 1974, 2nd ed., 1979), the first college text in this field. Dr. Goldhaber has directed communication studies of manufacturing, educational and governmental organizations, including the U.S. Senate. A frequent lecturer on communication, Dr. Goldhaber has spoken throughout the United States and Canada as well as in England, Germany, Mexico, Japan and Belgium. He was Vice President of the International Communication Association and chair of its Organizational Communication Division and is a member of the Academy of Management and Industrial Communication Council. Dr. Goldhaber recently became President of McLuhan, Goldhaber and Williams, Inc., a consulting firm that primarily services decision makers in politics, television and the motion-picture industry.

Harry S. Dennis III is Chairman of the Board of The Executive Committee, a continuing education and business counseling organization that services CEO's from over 150 diversified, private and public corporations. Dr. Dennis is currently serving as Vice President of the International Communication Association and chair of its Organizational Communication Division. He also holds memberships in the Academy of Management and the American Psychological Association and has written a number of professional papers, articles, and an annual yearbook review of the state of the art in organizational communication. Dr. Dennis is Deputy Director of the ICA Communication Audit project and was one of its original developers.

Gary M. Richetto is Manager of Organization Development, Corporate Staff, The Williams Companies. Formerly on the faculty of General Motors Institute, Gary was Vice President of the International Communication Association and chair of its Organizational Communication Division. He is an Advanced Special Fields Member of the International Transactional Analysis Association, a member of the Academy of Management and the World Future society. Dr. Richetto has been a communication and organization development consultant to a variety of government, educational, military, and business organizations. His publications include articles and original chapters on organizational change, organization communication, transactional analysis, and videotapes on interviewing (with J.P. Zima) and effective business presentations, produced by Advanced Systems, Inc.

Osmo A. Wiio is Professor of Communication Theory and Organizational Communication as well as Director of the Institute of Communication Research of the University of Helsinki, Finland. He was a member of the Finnish Parliament and the chairman of its Defence Committee 1975–1979. Formerly a professor of organizational theory and management of the Helsinki School of Economics and Director of the Helsinki Research Institute for Business Economics 1972–1977. He has served as a member of the Board of Governors of the Finnish Broadcasting Company and the Executive Committee of the Finnish Academy (Science). He has been a frequent guest lecturer in European and U.S. universities and international meetings. He has also been a communication development consultant to a large number of business organizations. He has served as a member of the Board of Directors of the International Communication Association, he is a member of the World Future Society and the International Institute of Communications. Dr. Wiio has written 26 books, produced several hundred radio and television programs. He is the originator of the LTT and OCD Communication Audit Systems which were developed in Finland parallel with the ICA Audit Project.

part one

The Nature of Organizational Intelligence

1

Information
Power

INTRODUCTION

Those of us who experience life largely within organizations—business, government, education—are living through a revolution. This revolution is unlike any we have experienced, unlike any we have heard about or read about before. This revolution has no political rhetoric, no impassioned oratory, no martyrs, no leadership in the conventional sense. This is a quiet revolution, a subtle revolution, an unconscious revolution. So quiet, so subtle, so unconscious, that most of us don't even know the revolution is in progress, let alone fully grasp our own roles within it.

Clearly charting the path of this revolution is difficult, if for no other reason than that the customary revolutionary evidence is absent. There has been no coup, no extortion of leadership through violence or threat. Rather, this strange revolution is constantly in process, constantly in the stages of becoming, and therefore often misperceived as evolutionary by individuals and organizations caught up in its momentum. But make no mistake. The revolution is indeed real. And its end result will be characteristic of all revolutions—the conclusive shift of power, authority, and control from one constituency to another.

The revolution about which we write is presently unique to industrialized (and emerging postindustrial) societies. Within this broad spectrum, however, the revolution is universal. It transgresses nations, cultures and economic sectors. It is in essence an *organizational revolution*, striking at the core of organizational life and the management function—the determination of decision-making power. It is a revolution whose aftermath will answer the questions Who will manage the organization? and Why will they have the right to manage the organization?

Resulting from a variety of intra- and extraorganizational forces, we are experiencing a revolution in which decision-making power is rapidly shifting from traditional decision makers (the line organization) to traditional knowledge workers (the staff organization). We are not resurrecting the 1950s and 1960s notions of line and staff conflict, however. What is happening in our organizations at present is far more complex than the traditional conflict between line and staff. In fact, the distinctions between these two organizational functions have become very much blurred in recent years.

Traditional staff activities such as legal, personnel, data-processing and so forth have gained such center-stage importance in contemporary organizations that to label them "staff" may be a misnomer. The *environment* within which the line organization now produces the product or extends the service has gained such importance in how the line performs its role that one must question the a priori assumption that the line organization is in control of the enterprise. We propose that those responsible for interpreting that organizational environment—staff—have emerged as the true controllers of the organization and that the future will, if anything, further solidify their organizational power.

To many line managers and administrators, what has been stated thus far may seem like heresy. To those managers and administrators who take pride in making decisions, in taking risks, in leading their organizations toward greater profits or higher-quality services, the suggestion that they are not in control may appear offensive. Those managers and administrators can take heart in the fact that their authority is not in question, nor is their accountability for results. But what this new revolution *is* shaking up is their means to these ends—control of the organization. For, as we will emphasize over and over again in this book, to have ultimate authority, ultimate accountability, is not necessarily to have control. Executive search files are full of one-time chief operating or chief executive officers who maintained their authority, their responsibility, but lost control of the organization—and their jobs— in the process.

Actually, the essence of what we're talking about is not really new— only amplified by the complexities of the modern organization in an environment of unprecedented, accelerated change. Let's move back momentarily to simpler times and places to illustrate our point.

AUTHORITY VERSUS CONTROL

David Berlo, past president of Illinois State University, recently shared some boyhood experiences with us that dramatize the authority-versus-control dilemma faced by contemporary management. It seems that some of Berlo's earliest role models for success in life came, as did many of ours, from watching movie Westerns in his hometown in Iowa. Every Saturday morning would find David and his friends watching the U.S. Cavalry score another victory against the Red Man. The clear-cut celluloid winners and losers in life were readily identifiable to David and his friends, even as children. Quite obviously, the guy to grow up being like was the Colonel. He had it all: the prettiest wife on the Post, the biggest house on the Post the best-groomed horse on the Post, the crispest uniform on the Post, and perhaps most impressive to aspiring young managers in the audience—he got to tell everybody else on the Post what to do.

Coupled with those perquisites was a relatively stable organizational environment—no EEOC (Equal Employment Opportunity Commission), no ERISA (Employee Retirement Information Security Act), no OSHA (Occupational Safety and Health Administration), no bargaining unit—and some straightforward management objectives—maintain the equipment, keep the Post looking neat, and kill the Indians. No doubt about it. If one wanted a role model for success, the Colonel was it.

So, like many of us, Berlo strove to be a Colonel—in his case the president of a large university—a university large enough to provide him the nicest house on campus, a university car in which to travel, the most impressive doctoral robes to wear at Commencement, and the right to give orders to lower-level administrators and faculty. Alas, then came the rub—the difference between life on the Post in the Wild West and life on campus in the late 1960s and early 1970s. For Berlo found, much to his dismay, that he could give orders, all right, but he was surprised at how frequently they were not listened to, surprised at his difficulties in gaining control of people and events.

Where had he gone wrong? Had he missed the Colonel's key to effective management? Had there been some managerial technique the Colonel employed which Berlo's childhood mind was unable to grasp at the time? Back to the movies.

After several reruns of those boyhood experiences, Berlo discovered something important. The Colonel wasn't really in control either—at least no more often than Berlo the university president had been. What Berlo the boy had missed, and Berlo the man found, was the key to control. Despite all the symbols of the Colonel's authority and responsibility, he wasn't always in control of his troops or his Post.

Well, then, who the hell *was* in control? Berlo asked himself. And what's more, *why* was whoever was in control, in control? What was his power base? And that's when he discovered that control was not in the line organization, but rather in the staff organization. Berlo discovered the Scout!

He was there all along, of course. But he was so easy to miss. The Scout wasn't even married, let alone to a pretty wife (in more recent Westerns, of course, he overcomes this problem by seducing the Colonel's wife); he slept in the bunkhouse or in a tent; his horse was swift but filthy; his clothes seldom matched and were anything but crisp; and he didn't have authority over a damned thing. But he was in control. He was definitely staff, but he was definitely in control of accomplishing the most critical objective of the organization—killing the Indians—because only he knew where they were. Thus, the Colonel had a problem in fulfilling his greatest responsibility, in performing the mission for which he was most accountable. He didn't know where the Indians were or what they were doing most of the time. He did not have first-hand access to information critical to accomplishing his objectives. That information resided in the staff organization—the Scout. And to the extent that the Scout shared that information with the Colonel, he had power over the latter and his organization.

Obviously, the Colonel was not without power as well. He could in fact dismiss the Scout, but at significant risk. Rather, the Colonel did what any intelligent line manager would do; he settled for authority, accountability, responsibility, but wasn't foolish enough to believe he was in control of the situation. The end result was counterbalancing bases of power—one overt and institutionalized by higher authority and organizational symbolism, the other covert and reality-bound by knowledge and experience in the organizational environment.

Let's return to the more familiar twentieth century. Not surprisingly, the authority-versus-control issue is even more complex. Now, rather than personally observing events like smoke signals and tribal maneuvers—a limited and time-consuming data base from which to extract information—organizational scouts rely on vast and myriad data from personal, textual, visual, and electronic transactions. The environment is even more turbulent than Frontier America—technically, politically, economically, sociologically. But the nature of control of organizations has remained surprisingly constant. Control and organizational power still reside in one's ability to access, and subsequently share or withhold, information.

CLASSES OF ORGANIZATIONAL POWER

Information and Organizational Power

Manifestly, this book deals with the role of information-processing and communication systems (individual, relational, organizational) in organizational effectiveness. Latently, however, we are dealing with the heart of organizational power—the license to make the important decisions affecting the short-term performance and long-term survival of the organization. A distinctive quality of those organizations which survive the highly competitive and rapidly changing environments of the 1980s and beyond will be their performance capabilities and information-processing systems. Information and power will become increasingly synonymous.

This, of course, has not always been the case. Historians have provided us ample chronicles of organizations, cultures, even whole societies which perished in large measure because of their inability or unwillingness to access information or abdicate "institutionalized power" to those who possessed information. Moreover, in earlier, less complex times, the environment-to-organization impacts were less volatile, more predictable, even manageable. Power resided in birthright, in lineages of ruling classes for whom information was not the "core" of organizational power.

The Nature of Organizational Power

Simply defined, *power* is the ability to gain compliance with one's will. In an organization, power is evidenced by one's ability to influence the organization's direction, its day-to-day activities as well as its longer-term destiny. The possession of organizational power is evidenced, in the final analysis, by outcomes. The extent to which one can "make things happen" in the organization is the extent to which one has power in that organization. The executive vice-president who becomes president (if, in fact, that is his goal) has power. The lab director who gains the increased budget for new product research has power. The committeeman who has one of his constituents reinstated with back pay for lost-time has power. Note that in each of these instances, however, the organization must be perceived by all parties as gaining, or at least not losing, in the process. A unique quality of organizational power is that its possessor must not threaten the survival of the organization.

Thus we see at the outset that power is as much a cultural artifact as it is anything else. That is, power and its source(s) depend upon, and evolve from, the value structure of the culture in which it resides and is executed. A shared value of an organizational culture is the recognition that the organization must survive. Only within the parameters dictated by that value system can the gamesmanship aimed at exchanges of power take place. Power struggles that threaten the organization's survival (and hence the survival of its members), once detected by those outside the immediate struggle, will not be tolerated. Information about the struggles and their destructive potential will be shared with those external power holders (board of directors, board of regents, stockholders, state governments, federal government, public at large) who are powerful enough to end the struggle.

Manifestations of Power

Power in organizations is manifested in various ways. Considerable research into the nature of organizational power suggests that power includes both the *personal* and *positional* attributes of the person possessing power. That is, not only is one's individual behavior toward others in the organization (open, trusting, well-intentioned, expert) of importance in manifesting one's organizational power, but so also is the person's hierarchical position (reporting relationships, organizational level, etc.).

We advance the notion here momentarily, and later in detail, that research of the future will discover one's *functional* attributes playing an increasingly important role in establishing one's organizational power. Because information and its dissemination will more and more determine power in organizations in the future, positional attributes will more and more give way to functional attributes as sources of power. Many powerful organizational members—particularly in terms of control discussed earlier —will oftentimes be found in less elevated boxes on the organization chart than their less powerful counterparts occupying boxes nearer the apex.

Power in organizations is difficult to define in terms acceptable to all parties. Yet ironically, all parties seem confident in their ability to recognize power when they see or experience its effects. Recent field research by Salancik and Pfeffer (1977) provides empirical evidence to support this notion. Writing in *Organizational Dynamics*, they contend:

> You can walk into most organizations and ask without fear of being misunderstood, "Which are the powerful groups or people in this organization?" Although many organizational informants may be *unwilling* to tell you, it is unlikely they will be *unable* to tell you. Most people do not require explicit definitions to know what power is.

Salancik and Pfeffer also report that people in organizations not only have little problem in recognizing power, but they are surprisingly in agreement in identifying power bases:

> People in organizations not only know what you are talking about when you ask who is influential but they are likely to agree with one another to an amazing extent. . . . So far we have studied over 20 very different organizations—universities, research firms, factories, banks, retailers, to name a few. In each one we found individuals able to rate themselves and their peers on a scale of influence or power. We have done this both for specific decisions and for general impact on organizational policies. Their agreement was unusually

high, which suggests that distributions of influence exist well enough in everyone's mind to be referred to with ease—and we assume with accuracy.

It would appear, then, that without formal definitions and their attendant semantic hassles, people in organizations not only recognize, but frequently agree upon, bases of organizational power. Research by Amitai Etzioni (1961) provides us with a taxonomy of these various power bases which may further clarify the nature of organizational power: (1) coercive, (2) reward or remunerative, (3) legitimate, (4) referent, and (5) expert.

Coercive power rests upon one's ability and willingness to use force in influencing another who perceives that, in fact, the person with power can and will physically or mentally punish him or her. In an age of enlightened management, we would like to think that raw, coercive power is very much on the wane in the modern organization. And it would appear to be. Given the external environment—be it intervention by the American Civil Liberties Union (ACLU), a government-subsidized economic floor for the unemployed, or changing sociocultural values that view coercion as an unacceptable form of control, this type of power is seldom found in contemporary organizations.

Perhaps the nearest we come to coercion in the modern organization are remarks such as "If you can't do the job, I'll find someone who can," or others aimed at depriving the person of his employment unless certain behaviors are modified. However, given the powers of collective bargaining, the protected age, racial, and/or ethnic groups under employment, the tenured nature of government employee systems, and so forth, firing or dismissal are, in the final analysis, usually not valid coercive stimulants. To be sure, considering the accelerated turnover of corporate chief operating and executive officers, university presidents, and heads of state, we are fast approaching an age in which there is probably an inverse correlation between one's hierarchical position and one's risk of termination. For most of us, however, out-and-out coercion as a base of organizational power is nonexistent.

Reward or remunerative power rests on the belief that someone is capable of, and willing to, extend positive sanctions for specific behaviors demonstrated.

Interestingly, here we find somewhat of a reversal of the "up the organization" phenomenon cited under coercive power. That is, the higher one moves in most organizations, while risk of dismissal increases, so also does one's ability to reward subordinates. It is in fact easier to "sell" a twenty- or thirty-thousand-dollar bonus for a subordinate in many large organizations than it is to "sell" a twenty- or thirty-dollar-a-week raise for a secretary.

One of the most difficult problems facing first-level and middle management in many organizations is that, essentially, they have no reward-power base. The organization, usually in response to pressures from the external environment, undermines their ability to reward. Blanket merit increases, cost-of-living adjustments, and the like—granted to all employees regardless of performance—have in large measure taken the power of economic reward out of the hands of most supervisory and middle management personnel. Thus, "people" skills—the ability to reward interpersonally and satisfy emotional needs for belonging, status, and acceptance—have become particularly critical to managers at these levels.

Legitimate power rests upon one party's belief that another party has the right to influence him or her. Etzioni refers to this power base as traditional, suggesting that the formal position of authority in and of itself (regardless of perceived competence) legitimizes the power relationship. The old military notion of "saluting the uniform—not the man" is characteristic of this power base.

Increasingly in our society, the traditional power base is declining. In an era of government when political figures are experiencing one of the lowest levels of public confidence, when an American president has resigned from office in disgrace, when heads of state are exposed in kickbacks and sexual scandals, when there has been a dramatic increase in investigative reporting revealing intraorganizational betrayals of trust (misuse of pension funds in one of the world's most powerful unions—the Teamsters) and interorganizational graft (Lockheed's and others' payoffs to heads of host countries)—all these have greatly shaken the public trust and have undoubtedly eaten away at acceptance of the traditional/legitimate power base.

And perhaps well they should. For in all but the least-educated, most archaic, most tradition-bound cultures, one's title is no longer enough to guarantee one's acceptance as influential. The bright side of the problems cited above is that more than ever before, one must *earn* power; one must *earn* influence; one must *earn* leadership. One's power base must more and more be founded on one's competencies. The environment is too turbulent, the survival risks too great, to tolerate traditional power as the moving force in the organization.

A postscript before leaving "traditional" power, however; it is still a viable and important power base in the sense that we are *initially* responsive to it. The programming of cultures and nuclear families for generations does not fade in a lifetime. When introduced to "Doctor" or "President" or "Director," our immediate reaction is to yield, to acquiesce, to subordinate ourselves psychologically. On the other hand, such yielding is far more tentative than it was in earlier generations. Traditional power is initially granted, but is also willingly tested and, if found without substance, more readily discounted than ever before.

Referent power is attributed to those charismatic leaders in our midst whose personal magnetism leads to our desire to identify with them. This form of power is difficult to sustain in a large, complex, bureaucratic organization. Division of labor, span of control, functional differentiation, and other principles of organization greatly inhibit this power base. An exception, of course, is during the birth phase of the organization. Here the charismatic leader is often essential. The organization requires a rallying point, a magnetic or dynamic personality serving as the catalyst for the direction of the enterprise.

After an organization has reached a degree of maturity, however, this power base begins to wane. Some of the most charismatic qualities so critical earlier may now be antithetical to the organization. Wheeling and dealing, risk-taking entrepreneurial qualities may no longer serve the best interest of the business organization which cannot sustain further growth. "Kill the pigs!" rhetoric may no longer be appropriate to the counterculture organization which has now gained political, economic, and legal impact in the community.

Expert power resides in the confidence that one has special knowledge or expertise considered valuable in satisfying individual and/or organizational needs. We submit that in future organizations this power base will take on the highest degree of relative potency, particularly in its impact on organizational control.

Moreover, we hypothesize that expert power will likely serve as the core construct for other forms of power, such as legitimate or referent power. In one sense, this book could be considered a primer in gaining and maintaining expert power. We intend to show conceptually in this chapter, and in later chapters operationally, that expert power is the only form of reality-bound power—power based upon accurate interpretation of organizational contingencies—available to the modern organization. Expert power also characterizes the Model II organization, an important, contemporary concept we discuss in Chapter 4.

We should note at the outset that expert power, despite tradition, is not the sole province of staff. We believe that line managers, though forced into generalist roles as they ascend the hierarchy, can nonetheless establish bases of expert power by developing personal and organizational systems of organizational intelligence. We will devote more to this notion of organizational intelligence later in this chapter and throughout the book. For the moment, we will consider organizational intelligence as the chief control mechanism of the organization—a systematically developed network of information sources, channels, receivers, and feedback loops—linked together within a conceptual grasp of organization-specific internal and external contingencies.

INFORMATION AND ORGANIZATIONAL POWER

Power as Cultural Artifact

We started our discussion of power with the statement that it is in large measure a cultural artifact. That is, power and its source(s) depend upon, and emerge from, the value structure of a given culture. It is this belief that supports our confidence in expert power—and organizational intelligence systems—as the driving power forces of future organizations.

Highly valued within our Western culture are decision-making and problem-solving capabilities. Whether they lead to the lightbulb, the cotton gin, atomic fission, or mechanisms for coping with international cartels, we value decisions which enhance the performance and long-term survival of our organizations. The possession and utilization of information which bears upon these decisions has become the source of organizational power.

Perhaps an even more important cultural norm than our admiration for the problem solver, however, is our faith in the democratic process. This broad-based cultural value is a potent force in the role of information as the source of organizational power. Despite the years-long national agony of Watergate and its related self-doubts, we have learned, once again, that the system works. Information regarding scandal at the highest levels of government was shared with two hundred million people of various emotional and intellectual competencies—and the result was *not* upheaval. The result was the systematic and rational removal of men from positions of traditional power.

Warren Bennis, former president of the University of Cincinnati and one of the most important intellects concerned with contemporary organizations, prophetically stated as early as 1967 that "democracy is inevitable." In *The Temporary Society* (1978), Bennis and Phillip Slater argued:

> Our position is, in brief, that democracy (whether capitalistic or socialistic is not at issue here) is the only system that can successfully cope with the changing demands of contemporary civilization. We are not necessarily endorsing democracy as such; one might reasonably argue that industrial civilization is pernicious and should be abolished. We suggest merely that given a desire to survive in this civilization, democracy is the most effective means to achieve this end.

A second cultural-bound factor in the emergence of information as power, then, is the empirically supported, Western experience of the *utility* of democratic organizational structures. As Bennis and Slater amplify:

> We will argue that democracy has been so widely embraced not because of some vague yearning for human rights but because *under*

certain conditions it is a more "efficient" form of social organization. We do not regard it as accidental that those nations of the world that have endured longest under conditions of relative wealth and stability are democratic, while authoritarian regimes have, with few exceptions, either crumbled or maintained a precarious and backward existence. (Italics added)

The "under certain conditions" clause in this quotation is extremely important: the "conditions" referred to here are the accelerated, constantly changing environments (economic, political, sociocultural, technological) within which social organizations function. The more volatile the external environment, the greater the demand for effective information flow up, down, across, and diagonally within the organization—essentially, the greater the demand for democratic organizational structures. Again from Bennis and Slater:

Democracy becomes a functional necessity whenever a social system is competing for survivial under conditions of chronic change.

External Environmental Contingencies

A cultural bias toward democracy, coupled with accelerated environmental change, has resulted in a free economy of information. More and more members of contemporary organizations, regardless of hierarchical level or function, have greater access to internally and externally generated information than ever before. At the micro level, this accessibility is the result of individuals' beliefs that they have the right to information as members of a democratic social system. At the macro level, however, such accessibility is less a right than a demand. The incredible pace of the organization's environment, in and of itself, requires that more and more members of the organization process more and more information to guarantee the organization's survival.

We stress the importance of the pace or rate of change in the organizational environment. This is the singularly most important difference between contemporary change and that of earlier societies. After all, change in and of itself is not new. What is new—as expressed in Table 1-1—is the *logarithmic rate of change*. This is the real message of Bennis, Toffler, Drucker, and McLuhan—this is the real "generation gap" between our parents and ourselves, and ourselves and our children.

At the core of change in industrialized society, as dramatically evidenced in Table 1-1, is science and its applied counterpart, technology. When we contrast those arenas experiencing the greatest with those experiencing the slowest (yet nonetheless rapid) rates of change, we see an important discrepancy. It appears that our social systems are falling—and

TABLE 1-1. SOME DIMENSIONS OF CHANGE IN THE LAST HUNDRED YEARS

Dimension	Increase Factor
Speed of communication	10^7
Speed of travel	10^2
Speed of data handling	10^6
Use of energy resources	10^3
Power of weaponry	10^6
Ability to control disease	10^2
Population growth	10^3

SOURCE: Schmidt (1970). Reprinted by permission of Wadsworth Publishing Company.

will continue falling—farther and farther behind our technological systems as we move into the future. Such lag-time will likely place greater burdens on individual and institutional coping mechanisms—chief among which is the ability to process vast, often conflicting, and continually growing amounts of information. (The potential for information overload, implicit within this scheme, will be discussed throughout Part Two.)

Further complicating this environment of unprecedented, rapid change are the synergistic effects of environmental components acting in combinations. Stated more simply, organizations are feeling more and more pain from the environments within which they function, and it is becoming increasingly difficult to determine from precisely which environmental component the pain is coming.

William Whyte has developed a graphic model which is helpful in visualizing this fusion of environmental components (see Figure 1-1).

In this model, Whyte describes the environment as having four broad components: (1) technical and physical, (2) economic, (3) legal, and (4) social and cultural. Within this environment is the formal organization (the pyramid in the center of the model). Within the pyramid are individual organization members; their existence is stratified into "I" (interaction/communication patterns), "A" (activities/tasks), and "S" (sentiments/feelings/attitudes). The arrows in the model depict influences, direct in the case of the solid arrows, indirect in the case of the dashed arrows.

The model suggests that various components of the environment directly or indirectly influence the organization and the individual organization member by affecting his or her communication patterns, tasks, or feelings, first individually and then collectively. That is, to change the task will mean affecting the attitudes and communication patterns; or to change the attitudes will mean affecting communication patterns and task performance; and so forth. We will deal with these individual variables in depth in later chapters. For the moment, we are concerned with the model's macro-level qualities.

FIGURE 1.1. WHYTE'S INTERACTION ANALYSIS MODEL

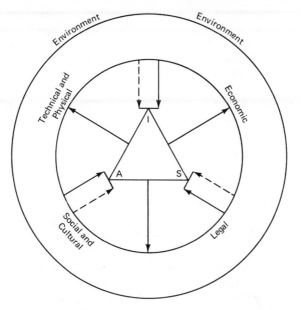

SOURCE: Whyte (1968). Reprinted by permission of John Wiley and Sons, Inc.

While Whyte's model clearly portrays the organization-to-environment interface and the impact of that interface on organizational behavior, it does not appear to reflect a compounding problem of environmental change to organizations. That problem emerges from the synergistic impact of the four broad environmental components on one another. That is, when does the pain start coming not from one component, but from two or more simultaneously? How can decision makers in organizations determine the extent to which a technological impact (such as a new computer system) is likely to take on social or legal significance? When does a social and cultural phenomenon (such as a black woman's refusal, metaphorically, to step to the back of the organization) become translated into legal action (civil rights, EEOC, affirmative action), and ultimately affect bottom-line, economic organizational issues (dollars spent on legal fees, training, development, recruitment)?

A missing factor in many discussions of environmental change, then, is the failure to recognize and sort out the synergistic impact of environmental components. This fusing or merging of components makes organizational environments more difficult to perceive, diagnose, and respond to accurately. And yet, there is some evidence that we are becoming increasingly more sophisticated in both making sense of, and developing strategies for influencing, our organizational environments.

A case in point is the actions of Irene McCabe and her associates in founding the National Action Group (NAG) in 1969. Describing herself as "just a concerned mother and housewife," McCabe and her friends launched a relatively sophisticated strategy of "street politics" that nearly brought a division of General Motors Corporation to a grinding halt.

During the fall of 1969, the city of Pontiac, Michigan (in which McCabe and her friends lived) embarked upon a busing plan to establish racial parity in the public schools. As in many cities across the country at that time, there were public outcries (mostly from whites) against the busing policy. Where others merely complained, however, McCabe took action—action which reflected an understanding of environmental components and their potential impact on one another.

McCabe saw important relationships between the private and public sectors of her environment. Her belief was that manipulation of the private sector (General Motors) could provide leverage for manipulating her ultimate target (state government), and hence accomplish her objective (to stop the busing). McCabe and her group began a campaign among family and friends (all employees of General Motors Pontiac Division) to "strike" the company unless it intervened by applying pressure on the state to abandon the busing program.

McCabe recognized (*a*) the incredible economic power of GM throughout the state, by far the greatest contributor to state tax bases and payrolls (when a GM executive asked, "Why *us*?" McCabe replied, "When you've got GM in a town, you don't strike Dairy Queen"); (*b*) the importance to GM of an uninterrupted work flow at its peak production cycle; and (*c*) the most vulnerable point of the corporation—its pocketbook. As a GM friend of ours has often said, "In General Motors, profit is not a goal—it's a goddam necessity."

Ultimately, McCabe's and the National Action Group's strategy was unsuccessful. What is important, however, is to recognize that in another era, another "Mrs. McCabe" and her colleagues would likely have marched to the School Board offices, vented their hostilities, received patronizing smiles and head-nodding (perhaps even some tea and cookies), and returned home—powerless—to another day of car-pooling kids, keeping house, and solving other peoples' problems on "As the World Turns."

Those days are likely gone forever. People are beginning to understand their organizational environments and are using that understanding to establish their power bases. The models for street politics provided by college students and blacks during the 1960s have been assimilated within our cultural psyche. The free-information economy—and with it the means for understanding the organizational environment—is as accessible to the "concerned mother and housewife" as it is to the chairman of the board.

ORGANIZATIONAL INTELLIGENCE:
"REALITY-BOUND" POWER

Thus far we have contended that power in the organization will more and more be dependent upon the obtaining, processing, and disseminating (or withholding) of information. Information is the foundation of organizational power. The instrumentation of power, however, will demand that managers and administrators do more than process information. They must develop an intelligence network—linking together information sources, bits of information, channels, and feedback systems—to form a system of exceptional, reliable, and timely input from which to make decisions critical to the survival and performance of the organization.

This development of organizational intelligence networks is something quite apart from processing information or establishing channels of communication. It requires that the manager or administrator become expert in diagnosing the information-processing abilities of subordinates, peers, and superiors alike. It requires that the manager become expert in recognizing relationship problems between individuals or organizational subunits which may impede the processing of accurate, timely, reliable information —intelligence. It requires that the manager become expert in recognizing the built-in structural obstacles to intraorganizational information processing. Finally, it requires that the manager begin to identify organizational members and departments who are in optimum liaison or interface roles with respect to the organization's environment—those in a position to most accurately perceive and diagnose the probable impact of extraorganizational phenomena on the organization.

In short, the manager must begin merging what is known about communication and what is known about organization into an integrated whole. We will attempt in following chapters to provide the roots for this integration. By describing specific information-processing behaviors of individuals, groups, and organizational subunits, we will attempt to identify the variables involved in merging communication knowledge and organization knowledge into a pragmatic strategy for developing a system of organizational intelligence. We will further describe specific techniques for assessing the operational characteristics of that intelligence system, once established in the organization.

In essence, we hope to provide a theoretical and pragmatic framework for reality-binding management's power in the organization—power that relies not simply on tradition, or coercion, or remuneration, but on one's ability to extract, from a myriad of information sources, the salient pieces of intelligence which can be brought to bear on making those decisions critical to the survival and effectiveness of the organization.

Organizational power is reality-bound to the extent that its base is organizational intelligence. And organizational intelligence is the function of a manager's ability to assess both impersonal/rational and personal/irrational kinds of information. We will discuss information and its characteristics in depth in Chapter 3. For the moment, however, it is important to recognize, as Drucker (1973) points out, that information is objective, logical, formal, and specific. In contrast, communication is process; it is subjective, perceptual, nonverbal as well as verbal, and general or contextual, rather than specific. An effective organizational intelligence network accurately diagnoses both information and communication phenomena. An effective intelligence network considers both content and context—both rational and irrational—inputs in grasping the meaning or significance of data to be used in making decisions.

In an era of political/military fiascoes like the Bay of Pigs, the escalation of bombing in Vietnam, and the national tragedy of Watergate, the very term *intelligence* has taken on a negative connotation. (In fact, as authors, we debated among ourselves the negative potential of using the term *organizational intelligence* in the writing of this book.) And yet, as we will see, intelligence means nothing more than the obtaining, digesting, and utilizing of knowledge by which to increase the effectiveness of decision making. The intelligence function is perhaps the most legitimate source of organizational power. At its core, organizational intelligence relies upon one of our most cherished values—trust—in the loyalties, competencies, and motivations of members composing the intelligence network.

The often inaccurate stereotype of the intelligence function as only a control function likely accounts in large measure for our relative ignorance and lack of empirical research into this vital organizational system. As Harold Wilensky (1967) notes:

> Failures in intelligence, which have received so little scholarly attention, can be more fateful than lapses in control, which have preoccupied students in the sociology of organization. The former may bring sudden death; the latter, no more than slow decline. If an auto manufacturer mishandles his labor relations, he merely suffers increased labor turnover or an unnecessary strike; if he miscalculates his consumer market and produces an Edsel, hard upon the heels of a Mercury, a whole division is finished. . . .
>
> The obvious significance of the intelligence function in government and industry has not resulted in the long bibliographies of solid sociological studies typical of other areas of organizational theory and practice. It is strange that social scientists, who are by profession devoted to the application of reason to man's affairs, have been more impressed by the use and misuse of power than by the use and misuse of knowledge.

Wilensky's final sentence is of critical importance here. Is it possible that since the 1960s (when he wrote) the knowledge function and the power function have become more closely identified with one another? And, more important, will their mutual identification in a postindustrial, knowledge-based society grow even stronger? Is it possible that, increasingly, to study power is to study the absorption, digestion, and utilization of knowledge—intelligence? Is it possible that by focusing on the use and abuse of organizational intelligence, we are more and more focusing on the use and abuse of organizational power? We believe so. What is more, we believe this fusion of intelligence and power—information power—to be the core of democratic industrial, goverment, and educational institutions of the future. We see a change in the nature of organizational power in the 1980s, '90s and beyond—away from its reliance upon reward or tradition or coercion and toward a reliance upon organizational intelligence.

Distinguishing Between Information and Intelligence

A management client of ours recently crystallized the information-versus-intelligence paradox. To one of our interviewing questions regarding the biggest communication problem he faces, he responded:

> "Communication problem? I'll tell you my biggest communication problem. Just look at this desk! Reports, computer printouts, telephone messages, letters, journals, telegrams. My biggest communication problem? I'm overloaded. I'm getting so goddam much information from so goddam many people I can't see the top of my desk! I'm drowning in paper; drowning in information."

And to our follow-up question regarding his "second-biggest" communication problem, he said: "I never know what the hell is going on around here!"

The greatest communication paradox facing those who manage today's increasingly complex organizations was captured in those intuitive, seemingly contradictory observations—too much information, too little intelligence. We will explore the information-overload phenomenon in terms of its impact on organizations and individuals in later chapters. For the moment, however, it is important to grasp the differences between information and intelligence. We mentioned earlier that information is static, impersonal, logical, nonhuman. In contrast, we said that communication is process, not necessarily rational, necessarily human. Organizational intelligence combines these concepts.

A manager having an effective organizational intelligence network has built that network by accurately diagnosing both its informational and human qualities. Such a manager recognizes that information, without taking into account its human source or generator, is meaningless. Such a manager recognizes that, as Drucker (1973) contends, "There are no facts

—only opinions." Such a manager processes not only the "what" of communication, but the "how" as well. Aware of the infinite potential for distortion, misperception, and other human fallibilities in his intelligence network, he rarely takes action on information from a single source without contrasting that information with that from other sources, thereby manufacturing (perhaps "discovering" would be a better term) organizational intelligence.

Information and intelligence, then, are interdependent. Information constitutes the broader term—for one often has access to information from which little or no intelligence can be extracted.

At the broadest level, we see the process of communication. This process involves the source, message, channel, receiver, and feedback functions necessary to the exchange of information. At a second level of analysis, we see the extraction of intelligence—the filtering of information itself, coupled with the knowledge of human variables at work in the source, message, channel, receiver, and feedback mechanisms—to be used in the decision-making process.

Time is also an important variable in this intelligence-producing/discovering process. The model suggests that an effective organizational intelligence network is developed over time. The user of intelligence has learned over time what human and/or system variables must be taken into account when processing information for its intelligence value. And the more rapidly the user/manager can accurately diagnose those human and systems variables, the more efficiently he or she can construct an intelligence network. Thus, by developing an intelligence system, a manager is using *information power* to control both personal performance and the organization's overall effectiveness.

BARRIERS TO DEVELOPING ORGANIZATIONAL INTELLIGENCE

Despite the importance of effective organizational intelligence systems in controlling short-term performance and long-term survival of organizations, a variety of individual, relational, and organizational barriers impede the development or organizational intelligence. The remainder of this book will be devoted in large measure to sharing theoretical and empirically based knowledge for overcoming these barriers. We will systematically investigate both environmental and organizational contingencies as well as individual communication variables to determine their potential impact on organizational intelligence. In this initial chapter, however, we will focus on broad, generic barriers related to processing information—the raw material for developing the intelligence function—at personal, relational, and organizational levels of analysis.

Personal Barriers to Developing Organizational Intelligence

One personal barrier to developing effective information-processing and organizational intelligence networks is the advent of the "mobile manager." Fewer and fewer top-level executives are winding their tortuous paths up the organization. Rather, they are making lateral or diagonal moves from one organization to another—hired from the outside to fill a specific internal void in leadership. This also explains in part the relatively rapid turnover of even highest-level executives in the modern organization. They are often hired away from a competitive or similar organization because they are perceived as highly successful. Their success, however, is likely due in large measure to the organizational intelligence networks which they develop—and which they must now attempt to duplicate under more difficult conditions in the unknown political environment of the new organization.

From the organizational intelligence standpoint, the problem here is that such systems take time to develop. The political nuances of the organization are far more difficult to grasp than are the requirements of a job description. While an Ed Cole in General Motors Corporation could still visit the "folks back at Cadillac," even as president, and have access to information from the bowels of that organization, from the old-timers who still remembered his first days as a time-and-motion-study man; or while a Werner von Braun at NASA could rely on intelligence from the "Peenemunde Team"—the same staff with whom he'd worked on the V-2—these leaders are more and more a rarity in both the private and public sectors.

More typical now are the likes of William Agee, the young president and chief executive officer of Bendix Corporation.* Here is an instance in which an executive was thrust into an organization at a very high level and within a few short years was at the helm. The difficulties involved in developing an intelligence network like that used by Cole and von Braun are overwhelming. Data on executive mobility suggest that Agee's career path is more likely to be the norm for organizations in the future.

Today's mobile managers (who statistics tell us will have from four to six extraorganizational career moves) may have considerable technical competence, yet fail if they lack the interpersonal skills to gain acceptance at multiple levels of the new organization. More often than not, failure at the highest of organizational levels results from the lack of interpersonal (as opposed to technical) competencies. Even in technically based industries or government agencies, engineering or scientific skills become secondary to interpersonal, behavioral, communication skills as one ascends the hierarchy. The learning curve required of today's mobile

---

*For a fascinating report about what Bendix has done to insure that its business is conducted in a moral and ethical manner, see Agee (1978).

manager in developing an organization intelligence network is far steeper than that of his predecessors.

A second personal barrier to developing organizational intelligence networks is the demands of role change and role reversal. As the individual moves from one group or organizational context to another, he or she takes on a new communicative role, demanding different kinds of communicative behavior. A strain on many managers, for example, is the need to psychologically move from the leader to the follower role in dealing with staff expertise. That is, while superior in the organizational hierarchy, sometimes the administrator or manager is subordinate to staff on a given subject matter. Managers require a psychological flexibility that many find taxing. Particularly in highly structured organizations such as the military, highly dysfunctional behaviors can result.

Victor Thompson has coined the term *bureaupathic* to describe the aberrant behavior many line managers display when confronted with the need to acquiesce to the technical expertise of subordinates. Senior-level officers in the military, for example, during a tour of duty at the Pentagon or any other assignment in which they are confronted by highly skilled junior-level officer personnel upon whom they must depend for information may well show the symptoms of bureaupathology. We have frequently witnessed versions of the following scenario:

> An Army colonel, combat branch, is assigned to a high-level staff activity in the Pentagon. Presently middle-aged in 1969, he has had little or no experience in data-processing systems beyond that of user of basic personnel accounting or staffing reports. Suddenly, he is thrust into an environment in which complex computer modeling of weapons systems, war games, and the like are commonplace. He is now very dependent upon junior-level officers four and five ranks below his own for their expertise.
>
> If, indeed, suffering from "bureaupathology," how is he likely to behave toward the first lieutenant with the M.S. in computer science from Stanford? More than likely, he will attempt to maintain his superiority by falling back on the accouterments of institutional power. That is, before he will even listen to the junior officer (who probably compounds the problem by refusing to speak in language other than the computerese with which only he and a handful of colleagues are familiar), he will check the shoes, polish on the brass, length of the sideburns, and so forth. Thus, feeling threatened at the psychological or intellectual level, the colonel will revert back to field experience and military bearing to obtain equilibrium.

Such behavior is of course not unique to the military. Scenes similar to the above repeat themselves daily in business and educational organizations as well. The rules of the game may change from one organizational context to another, but the game itself remains constant. Whenever those in authority feel momentarily not in control and cannot cope with such feelings, we are likely to find symptoms of bureaupathic communication behavior.

A third personal barrier to developing effective organizational intelligence is the apparently natural human tendency to withhold or distort upward communication of the negative variety. The nature of the corporate creature is not to show weakness to higher levels. Thus, any information which even suggests one's inability to manage his or her own shop is likely to be suppressed.

Moreover, this phenomenon is repeated at each higher level of the organization. Thus, rather than the broad visibility which one would expect to find at the top of organizations, one often discovers that the apex of the pyramid is among the poorest informed, particularly on negative aspects of organizational performance. As Bobby Kennedy once remarked regarding U.S. Army killed-in-action and weapons-exchange ratios, "Were we to believe these figures, we would have to conclude that we have totally incapacitated the male population of North Vietnam." The problem, of course, was that every major advisor in a district wanting to make lieutenant colonel, and every lieutenant colonel advisor in a province wanting to make colonel, felt it potentially career-damaging to pass up information which suggested we were losing the war—that "pacification" was not working. The result, of course, was poor aggregate data upon which the Joint Chiefs of Staff and our commander in chief based their collective confidence in the "light at the end of the tunnel"—the "light" which, a comedian was later to explain, was "actually a train coming the other way."

Again, while perhaps more visible, such communication behavior and its end results are not unique to the military. Another example is General Dynamics' multimillion-dollar loss on one of their airplanes which reportedly bench-level draftsmen and engineers knew to be "aerodynamically unsound"—information no one would, or perhaps could, send up to levels empowered to take corrective action. Some of NASA's early failures in rocketry are also documented examples of the same phenomenon.

Relational Barriers to Organizational Intelligence

In Chapters 4 and 5, we will identify and discuss a full range of relational communication variables bearing on the development of organizational intelligence systems. For the moment, however, we wish to focus on a more generalized relational barrier to forming organizational intelligence which Irving Janis (1971) has termed "groupthink." For the past several years, Janis has studied the group dynamics of high-level decision-making groups in government. Focusing on (1) the Bay of Pigs fiasco during the Kennedy administration, (2) U.S. failure to prepare for the attack on Pearl Harbor, (3) the no-win stalemate during the Korean conflict, and (4) the escalation of U.S. involvement in Vietnam, Janis was amazed to find a recurring theme: the tremendous power of social conformity in rendering individual judgments impotent. As Janis says:

> I use the term groupthink as a quick and easy way to refer to the mode of thinking that persons engage in when concurrence-seeking becomes so dominant in a cohesive ingroup that it tends to override realistic appraisal of alternative courses of action. Groupthink is a term of the same order as the words in the newspeak vocabulary George Orwell used in his dismaying world of *1984*. In that context, groupthink takes on an invidious connotation. Exactly such a connotation is intended, since the term refers to a deterioration in mental efficiency, reality testing and moral judgments as a result of group pressures.
>
> The symptoms of groupthink arise when the members of decision-making groups become motivated to avoid being too harsh in their judgments of their leaders' or colleagues' ideas. They adopt a soft line of criticism, even in their own thinking. At their meetings, all the members are amiable and seek complete concurrence on every important issue, with no bickering or conflict to spoil the cozy, "we-feeling" atmosphere.

In short, groupthink serves as a tremendous obstacle to the development and utilization of effective organizational intelligence. Moreover, frequently the higher the level of the decision-making group, the greater the tendency toward groupthink. That is, the more prestigious the group, the greater the desire of individual members to be accepted, and thus the greater the willingness to suppress their own dissenting views.

Janis identifies eight symptoms of the groupthink phenomenon which emerged from the decision-making groups he studied: (1) invulnerability, (2) rationale, (3) morality, (4) stereotypes, (5) pressure, (6) self-censorship, (7) unanimity, and (8) mindguards.

Invulnerability. Those at the apex of the pyramid suffering from groupthink can apparently delude themselves into a posture of invulnerability. "Nothing breeds success like success," the saying goes. While this may in part be true, as often as not success can also foster an invalid feeling of confidence—of immunity from failure. By definition, those at the highest levels of organizations have been successful in pursuing individual careers. Merge such stars into one top-level clique, and there is sometimes the temptation to think, "If this group can't accomplish it—no one can. After all, the most experienced, most knowledgeable, most 'track-proven' performers in the organization are assembled around this table." Such thinking can lull decision makers—all of whom desire to remain part of this elite—into a false psychological posture of superiority.

Rationale. A second symptom Janis identified in groupthink decision making is the tendency for the group to discount earlier bad decisions. This is a collective tendency toward the individual behavior of rationalization. Negative feedback regarding the outcomes of such decisions is avoided or discounted. Rationalizations are stated individually and reinforced by others in the group to explain away earlier behavior. For example, a reduction in force, even though it stripped the organization of some of its finest young talent, can be confirmed as an "unfortunate necessity"—or in its worst form, the posture of "hell, they weren't all that good anyway." Or the acquisition that must be sold at a substantial loss because of its poor profit picture is seen as a problem of "timing," rather than a failure to fully investigate its potential in the market with valid criteria.

Rationalization allows individuals in the group to diffuse their own responsibility by sharing it with the group. The group, in turn, legitimizes such behavior through its consensus that, indeed, they had performed correctly, given the circumstances.

Morality. Focusing on government and political decision-making groups, Janis determined that the groups he investigated took on a moralistic posture that served to further legitimize their behavior. That is, not only did such groups reinforce and support one another's decision-making inputs, but seemed to believe that "God is on our side"; or that what was being decided was "for the ultimate good..." of Mankind, the Country, the Party, or whatever. As Janis points out, this symptom emerges not so much through specific comments or actions, but rather by the things *not* said or done. The morality of the group's actions is simply assumed, not questioned or challenged.

The likelihood that this symptom is not unique to government is evidenced by recent admissions of corporate payoffs to foreign countries and questionable industrial political contributions—a phenomenon satirized by the *New Yorker* cartoon showing a group of executives seated around a mahogany conference table, the chairman of the group, cigar in hand, saying, "Gentlemen, it has been moved and seconded that we obey the law..."

Stereotypes. A fourth symptom of groupthink behavior is that of stereotyping the opposition, particularly its leadership. Here, the group operates on the collective stereotypes of "big labor," "big business," "the Communist conspiracy," or other convenient labels with which to categorize opposing views and individuals. The group's solidarity is thus reinforced by forming outgroup stereotypes of the "enemy"—student, blue-collar worker, the union, the country club set—and operating on those stereotypes as "reality."

Pressure. Another symptom of groupthink is the high degree of pressure placed on group members whenever they show signs of questioning the group's decision-making posture. According to Janis, the pressure may be subtle, even tinged with a degree of humor, such as President Johnson's reference to Bill Moyers (one of the few members of his administration to question the bombing escalation during the Vietnam conflict) as "Well, here comes Mr. Stop-the-Bombing." One can imagine the impact of this comment on Moyers's standing within the group, particularly since its source was the commander in chief.

On the other hand, such pressure can be quite obvious, and applied directly rather than obliquely. Janis reports that former attorney general Robert Kennedy, in talking to Arthur Schlesinger, who questioned the United States' plans to invade Cuba, said "You may be right or you may be wrong, but the President has made his mind up. Don't push it any further. Now is the time for everyone to help him all they can."

Self-censorship. One of the more cancerous qualities of groupthink is what it does to the individual "cells" in the group. Individuals apparently begin to censor their own behavior—even without overt pressure from others to do so—rather than run the risk of jeopardizing their positions in the group.

A company which has committed large budgets to a new product line, for example, may find individual directors of marketing, manufacturing, advertising, or research and development blinding themselves to data which suggest the product's potential may be less than originally envisioned. Executives in Ford Motor Company have suggested there was evidence that the Edsel was a loser a full year or more in advance of its introduction to the marketplace. Nonetheless, the loser was produced—in part due to irretrievable costs in design, tooling, and preproduction allocations—but also, perhaps, due to the self-censorship of Ford executives.

Unanimity. Interestingly, one seemingly positive quality of groups suffering from groupthink proves to be an illusion—the "we-feeling" Janis mentioned earlier. Apparently, so great is the need for "we-ness" in groupthink decision-making teams that individuals perceive more agreement than actually exists in the group. Janis contends that this illusion of unanimity emerges in part from the groupthink symptoms cited above. These symptoms form a false belief within the individual that everyone else in the group sees things the same way.

Here again is an example of groupthink's being more than the sum of the parts—a collective whole, distinct from its individual human components—in which individual behavior is suppressed by the group's drive toward consensus. Much like early experiments by Solomon Asch, in which group estimates of light "movement" in a darkened room affected individuals' later judgments of such "movement" (actually the light remained stationary—the movement was an optical illusion), individual views in policy-making groups may differ significantly from that of the group, yet nonetheless be withheld, resulting in unanimity which is then sacrosanct.

Mindguards. Finally, Janis contends that some individuals experiencing groupthink often emerge in policing roles—controlling the flow of information to those with ultimate responsibility. These "mindguards," as he calls them, may not necessarily be Machiavellian personalities attempting to manipulate others or to seize control of the decision-making process. More often than not, they are just the opposite—blindly loyal to the leadership, screening the leader to protect him or her from negative or disconfirming feedback from subordinates or external sources.

Perhaps more than any other symptom of groupthink, this mindguard quality is most difficult for the chief executive or chief operating officer of an organization to see. A seemingly inherent quality of formal organizations is for those nearest the apex to insulate, often unintentionally, their leader from bad news.

Peter Drucker (1973) suggests that executives keep a diary on themselves, to "gain insight into how they spend their time." They might also discover something else about themselves during that exercise—namely, the surprisingly small number of people within their organizations upon whom they rely for information about how the organization is functioning. They would gain insight into their few primary sources of organizational intelligence—and be faced with the question, "Is this as complete an intelligence network as I need?"

A Word About Conflict. Before leaving the area of relational barriers to effective organizational intelligence, let us focus on one important antidote to groupthink: the role of healthy conflict in the making of decisions and the functioning of effective organizations.

Conflict is a necessary quality for optimum decision making. As Drucker has contended for years, "Without conflict, there is no decision." We commented earlier that a strong cultural value in Western societies is the trust of the democratic process. Part and parcel of democracy is dissent and conflict, within certain political and legal parameters.

Given the impact (and misunderstanding) of the human relations movement of the past few years, some organizations have been lulled into thinking that effective, efficient organizations are those without conflict. Quite the contrary. Conflict should be built into organizations to ensure effectiveness and efficiency. For example, conflict between production and quality control is healthy conflict, resulting in product and volume optimization. Conflict between the controllers' function and profit centers or staff activities is healthy conflict, resulting in optimizing expenditures and cost savings. Conflict between the personnel department's affirmative action efforts and the line organization is healthy conflict, resulting in a more socially responsible enterprise (not to mention one which saves court costs and class action suits).

Recognizing the need for conflict in decision making is one trait of an effective manager. In the *Effective Executive*, Drucker (1966) describes a meeting of the Board of Directors of General Motors Corporation which dramatizes the importance of conflict in good decision making. "Old man Sloan" was in the chair, Drucker reports, and someone presented an idea regarding a potential acquisition, new product line, or whatever. After the presentation Sloan queried each of his lieutenants around the table for an opinion. To a man, according to Drucker, no one gave a dissenting view. No one saw any possible reason not to move on the idea at the earliest opportunity. Finally, Sloan looked at the other board members and said something like, "Gentlemen, I don't see any reason not to adopt the idea either. Therefore, I suggest we postpone this decision for thirty days while we do some more thinking." Thirty days later, the board decided against the plan—having ample evidence of its liabilities.

Organizational Barriers to Developing Organizational Intelligence

Organizational variables impinging upon the intelligence function will be considered in depth in Chapter 6. Such variables will be presented in an integrative model that shows how human input at the personal and relational level utilizes formal and informal communication systems to process the information needed to accomplish desired organizational output. Here, as with our treatments of personal and relational barriers to developing organizational intelligence networks, we will use a more generalized model of organizations in order to provide a framework for later, more refined discussion of organizational barriers.

Perhaps chief among the organizational parameters affecting organizational intelligence is *structure*—the arrangement of functions and responsibilities for optimizing organizational performance and survival. For nearly two thousand years, organizations have been structured in pyramidal form, with organizational subunits structured into minipyramids within the whole. This basic structure has transgressed organizational cultures—from the Roman Catholic Church, to the United States Army, to IBM—with a high degree of success in terms of both survival and efficiency of performance. Closer investigation would indicate, however, that during times of environmental stress—during threats to organizational survival—many of the principles of this bureaucratic organization (chain of command, formalization of communication channels, span of control) have been breached because, rather than being helpful, such principles greatly inhibited the organization's ability to adjust to environmental change.

This observation, while not new, has taken on increased importance in contemporary organizations because of the volatility of their environments. The bureaucratic structural model is an efficient one under conditions of relative environmental stability. But, as discussed earlier in this chapter, we are simply running out of stable organizational environments. Whether in business, governmental, or educational institutions, the environment is constantly attacking stress points within the organization, constantly making demands which require rapid internal change and built-in flexibility. In most organizations, such flexibility is attempted through chronic reorganization. Nor is reorganization a modern-day malady:

> We trained hard, but it seemed that every time we were beginning to form up into teams we would be reorganized. I was to learn later in life that we tend to meet any new situation by reorganizing; and a wonderful method it can be for creating the illusion of progress while producing confusion, inefficiency, and demoralization. (Petronius Arbiter, 213 B.C.)

Though we hear a great deal about matrix organization (see Chapter 6), temporary systems, and the like in the literature of organizational theory, it would appear unlikely that the pyramid will be altogether replaced as the basic form of organization in the near future. Rather we will more likely see our energies expended on ways to make this basic structure more organic—more capable of responding to an environment of accelerated change. We are likely to see managers and administrators devoting time and dollars to *diagnostic* activities, to *sensing* activities, aimed at better understanding intraorganizational and extraorganizational environments. We are likely to see managers and administrators attempting to form *proactive* (as opposed to *reactive*) postures in managing the organization. Those who ascend to the highest managerial and administrative levels are likely to be those who are most comfortable with uncertainty, with ambiguity, with contingency-based strategies for optimizing organizational performance. And such managers and administrators will rely upon organizational intelligence as their primary resource.

A CONTINGENCY-BASED ORGANIZATIONAL
PERSPECTIVE

Paul Lawrence and Jay Lorsch of the Harvard Business School have developed a conceptual framework for diagnosing an organization's structural requirements (Lawrence and Lorsch, 1967) that is particularly relevant to our discussion here. Moreover, their model and research fit our biases toward contingency-based strategies for designing organization structures and developing organizational intelligence networks. Essentially, they contend that there is no one best way to structure an organization. Lawrence and Lorsch's answer to "How should we organize?" would be, "It all depends on (1) the nature of human inputs and tasks under consideration, and (2) the nature of the organizational environment in terms of predictability." For, as their research has indicated, *under certain conditions*, the mechanistic, highly bureaucratic organization with its commensurate, built-in routines and rigid policies is the optimum form of organization. Conversely, this bureaucratic model is doomed to at least a slow, decaying demise under other conditions. Earlier we described organizational intelligence systems as taking into account both internal and external contingencies to optimize decision making. We find the Lawrence and Lorsch model invaluable in providing the conceptual framework within which to consider such contingencies, particularly those related to organizational structure.

The Lawrence and Lorsch framework is a response to a felt need in organizational theory. This need results from, first of all, the shortcomings of the bureaucratic model—ideas for structural design built around the notions of division of work, chain of command, span of control, and formality of communication systems. These ideas were advanced by classical organizational theorists like Henri Fayol, Luther Gulick, and Lyndall Urwick during the 1920s and 1930s and were later given industrial engineering refinements by Frederick Taylor. Secondly, the need for a new framework arises from the shortcomings of the psychological and social-psychological model—ideas for structural design built around the notions of needs for self-actualization, collaboration, job enrichment, and team building, ideas advanced by behavioral theorists like Rensis Likert, Frederick Herzberg, Douglas MacGregor, and others during the 1960s.

The primary shortcoming of the bureaucratic model is its failure to take into account the human element in any but the most cursory, simplistic sense. These theorists focused almost exclusively on the task to be accomplished—usually breaking the task down into its most routine, narrow components and then distributing or assigning these subtasks to individuals and departments. The bureaucratic model is concerned primarily, then, with technical and economic efficiency. This basic concern led to tremendous oversimplification of the role and nature of human resources in the system. Employees were seen as motivated exclusively by monetary rewards and as incapable of handling all but the most programmable of tasks. The result, of course, was a highly efficient, machinelike organization capable of accomplishing its mission of producing goods and services, but ill equipped to handle unexpected, rapid change in its environment.

The behaviorists' model represents the flip side of the bureaucratic-mechanistic model. Here, recognizing the failings of bureaucracy, theorists suggested that tasks be enriched—made meaningful—because, in addition to monetary reward, employees are motivated by social and self-actualizing needs. A shortcoming of this model is the tendency to see all employees motivated by such interpersonal needs. As Lawrence and Lorsch state, "No attention is focused on the important differences in individual needs." Likewise, this model does not adequately address the real-world fact that *some* jobs in *some* industries appear to be nonenrichable; the only viable alternative here is automation and subsequent unemployment—an alternative not in the best interest of human resources.

Lawrence and Lorsch (1967) identify a broader shortcoming of both schools of thought:

> While each offers a particular prescription about how to design the basic structure of an organization, both approaches are offered as the one best way to organize. To the readers who have already been exposed to a systemic conceptual framework, it should be obvious that any blanket prescription is an oversimplification. ...Furthermore, recent research...suggests that the choices made in designing a basic structure depend on the task and human inputs involved.

We are not negating the important contributions of both the classical and social-psychological theorists to understanding organizations. For purposes of identifying organizational barriers to intelligence systems, however, we find Lawrence and Lorsch's contingency-based framework most appropriate. As we will see in later chapters, *within* Lawrence and Lorsch's "differentiation-integration" framework, the principles established by classicists and behaviorists are invaluable to organizational design.

In studying several organizations in several industries (plastics, consumer foods, standardized containers), Lawrence and Lorsch developed a scheme for determining optimum organizational structure whose primary strength lies in the matching of organization to environment. That is, their model suggests that by comparing an organization or subunit along certain dimensions with the nature of its environment, one can discover mismatches impeding organizational performance and, ultimately, threatening its survival.

Differentiation-Integration

Two concepts are central to grasping Lawrence and Lorsch's "differentiation-integration" model. The first, *differentiation*, concerns

> the differences in cognitive and emotional orientations among managers in different functional departments, and the differences in formal structure among these departments. (Lawrence and Lorsch, 1967)

In attempting to compare differences among departments in their applied research, Lawrence and Lorsch investigated:

1. Differences in the formality of organizational structure—for example, how rigidly structured they are in terms of communication channels, work schedules and work flows.
2. Differences in the interpersonal orientation of managers—for example, how aloof they remain from subordinates, how formal or informal their relationships are with subordinates.
3. Differences in time orientation—for example, whether the departments operate on close or longer-term deadlines.
4. Differences in goal orientations—for example, whether goals are clear and immediate (e.g., meeting production schedules) or longer-term and more diffuse (e.g., discovering new products or knowledge within a research function).

Second, Lawrence and Lorsch's model requires an understanding of *integration*, which they define as

> the quality of the state of collaboration that exists among departments that are required to achieve unity of effort by the environment.

At this stage, it might be helpful to view the need for integration as the x-axis and the need for differentiation as the y-axis of the graph in Figure 1-2.

The goal in devising an optimum organizational structure as portrayed here is to find that vector which most effectively combines the need for differentiation (in goals, formality, interpersonal styles, time orientations) with the need for integration (getting these diverse departments to coordinate their efforts) demanded by the organizational environment. Thus, environment becomes the third critical variable in the Lawrence and Lorsch model. As we move from an organizational environment of certainty (one whose demands can be predicted with higher probability) toward one of uncertainty (one of rapid change and lower predictability),

FIGURE 1.2. THE CONTINGENCY CONCEPT AND THE ORGANIZA-TION'S ENVIRONMENT

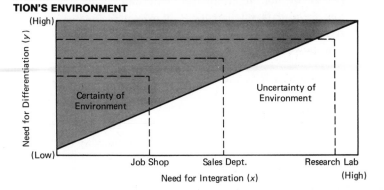

we must have greater differentiation within the organization. The more uncertain the organizational environment, the greater the need to have more organizational members in touch with different parts of that environment. The result is a "flatter" organization with broader spans of control and greater decentralization of decision making. Simultaneously, however, there will be greater problems in integrating these diverse organizational subunits with one another.

Conversely, in an environment of relative stability and certainty in terms of organizational demands, we would expect to find little diversity—differentiation—among organizational subunits. This would result in "taller" organizational structures with more narrow spans of control and greater centralization of decision making. Theoretically, given less differentiation, we would expect to find less difficulty in integrating organizational subunits.

We see, then, the structural paradox within the Lawrence and Lorsch model: the greater the uncertainty of the environment, the greater the need for differentiation among organizational units and, conversely, the greater the difficulty in integrating these units with one another. In a rapidly changing environment, the most effective organizations, then, are those which have both high differentiation *and* high integration characteristics.

We believe that more and more organizations are caught up in environments characterized by uncertainty, rather than certainty. This trend is likely to continue, perhaps at an even more accelerated rate. This places significant demands on those who manage such organizations to understand both the internal dynamics of the organization and the external dynamics of the environment; to develop administrative and structural contingencies through which to better ensure organizational survival; to develop organizational intelligence systems capable of providing insights into the workings of the organization and the effectiveness of its organization-to-environment interfaces. And those managers and administrators who can best sift through internally and externally generated information, drawing from these data intelligence with which to make their decisions, will be those who succeed in leading the organization—in establishing organizational power. As Bennis (1976) states:

> ... information itself is the chief lever of power ... and the men who get power are the ones who learn how to filter the incredible flow of information into a meaningful pattern.

An important organizational barrier to developing organizational intelligence, then, is the structure. To the extent that the organization is structured in a fashion which complements its environment—be it one of certainty or uncertainty—the individual manager or administrator can more readily identify his or her sources of information and begin to build his intelligence networks. In instances in which the organization's structure is out of step, mismatched with its environment, the establishment of the intelligence network is far more difficult, for despite the individual capabilities of members of the network, their basic commodity—information—is not available to them.

We wish to reinforce the Lawrence and Lorsch model's value as a diagnostic tool—as a conceptual framework for thinking about organizations in conjunction with their environments. The initial step in developing organizational intelligence systems is to accurately diagnose the nature of the environment within which the organization functions. The demands of this environment should determine those people and functions within the organization whose power is reality-bound—based upon their access to, and competencies in accurately perceiving, those demands. These are the legitimate leaders, legitimate controllers of the organization's direction. These are the managers, administrators, and staff specialists whose power base evolves from knowledge, from expertise, from networks of organizational intelligence.

The Problem of Institutionalized Power

What happens when power in the organization is not reality-bound, not legitimized by complementary environmental demands? This question leads us to one more generic barrier to developing effective organizational intelligence—the tendency for organizational functions, disciplines, or specializations to institutionalize their power, once having gained it.

Ideally, power within the organization should shift from source to source as the organization's environmental demands shift from one component (technological) to another (sociocultural). Those who ascend to positions of power within the hierarchy are those whose expertise is required by the organization *at a particular point in time* in order to survive and perform in its environment. And in those organizations which have not only survived but flourished, this has usually been the case.

We need only to look at the career paths of chief operating or chief executive officers in major business corporations over the past few decades to see evidence of this phenomenon. Initially, one will see degrees of experience in engineering—reflecting the firm's earliest environmental demand: producing the product. Later, one will see degrees or experience in marketing and in distribution—reflecting the second-generation environmental demand: delivering the product to consumers in a highly competitive environment. Third-generation (present-day) leadership reflects the most recent environmental demand—massive amounts of capital to sustain growth, resulting in the ascension of financial officers to the highest organizational levels. Fourth-generation environmental demands would appear to lie in increased government intervention and regulation of industries—likely thrusting legally trained executives into the seats of power.

Unfortunately, once in place, the tendency of functions of individuals in power is to institutionalize their power. Salancik and Pfeffer (1977) explain:

> ... By institutionalization we mean the establishment of relatively permanent structures and policies that favor the influence of a particular subunit. While in power, a dominant coalition has the ability to institute constitutions, rules, procedures, and information systems that limit the potential power of others while continuing their own.

We see such institutionalization as unfortunate in that it ultimately threatens the organization's survival, while impeding organizational performance in the interim. Having financial power institutionalized, for example, when marketing expertise is demanded by the environment greatly hinders the organization's ability to compete. Having technological power institutionalized when financial know-how is demanded by the environment likewise cripples organizational performance, and so forth.

An important antidote to institutional power should be recognized. As Salancik and Pfeffer point out, those attempting to institutionalize their power in the organization may begin to restrict or control the flow of information. Given the free-information economy about which we have spoken, however, it is apparent that sources of institutional power can control only *internally generated* information. Thus, reality-bound, information power can still emerge in the organization through the development of organizational intelligence networks which focus primarily on *externally generated* information. Such networks can identify discrepancies between events in the organizational environment and decision-making processes within the organization. Thus, a source of organizational power with which to combat institutionalized power is intelligence which reveals shortfalls between environmental demands and organizational actions. As Salancik and Pfeffer state:

> ...we suspect [institutionalized power] is an important condition that mediates between the environment of the organization and the capabilities of the organization for dealing with that environment. The more institutionalized power is within an organization, the more likely an organization will be out of phase with the realities it faces.

The most vivid recent contrast of intelligence-based power with institutionalized power is, of course, Watergate. Despite considerable pressures by those in power to suppress internally generated information, external demands—first from investigative reporters, then from the public at large—resulted in the demise of institutionalized power. The bureaupathic behavior of "hunkering down" and "stonewalling" served only to dramatize just how out of phase the Nixon enclave had become with its organizational environment.

SUMMARY AND PROLOGUE

In this initial chapter, we have described a revolution at work in contemporary organizations. This is a revolution whose end result promises to be the dramatic shift of organizational power—particularly control—from one organizational constituency to another; a revolution in which the right to make decisions is gravitating from traditional decision makers (the line organization) to traditional knowledge workers (the staff organization).

We have also contended, however, that line and staff functions have become so blurred over the past decade, that their initial meaning has been lost. They have been replaced by a distinction between those responsible for diagnosing the organizational environment (formerly staff alone) and those responsible for providing the product or service (formerly line alone). Thus, traditional line managers can learn to diagnose the organizational environment, and traditional staff workers can learn to diagnose the internal workings of the organization. Those who will ascend to positions of power in the organization, however, will be those who can sort out both internal and external contingencies by establishing networks of organizational intelligence.

These intelligence networks will merge knowledge about human communication behavior with knowledge about organizational theory and organizational environments. Such knowledge will form a legitimate, reality-bound base of power through which to control the short-term performance and, more importantly, the long-term destiny of the organization.

Given the fact that power (organizational or interpersonal) is a cultural artifact emerging from the value base of the culture in which it operates, those who gain control of organizations of the future may or may not occupy the highest levels on the organization chart. For our Western industrialized (and emerging postindustrial) culture values democratic social structures, resulting in a free-information economy accessible to all who desire exposure to it. Thus, more and more, information and organizational power will become synonymous. And those who can refine bits of information into the currency of intelligence with which to affect decision-making processes will be those who become the most powerful of all.

Finally, we have investigated some of the broadest, most generic barriers to developing effective organizational intelligence networks at the personal, relational, and organizational levels. The remainder of this book will be devoted, in large measure, to the further identification of those variables acting as catalysts and impediments to the development of organizational intelligence.

In the following chapters of Parts One and Two, we will focus on communication contingencies (internal and external) and communication variables (personal, relational, organizational) bearing on organizational intelligence. In Part Three, we will deal with the measurement or diagnosis of organizational intelligence systems. Our focus will be both on types of tools to be employed at the personal, relational, and organizational levels of analysis and on the application of such tools in ongoing organizations, describing administration of instruments, results, and normative data.

In Part Three, we will also discuss the renewal of organizational intelligence systems, describing the use of feedback to reflect the effectiveness of present systems, indicate recommended actions for improvement, and install new components within systems. Finally we will apply our theory to the recent work experiments conducted at the Saab and Volvo plants in Norway and Sweden.

Communication Contingencies

Whatever else organizations may be, they are political structures. This means that organizations operate by distributing authority and setting a stage for the exercise of power. (Zaleznik, 1970)

Knowledge is Power. (Sign on an eighth grade blackboard in 1957)

INTRODUCTION

Les had supervised his department for the last twenty years, but was now getting ready to retire. One of the candidates for his job, Jim, had been interviewing several different managers in order to get a perspective on the status of Les's department. One manager replied to Jim, "Oh, *Les* is a terrific manager! *He's* been here for a long time. *He's* accomplished some significant things." Another stated, "You know, whenever I think of that department, I think of *Les*." Still another said, "I just can't think of anything about the department, now that you ask, except that 'good old Les runs it.'"

Radenko Sainovic has also been involved in running his department, but unlike Les, Sainovic was a worker, not a manager. As reported in *Newsweek* in 1971, he had been involved in charting his Yugoslavian "firm's wage policies and in planning new investments amounting to about $2 million to expand production of a new line of plastics for the construction industry." As a member of the worker's council, Sainovic stated, "We studied the market carefully... and all the workers were informed about the investment. We thought it over many times before approving it. Even when snap judgments must be made by the Grmec directors, the [workers'] council has full power to review—and reverse—their decisions."

Les may have been a good manager, but was his *department* operating at maximum effectiveness? Probably not. Les had become institutionalized, and when he leaves his department may be just as helpless as the widow whose late husband had never shown her the checkbook. Sainovic's department, given the amount of shared information processing, was more able to cope with the changing needs of its environment. We would conclude that Sainovic's department, given the shared information processing, has the organizational intelligence needed to cope with its changing environment.

Our industrial society has become an information society. One out of every two workers is now employed in some aspect of information processing. Organizations need more machines, better systems, and more highly trained people not only to remain competitive but just to stay alive. As discussed in Chapter 1, Lawrence and Lorsch's contingency theory indicates that since factors in the environment are changing so rapidly, there is no one best way to run an organization. Kast and Rosenzweig (1973) summarize this position:

> The contingency view seeks to understand the interrelationships within and among subsystems as well as between the organization and its environment and to define patterns of relationships or configurations and attempts to understand how organizations operate under varying conditions and specific circumstances. Contingency views are ultimately directed toward suggesting organizational design and managerial actions most appropriate for specific situations.

Just as there is no one best way to manage, so is there no one best way to communicate. The communication process is influenced by many internal and external constraints of the organization and its subsystems. The constraints determine the status of the organization or its subsystems at any given time. The constraints are dependent on the situation: the state of the environmental suprasystem and the states of the subsystem. The communication process is thus contingent upon external and internal stimuli and upon the degree of freedom of states of the system allowed by the organizational constraints. Just as a person is not the same person when he talks with his spouse as when he talks with his boss, so are organizations different when their communication contingencies change.

Studies by Wiio (1975, 1976, 1977) in Finland and by Goldhaber and others in the United States and Canada have provided strong evidence to support such a contingency view of organization communication. Using data collected in over thirty five organizations, representing over forty thousand workers, both Wiio and Goldhaber found differences in communication effectiveness as a function of both type of organization and composition of the work force (age, sex, education, tenure). To quote Wiio (1974), "In different organizational contingencies, different demographic variables showed significant relationships with communication variables."

OVERVIEW OF
CONTINGENCY AND INTELLIGENCE CONCEPTS

One's ability to cope with the contingencies affecting an organization's communication system allows one to control his information system. This results in organizational intelligence—the tactics, strategy, and logistics for confronting an uncertain environment. The organization with intelligence has information power, which facilitates decision making and overall effectiveness. To the extent a manager is low in information power, he is more susceptible to such problems as receiving too little information about major decisions, irrelevant information which doesn't answer his questions, and information in the wrong form or with too much detail or frequency. In short, he might rapidly succumb to the most troublesome communication problem plaguing managers today—information overload. The paradox of organizational intelligence is how to simultaneously avoid being overloaded with the unnecessary and being underloaded with the vital. Developing information power through organizational intelligence helps eliminate that paradox.

The matrix in Figure 2-1 illustrates the interface between communication contingencies and communication variables. Our division of contingencies into those external and those within the organizational system is consistent with the view of Luthans and Steward (1977), who state:

> External environmental variables, such as federal legislation, are considered to be outside the organizational system. Internal environmental variables are also beyond the direct control of the manager in question, but are within the control of the formal organization.

FIGURE 2-1. ORGANIZATIONAL INTELLIGENCE MATRIX

Contingencies	Communication Variables		
	Personal Variables	Relational Variables	Organizational Variables
Internal Contingencies			
External Contingencies			

The communication variables are further divided into those which are most salient to the manager's personal frame of reference, to his interpersonal relations with others, and to the organizational system at large.

Since we will later deal with ten contingencies and seventeen communication variables, the complexity of possible situations confronting the manager and his intelligence system is apparent: when we add the possible interactions among the contingencies and variables, we rapidly approach several thousand different communication situations (and there are even more variables and contingencies we simply chose not to describe). Is it any wonder that managers have difficulty coping with the communication environment?

Table 2-1 identifies those internal and external contingencies which most directly affect the communication system and ultimately the amount of organizational intelligence available in a system. When an organization has maximized the effectiveness of its communication system, it is in the best position to cope with the potentially unstable environment, both internal and external to the organization. As can be seen in Figure 2-2, the amount of intelligence needed by an organization depends upon the status of the contingencies. Conditions of rapid change will require more organizational intelligence. As can also be seen in Figure 2-2, the amount of intelligence possessed is a function of the quality of the communication system—the lower the quality, the lower the intelligence. The gap or difference between the intelligence needed and the intelligence possessed is the information power gap; the greater this gap, the less the manager's chances for coping with the environment. The condition of maximum danger to the organization occurs when a high rate of change in contingencies is coupled with an ineffective communication system. This condition results in the largest gap between intelligence needed and intelligence possessed, greatly reducing the information power the organization has to cope with its probably overloaded state.

TABLE 2-1. COMMUNICATION CONTINGENCIES

Internal Contingencies	External Contingencies
1. *Structural:* degree of formality and type of structure chosen to organize the functions and relationships in the organization.	1. *Economic:* amount of stability in current market/competition.
2. *Outputs:* amount of diversity and degree of quality in the products/services.	2. *Technological:* degree of innovation with equipment, science, research and development.
3. *Demographic:* degree of variation among employees in such characteristics as age, sex, education, tenure, supervisory status.	3. *Legal:* local, state, and federal regulations, guidelines, and laws.
4. *Spatiotemporal:* degree of variation in both spatial (design, amount, location, distance) and temporal (timing, timeliness) matters.	4. *Socio/political/cultural:* social, cultural, and political considerations.
5. *Traditional:* degree of conformity with organizational norms, history, and script.	5. *Environmental:* climate, geography, population density, and availability of energy.

FIGURE 2-2. CONDITIONS OF ORGANIZATIONAL INTELLIGENCE

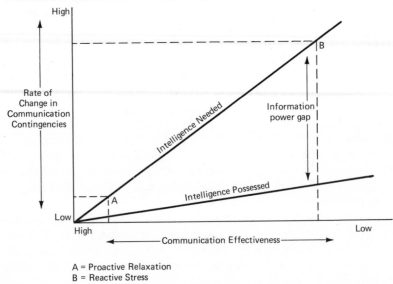

A = Proactive Relaxation
B = Reactive Stress

Analyzing Your Organization's Position

Table 2-2 summarizes the four typical conditions possible for an organization facing varying degrees of contingency shifts and varying effectiveness in communication systems:

1. Proactive relaxation (the "honeymoon"). In this state the environment is generally stable and the communication system is very effective. Because of its certain environment, the organization, possibly a small system with a single product line, does not have many information demands placed upon it. It is ready to cope with changes in its environment because of its effective communication system, which can handle potential information overload. It is *proactive* because it is in a state of readiness. It is relaxed because of the stable environment. This type of organization needs very little organizational intelligence under current conditions—until the honeymoon is over.

2. Proactive coping (the "marriage"). Here the environment is highly uncertain. Conditions both within and outside the organization are rapidly changing, and the effects of the changes are felt directly on the organization. However, due to a highly effective communication system, the organization is ready and able to cope with these changes and their potential information overload. It is proactive because of its readiness; it is coping because of the rapid shifts in contingencies. Just as with the oil refinery which ran smoothly for a year despite a strike, our conclusion is that this type of organization requires little additional organizational intelligence: it has all that it needs.

**TABLE 2-2. STATES OF ORGANIZATIONAL INTELLIGENCE
AND INTELLIGENCE NEEDS**

When: Rate of change in communication contingencies is:	And: Effectiveness of the communication system is:	Then: The organization's current condition is:	And: The organization's current intelligence needs are:
1. Low	High	Proactive relaxation the ("honeymoon")	Low
2. High	High	Proactive coping the ("marriage")	Low
3. Low	Low	Reactive hibernation the ("time bomb")	Moderate
4. High	Low	Reactive stress the ("explosion")	High

3. Reactive hibernation (the "time bomb"). Here the environment is relatively stable but the communication system is very ineffective. This is potentially very dangerous because the organization may be lulled by the quiet of the environment into thinking that it can cope. Typical of this type of organization is the presence of institutional power, that is, people controlling others by virtue of title, role, or tenure. When the environment changes, this type of organization will resort to the crisis management of putting out brush fires rather than prevention tactics. Consultants who strongly advocate a particular intervention, despite the client's needs, fall prey to reactive hibernation by ignoring the contingencies which are currently critical to the organization. Our conclusion is that this type of organization needs moderate amounts of organizational intelligence due to its inability to cope with future needs.

4. Reactive stress (the "explosion"). Here the environment is highly unstable; contingencies affecting the organization are changing at a rapid rate. However, the organization is unable to cope with the overload associated with the environmental uncertainty because of its weak communication system. This is extremely dangerous and will mean the death of the organization if left unchecked. For example, a secretary with sole knowledge of virtually all of an organization's external contacts quit in the middle of a strike, leaving the system in a state of collapse. The explosions that occur result typically in a call to bring in the consultant. Our conclusion is that this type of organization needs very high amounts of organizational intelligence if it is to survive in its present form.

These four states of organizational intelligence will become clearer after we present the most salient of the internal and external contingencies affecting communication. We will describe the contingencies, show the communication implications for each one, and give some examples of how they may lead to some of the above states. Chapters 3, 4, 5, and 6 will then focus on the personal, relational, and organizational communication variables of the intelligence system.

INTERNAL COMMUNICATION CONTINGENCIES

Structure

Structure refers to the network of relationships and roles existing throughout the organization. Structure enables the organization to meet its objectives effectively and in an orderly manner. Thus, structure provides the stability, predictability, and regularity necessary for an organization to function without anarchy. Structure also provides an interesting communication paradox. Some structures, because of their extreme formality or cumbersome size or bewildering complexity, act as communication blocks, filtering and distorting potentially useful information. On the other hand, more informal structures tend to allow more information to flow across its network paths than people can handle, leading to overload. The major communication implication of structure, then, is what kind of structure is most suitable for present organizational needs such that important information flows freely without overloading relevant decision makers.

In the 1950s, one of our client organizations, a midwestern university, was relatively small—a few thousand students and two hundred faculty. Following a merger with the state system, the university changed its student clientele to a more nontraditional undergraduate (older, employed, female) and attracted several thousand additional students, most of whom wanted to attend at night. The existing organizational structure, a relatively informal, highly centralized network, centering around the offices of the president and academic vice-president, was no longer viable for the current growth needs of the system. The president, accustomed to the good old days, would still conduct much of his official business in the corridors where he would frequently roam to "see who was around." His staff, consisting entirely of one secretary and one administrative assistant, was constantly harried with frequent memos, letters, and phone calls, mostly from faculty and deans awaiting replies to earlier requests. To compound matters, the president spent 60 percent of his time lobbying for funds from the state legislature, but he retained final authority on most academic decisions. The academic vice-president and his staff (one secretary and one assistant), perhaps intimidated by the president and his style, rarely made a major decision without "checking with the boss." The Council of Deans met frequently, but usually only to debate the trivial and inconsequential. Out of desperation and frustration from lack of attention, faculty and administrators were constantly sending the president reprints, papers, and copies of extensive studies. When we interviewed the president, we found him bent over, picking up a stack of papers from the floor, where he had loosely filed and tossed several dozen documents sent to his office. His opening remarks to us were, "Look at all this stuff! I can't understand why they keep sending it to me."

For our president, life in the 1950s must have been reasonably pleasant —a state of proactive relaxation. His environment was stable and the structure of his university was suitable for his needs. He was so lulled by the peace that he failed to notice the rapid changes in his environment, thus inducing a state of reactive hibernation. His organizational structure, once adequate, was no longer appropriate; his failure to adapt, in time, led to the crisis we found him in—reactive stress. In short, the lack of formalized structures—gatekeepers, decentralized decision makers, additional staff—had created an unbearable overload situation in which little progress toward achieving goals was realized.

Sometimes a manager may believe he is coping with shifting environmental influences by adapting his structure—only to find he chose the wrong adaptation. Such was the case of a large commercial bank which undertook to compete more favorably with other banks that were now benefiting from new banking regulations. The bank decided to involve their several thousand employees in a campaign to attract customers by creating a new structure (called, coincidentally, a "communication network") in which relevant information from top management would be filtered through a "network person" to the employees. The bank, however, neglected to adequately prepare the network personnel for the large volume of additional information, the new tasks of reading, synthesizing, translating, and the new behavior of meeting with employees in groups. The result was a disaster. The network personnel would typically receive their packets of information and promptly file them in the waste basket. Morale problems mounted among employees who felt left out of the network, and the bank's share of the market declined even more.

Again, we find an organization reacting to sudden shifts in its environment rather than planning ahead for the possible. The predictable reactive stress explosion occurred because they hastily implemented a new structural artifact *after* new banking regulations affected their market status.

Another financial institution is now in a state of reactive hibernation. They currently enjoy a large share of their market, but have an ineffective communication system. The top six executives who run the two-thousand-person organization recently designed and implemented a corporate plan outlining the financial and management goals for the coming five years. Amid the plaudits fed back for "finally telling us where we're going" were several comments from subordinates questioning "where do we fit into this plan" and wondering out loud, "Why weren't we asked for our opinion on this matter?" Such are the cues that forecast a limited upward-directed input system. Such are the cues that indicate a top management group that acts in secret and may not be willing to listen. Adherence to highly formal structures, a common practice in financial institutions, may work in times of low uncertainty, but watch out when the prime lending rate is dropped 1 percent!

In another case, a U.S. senator's office with only thirty people in it had a surprisingly high degree of differentiation among its personnel, without any significant integrating mechanisms. As a result, the press secretary rarely knew what constituent requests an aide was working on because the latter infrequently told him. On one occasion, the aide had just completed a difficult constituent request, which the press secretary heard about at lunch from a friend of an aide in another U.S. representative's office. When we asked the aide why he never checked with the press secretary, he replied, "He's too busy—and what I'm doing isn't that important." More reactive hibernation awaiting an explosion around election time!

As an example of an organization practicing proactive coping, one of the two hundred largest industrial corporations in the United States, with assets in excess of $2 billion and over thirty thousand employees in North America and Europe, recently adopted a matrix organizational structure. (We discuss the matrix further in Chapter 6.) Since a matrix is a powerful way of organizing resources to focus on relatively short-term projects, and since this corporation is a large diversified system confronting a rapidly changing market, the matrix seemed like a good structure for their current needs. Notice in Figure 2-3, which illustrates their matrix, how a member of the manufacturing department would report both to the corporate manufacturing head and to the head of profit center A. This dual reporting function is typical of the matrix system. It also serves notice to those who use it of potential problems in authority, power, communication delegation, and control. Conflicts typically arise from the above ambiguities which tax the interpersonal skills of most managers, requiring negotiation and confrontation instead of avoidance.

To illustrate their ability with proactive coping, this management group implemented a three-phase renewal effort involving confrontation meetings, intergroup development efforts, and team building. All of these activities were designed to reduce the overload upon the matrix participants so that the change in organizational structure would maximize organizational intelligence.

Coping with Structural Changes. Managers and organizations who desire to become more proactive in coping with potential shifts in organizational structure which may influence their communication systems should consider some of the following questions, some of which are adapted from Farace and Danowski (1973).

At the system level:

1. Does the current structure of the organization allow it to meet its objectives? Can alternative structures better facilitate communication flow and organizational effectiveness?
2. What are the major sources of information that form the environment? Can organization-environment stresses be alleviated by

FIGURE 2-3. SAMPLE MATRIX ORGANIZATION

Corporate unit	Profit Centers (PC)				
	PC 1	PC 2	PC 3	PC 4	PC 5
Manufacturing					
Employee Relations					
Administration/Finance					
Technology (R/D)					
Marketing					

reducing redundant organization-environment links? Can alternative mechanisms be created for better communication flow between the organization and its environment?

3. Do the work, innovative, social, and grapevine networks of the organization differ? In what respects are these differences, if any, beneficial or harmful to organizational effectiveness?

4. When discrepancies occur between actual and expected networks, should (*a*) new groups be formed? (*b*) current groups be changed or their functions eliminated? (*c*) current groups remain extant because they serve useful integrative functions?

5. Which groups are well connected to each other? Which aren't? Should they be isolated? integrated? Are those groups which are isolated from the total organization experiencing information underload? Are certain groups too highly connected to other groups in the organization—perhaps raising problems of information overload? Are there too many links through which information must pass to reach certain groups—increasing the likelihood of information distortion?

At the group level:

1. Are certain groups too large—or too small? Are the internal communication patterns of the group too restricted for optimum task accomplishments or member morale? Is the group too dominated by one or two individuals? Or is the internal communication pattern too loose and unrestricted for the accomplishment of particular task objectives?

2. Is there enough centralization of the group structure? Are the shortest paths of communication between any two group members sufficient? excessive in length?

3. If a group is dominated by a few individuals, do these people have the necessary communication skills and training to serve this role?

At the individual level:

1. Who are the key communicators in the organization? Are their patterns of communication consistent with their prescribed job functions? If not, why not? Should their functions be changed? Should their skills be changed?

2. Who are the liaisons?* Are the persons performing these roles those who are expected to do so by organizational chart placement

---

*A *liaison* is a person who functions as a connecting link between two or more groups in the organization, but does not hold membership in these groups. We discuss liaisons further in Chapters 5 and 6.

or job description? Do these liaisons serve an integrative or supervisory function? If the liaisons are not in management roles, should their functions be changed? Do the liaisons need more responsibility or clearer authority or additional skills to best carry out their role? Are there sufficient number of liaisons to allow for the effective coordination of work group activities?
3. Who are the isolates? How many individuals are isolated from communication flows? Are certain individuals not communicating about work-related matters? Are new channels of communication needed to better integrate the isolates into the organization?

A final note about structure. Until now, we have been talking about the communication implications of organizational structure. The organization in a true state of proactive coping will ultimately let the communication system dictate the structure of the organization. Just as a wise landscape architect often designs a sidewalk where the grass has been downtrodden by footprints, so will the proactive organization cope with potential future overload by designing structures to fit existing communication patterns. Indeed, this is already happening with the research being done on "office landscaping" (or bürolandschaft) in Germany and "office locations" in England.

Outputs

... the total weight of the paper submitted was 35 tons—the maximum payload of today's C-141. It took more than 400 Air Force experts five months to read and evaluate that mass of data. This, to me, hardly represents progress in the management of management information. *One reason is that we didn't know exactly what questions to ask—so we asked far too many. . . .* (Estes, 1966)

The outputs of an organization are the result of what it produces. More and more we are viewing an organization as a network of interdependent relationships with different goals being fused to produce a unified whole (product or service). To the extent that an organization has clear and appropriate goals it will operate from a state of proactive coping. To the extent that it achieves these goals, it will be effective. As we will see, different types of organizations have different goals and levels of performance in achieving them, all of which influence the kind and quality of communication system.

Goals and Organizational Intelligence. A pants manufacturer in the Southwest operated on a quota system. After a mutually determined number of pants were agreed upon by work teams, a series of different colored flags were to be used to signal a group's status toward reaching its goals. For example, green flags denoted above-quota performance, red meant below, and yellow meant on target. These flags were posted near work benches along with monthly performance charts—for all to see as they walked by the work station. For several reasons this manufacturer demonstrated proactive coping. Although the competition was stiff (two other plants in the same town), the goals were communicated clearly in a language (charts/flags) understood readily by all, thus reducing potential perceptual disparity; also, the goals were realistic and tempered by past performance and experience with different workers.

Not all organizations behave this way with goals. Far too many rely upon the crutch of the job description, which is often inflated to enhance the importance of the writer. Our research has shown that job descriptions hardly ever indicate what workers do or think they're supposed to do. In stable environments, job descriptions (the wrong medium for communication) may lead to reactive hibernation; in uncertain times, organizations clinging to outdated descriptions may bring on *reactive stress*. We have found that when goals are not met, leading to reactive states, it is usually because of the following causes:

1. *The goals are unclear.* If goals were clear, why would MBO (Management By Objectives) be so popular today? This is of particular importance in the public sector where outputs themselves are not always clearly understood. For example, in a government agency, is the output the number of complaints processed? the number of visitors serviced? the number of letters answered? the amount of money overbudgeted? Framing specific goals is essential to later measurement of effectiveness. For example, the goal of the sales manager this year is to boost sales by 10 percent with a cost reduction of 6 percent. To achieve this goal, the manager will...

2. *The goals are not communicated.* In large organizations, top management may have a clear understanding of what it wants to accomplish, but it has failed, either deliberately or by oversight, to inform the rest of the organization of the plan. One printing company established specific goals for its workers and posted them on a bulletin board which nobody ever read.

3. *The goals are overcommunicated.* Occasionally, an overanxious manager may constantly stress "the bottom line" and the importance of "working as a team." If the goals are fair and appropriate, if the workers have sufficient input, undue stressing of the goals may lead to a negative reaction. A manager at a research office supervised his team by constantly walking into their offices unannounced with his checklist attached to a clipboard. As he'd ask for their status on the project, he'd check off their progress. All fifteen members of his team, Ph.D.'s from leading universities, threatened to quit within the first day of such treatment.

4. *The goals are not realistic.* Overestimating or underestimating what can be accomplished in a given time span may be caused by insufficient attention being paid to the details of determining exactly what it will take to reach the goals. One university department chairman set as his personal goal to recruit fifty new graduate students to his department. He did, but the university cut back on the number of his faculty, an effect of economic contingencies, leaving him with students but no teachers. Had he achieved a state of proactive coping, he would have realized the futility of organizational growth in times of financial retrenchment.

5. *The goals change too quickly.* One of our recent clients told us that "the only thing stable around here is change." He was talking about the constant revision, every six months, of his plant's newest goals. As Toffler (1970) has so aptly pointed out, too much change creates stress which may be unmanageable.

6. *The goals are wrong.* When all else is said, the organization may decide to embark upon a course of action that is morally, ethically, or legally wrong. Illegal donations to politicians, bribes to foreign nations, withholding of energy products from the market to boost prices, exchanging one automobile engine for another—all are examples of organizational malfeasance. As we pointed out in Chapter 1, the individual's voice may not be heard to object due to personal jeopardy or "groupthink," thus contributing to the formation of the wrong goals.

7. *There are no goals.* Naturally, all of the above assumes that the organization has articulated either explicitly or implicitly a set of goals. This is not always true. As perfect evidence for reactive thinking, many leaders may simply state, "My goal is survival." Politicians often behave in this manner. One U.S. senator, after serving half his term, realized he had not been identified with any single piece of major legislation. He had decided to run for reelection, but was frightened by the absence of an issue.

Effectiveness. The degree to which an organization achieves its goals is the degree to which it will be judged effective. Often achieving the goal is not enough if the quality of the product or service reduces the value of the obtained goal. Thus, the pants manufacturer's goal of 14 percent more pants during the first quarter may have been achieved, but the expense of replacing .5 percent of the pants with new zippers may have reduced the overall effectiveness of the company. This is precisely why most organizations have the equivalent of a quality control unit which monitors such things as work errors, accidents and safety records, number of complaints, and so forth. Of course, one way to produce goods and services with fewer errors is to redefine the level of performance associated with an error. Reducing standards has a corollary effect: the amount of information required to coordinate resources will decrease as performance levels are reduced.

Common ways to measure organizational effectiveness, depending upon the type of organization, are (according to Kilmann and Hermann, 1976):

1. Employee turnover (the U.S. volunteer Army)
2. Absenteeism (the Finnish automobile industry)
3. Number of grievances (a school union)
4. Employee attitudes (a manufacturing company's morale study)
5. Organizational climate (a large bank)
6. Employee commitment (purchase of ESOPs [Employee Stock Option Plan] in a large industry)
7. Interpersonal relationships (a counseling center)
8. Community satisfaction with organization (complaints to an airline)
9. Satisfaction of supplier with organization (number of orders sold to chemical company)
10. Consumer satisfaction (number of complaints to department store)
11. Ability to identify problems or opportunities (number of suggestions rewarded in manufacturing company)
12. Social responsibility (amount of money donated to community symphony by computer company)
13. Quality of life (number of employees and families educated in graduate school by large industry)
14. Environmental impact (amount of pollution produced by steel company)

Whatever measures are most appropriate for your organization and its goals, effectiveness must be assessed in order to achieve a state of proactive coping.

Types of Organizations and Organizational Intelligence. Diversity of outputs leads to differences in types of organizations. We have found that differences in organization type lead to differences in perceived information requirements. The following summarizes our findings on organization type:

1. Government organizations have a greater need to receive information than other types of organizations.
2. Government organizations have a greater need to send information than other types of organizations.
3. Government organizations have a greater need to receive information from a variety of communication sources than do other types of organizations.

4. Workers in government organizations tend to be less satisfied with organizational outcomes than those in other organizations; satisfaction is highest among workers in private sector organizations.

A word of caution: although the above findings tend to support contingency theory, and although the sample included thirteen organizations, the sample within any one organizational category is small. Further, the apparently negative results about governmental organizations, while possibly representative of the greater population of government organization, was collected in great part from a paramilitary police agency. A better understanding of the above findings will come when we analyze them in conjunction with another internal contingency—demographics.

Demographics

> Business' biggest single cost is *labor*, yet that's the one expense that's left essentially to chance. Personnel departments really don't give any more than lip service to the subject. With rare exceptions, business doesn't know how to select the right people, how to motivate them— or how to develop them to grow with the business. (Ginzberg, 1976)

If Ginzberg is right in his analysis, then the situation has grown even more tenuous for personnel departments because the labor force has changed even more since he said this. It is younger, and turnover is growing higher. Younger workers are better educated and more sophisticated than their older counterparts. They want more of a challenge in their jobs, and their sheer numbers make them a force which any manager should notice. (In the Appendix we will show an alternative to the assembly line which seems to have increased worker satisfaction in Finland and Sweden.)

Problems of managing the labor force do not exclude executives. Executive turnover has risen fivefold since 1950, particularly among college-trained personnel who seem to ignore power, money, and position as they move upward from organization to organization. Eugene Jennings (1970) called these executives "mobicentric man" for whom "success is represented less by position, title, salary or performance than by moving and movement." Job turnover by middle and top management is also high. Although sometimes associated with dissatisfaction caused by poor relationships, inept supervisory style, unsafe or uncomfortable working conditions, salary discrepancies, or poor job design, much of the turnover is simply the mobicentric man trying to get ahead.

Since this is not always bad for the organization, the problem for managers is to distinguish turnover associated with dissatisfaction from that related to upward mobility. The former may be managed; the latter may not matter and may have positive benefits for an organization—unless the turnover rate becomes too high. Very low turnover may indicate you are holding on to deadwood; fast-track people may be held back along with their exciting ideas. As Salancik and Pfeffer (1977) have pointed out, very low turnover may lead to institutional power which typically puts an organization out of phase with the realities it faces: "To the extent that organizational influence structures become institutionalized, there would be some lag between the external contingencies faced by the organization and the recognition of these contingencies in the organization leading to changes in chief executives."

Peter Drucker (1973) has applied this concept to the university setting and concluded that the university tenure system, while institutionalizing its faculty, may be composed of stagnant, stale, and putrefied groups. Although 10 percent turnover is often given as a rough index by which to gauge your organization (above 10 percent may indicate people problems, below 10 percent may indicate deadwood problems), these figures tend to vary from organization to organization, as shown by recent averages published by the Administrative Management Society (1977):

> Advertising, printing, publishing—19%
> Banking, insurance, finance—16%
> Education—15%
> Government agencies—11%
> Manufacturing—12%
> Oil, mining, lumber—12%
> Public utilities—7%
> Retail sales, distribution—16%
> Service—19%
> Transportation—10%
> Wholesale sales and distribution—18%

Their figures also vary according to size of office:

> 1–25 employees—18%
> 26–100—19%
> 101–250—19%
> 251–500—17%
> 501–1000—15%
> 1001–5000—12%
> Over 5000—7%

Apparently turnover is highest with smaller organizations. We agree with Salancik and Pfeffer that some turnover is essential to prevent institutional power from replacing information power. Further, we contend that:

1. The longer a manager remains in office, the greater the amount of institutional power.
2. The greater the institutional power, the greater the uncertainty in coping with the critical contingencies facing the manager and his organization.
3. The greater the uncertainty, the greater the information overload and the lower the intelligence.
4. Greater overload and lower intelligence will lead to states of reactive hibernation and stress.

Demographics and Organizational Intelligence. We have collected data in both Finland and the United States and have concluded that *there do not seem to be any general relationships between demographic and communication variables.* We have, however, found significant relationships in different types of organizations and in different contingencies:

1. *Sex* does not seem to be a very strong demographic factor in organizational communication behavior. It seems to be somewhat important in upward communication improvement; in banks, and in hospitals, it is important regarding economic education.

2. *Age* seems to have more influence than sex: younger employees tended to receive less and want more information than older employees; younger employees were in general more satisfied with their relationships but less satisfied with their jobs.

3. *Job tenure* was also strongly related to communication behavior, indicating that those workers with the longest tenure needed less and received more information while enjoying higher morale. (They may have been receiving more of the useless information, leading to overload.)

4. *Shift of work* was not strongly related to communication behavior and was very selective among types of organization, particularly service organizations.

5. *Organizational level* seems to be generally important (more so in manufacturing industries than elsewhere); the higher the level, the more information received, particularly about economic matters.

6. *Level of education* is most important in public administration, the service branch, and manufacturing industries. It influences satisfaction with upward and downward communication and the availability of economic information. As education increases, the need to send information decreases, better relationships are enjoyed, and satisfaction with organizational outcomes increases. Those who were the least *and* most educated wanted and needed the most information.

7. *Union membership* is again very selective: it seems to be most important in manufacturing industries and to a minor degree in the service branch. In the printing industry it is relevant in connection with organizationwide information, and in banks and insurance companies in connection with economic information.

Since demographics tend to vary so greatly among organizations in terms of their impact upon communication behavior, the proactive manager who desires to cope with this uncertainty must maintain up-to-date descriptive measures of his or her labor force. In this way he or she can maximize the amount of intelligence needed to make effective decisions.

Spatiotemporal Factors

Space and time both affect the kind, frequency, and quality of communication within an organization. Knowledge of variations in both will increase your organizational intelligence.

Space. Space may be viewed physically by looking at the actual distances between people, offices, and buildings, or psychologically by studying the role distances create by scalar and functional distinctions.

Physical space. Entire books have been written about differences in personal space, power seating arrangements, office design, and building ecology.

Space has been linked to organizational status: personnel with high status will typically have greater amounts of space, protect their space better, and more frequently invade the space of lower-status personnel. Space has been linked to power: sitting to the immediate left or right of a hostile person at a meeting is more likely to allow you to control that person's influence. Space has been linked to productivity: workers in "open environments" (buildings without walls) tend to work at higher productivity levels.

Space has been linked to communication costs: office relocations outside major metropolitan areas (to save money in rent or salary) may increase communication costs sufficiently to offset other savings. Several studies have been done in Europe in the last ten years which confirm this point. Thorngren showed in Sweden and Goddard in England (1977) that after relocation, most workers retained 30 percent of their old communication contacts. The Communication Studies Group in London has estimated that on relocation "a civil servant's telephone costs would increase by about 50 pounds per year" (Pye, 1977). Pye developed a model for computing the approximate extra travel costs involved when relocated employees travel back to their old city for business meetings. Pye concluded that "the increased economic benefits which are, in general, obtainable from longer distance moves do not offset the greater costs of communication." Naturally, communication costs can be reduced if the need for the old contacts is diminished by regional decentralization of decision making, such as that done by the Prudential Insurance Company in the United States. Another alternative, currently being experimented with in both England and Canada, is to substitute telecommunications alternatives for needed travel. Preliminary findings (reported by Elton, 1976) indicate that about one-third of current meetings consist of "activities whose outcome is not significantly affected if the meeting is conducted via audio teleconference devices. . . . an additional 10% of existing meetings consist only of tasks the outcome of which would not be affected if conducted by television-type visual teleconference devices. . . . " This still leaves a majority of the meetings to be accounted for in communication costs affected by new spatial arrangement, but the proactive coping manager would probably figure out his own organization's needs and balance them against potential costs.

Role Distance. Our recent studies of American and European organizations has confirmed a significant impact of role distance on organizational communication behavior. Both dissatisfaction with organizational communication and need for communication improvements increase with organizational distance. We have also found that organization members seem to be less satisfied in the role of information receivers than in the role of information senders. Some of our specific conclusions (derived from studies in thirteen U.S. organizations, with samples approaching four thousand employees) related to distance are:

1. The farther up the organizational hierarchy, the less the follow-up, particularly related to information sent to top management.
2. The best sources of information are those closest to employees (co-workers, immediate supervisors), and the worst are those farthest away (top management, boss's boss, formal management presentations).
3. Information from top management is of lower quality than that from other key sources.
4. The immediate communication climate is excellent and healthier than that of the organization at large (which limits openness, lacks sufficient incentives and rewards, and minimizes input, influence, and advancement opportunities).

Additional studies done in Finland (reported in Tables 2-3 and 2-4) both support these conclusions and provide additional data about our earlier statement about communication role (sender/receiver).

TABLE 2-3. COMMUNICATION SATISFACTION (TOPICS RANK-ORDERED NEGATIVELY WITH RESPECT TO SATISFACTION)

Rank	Percentage	Question: How much information do you get about your organization from:
1	69	Other superiors (management)
2	58	Members of joint committee
3	53	Your immediate superior
4	50	Shop steward or liaison officer
5	27	Fellow employees

These rank orders are very consistent across different types of organizations and organizational levels. Thus, we feel justified to suggest the following conclusions:

1. Dissatisfaction with organizational communication seems to increase with organizational *distance* between the source of information and the receiver.
2. *Direction* of communication has an effect on organizational communication satisfaction. Organization members are less satisfied in the role of receivers of information than in the role of senders of information.

In communication, it seems better to get than to give. "There is nothing wrong with my communication, I just don't get enough information." This seems to be a very general attitude among members of organizations. They feel that they themselves give enough information; the problem is "other people." If there is dissatisfaction in the outgoing communication, it is in the belief that they are not allowed to express themselves freely or that their opinions are not considered.

TABLE 2-4. COMMUNICATION IMPROVEMENTS (TOPICS RANK-ORDERED POSITIVELY WITH RESPECT TO NEED FOR IMPROVEMENT)

Rank	Percentage	Question: In what respect would you like to see improved communication?
1	73	From management to personnel
2	71	From immediate superiors to personnel
3	64	From shop steward to personnel
4	63	From joint committee to personnel
5	62	From personnel to management
6	60	From personnel to immediate superiors
7	59	From personnel to joint committees
8	58	From personnel to shop steward
9	50	Among personnel

Space and Organizational Intelligence: The Distance-Direction Model.
In Figure 2-4 communication distance is indicated by the headings "Far"
and "Near." Communication direction is indicated by the headings
"Sender" and "Receiver"; in the sender mode the information flows away
from the organization member and in the receiver mode the information
flows toward the organization member.

According to the model in Figure 2-4, satisfaction with organizational
communication is greatest when communication distance is short and the
subject acts as an information sender. A little less satisfactory situation
exists when the communication distance is short and the subject acts as an
information receiver. When the communication distance is large and the
subject acts as a sender, there tends to be more dissatisfaction than
satisfaction. Dissatisfaction is even greater when the distance is large and
the subject acts as an information receiver.

The next obvious question is: how near is *near* and how far is *far*? In a
work group *near* means the immediate work environment, the work group,
and the immediate superior. In communication terms it means a communication system with frequent, interactive, transactional contacts. *Far*
means a communication system with infrequent, mostly one-way, and
often indirect contacts.

It may well turn out that the distance dimension can be divided into
several communication systems. There are some indications of that in our
data, but not conclusive evidence.

Our analysis suggests that there are at least these four different contingencies of organizational communication satisfaction from the
viewpoint of an individual member of an organization:

1. *Near-sender contingency.* In this contingency, the organization member is a sender of information to his immediate social environment, his
work group, his immediate superior, and his closest friends. In frequent
and interactive communication this contingency is sometimes difficult to

FIGURE 2-4. DISTANCE-DIRECTION AND COMMUNICATION SATISFACTION

Communication	Far	− +	− − +
Distance	Near	+ + +	+ −
		Sender	Receiver

Communication direction

separate from the near-receiver contingency. This contingency represents usually the greatest amount of communication satisfaction.

2. *Near-receiver contingency*. Here the organization member judges his chances to receive information from the immediate social environment. This communication is usually perceived as positive, but there is more criticism than in the first contingency.

3. *Far-sender contingency*. In general, communication outside the immediate social environment is perceived as more negative than with the immediate environment. In this contingency, negative attitudes, however, do not seem to be very strong.

4. *Far-receiver contingency.* This seems to be by far the most negative organizational communication contingency. Organization members seem to blame distant information sources for almost all communication failures. In contingencies 3 and 4 it is easy to make a distinction between the sender and receiver roles.

In addition to these contingencies there are, of course, many other situational communication systems. Moreover, demographic contingencies also play an important role in organizational communication satisfaction.

Time. In June and January, Japanese businesses typically declare bonuses, thus providing a tremendous economic boost to the Japanese economy. Throughout the country, workers rush to their closest department stores to spend their bonuses on gifts for business and social contacts. It seems that the entire country moves into high gear as part of this elaborate plan to infuse new revenues into the hands of workers—all on a precise schedule. The Japanese appear to manage their time rather than be managed by it, a lesson American businessmen would best heed.

Our studies have shown that information from most major sources in organizations is reduced in quality because of poor timing. Messages typically arrive too early or too late to be of use to employees. Although distant sources (top management) are most guilty, few escape the behavior or its consequences. It seems that "slow news travels down and fast news travels up the organization." In one organization, for example, a middle manager summed up the feelings of most of his colleagues: "It seems that whatever reports or memos I send upstairs just seem to float around and disappear." Our analysis revealed that highly overloaded top managers were deliberately filtering most messages and answering only the most pressing. This is an example of reactive stress because the morale was low and the turnover was rapidly increasing.

Just as *timeliness* has implications for intelligence, so does the *amount of time* spent in various activities. Symptomatic of information overload is the accompanying waste of time sifting through the irrelevant in order to apply the necessary. Such is the case with meetings. No meeting should last more than ninety minutes. After this, fatigue and inattention reduce the quality of decision making. To fully understand the implications of this statement, assume a meeting lasted three hours instead of ninety minutes. Attending this meeting were ten managers whose average salary was $15 an hour. Does the extra ninety minutes produce at least $225 worth of decisions or solved problems? And that's just to break even!

Reducing the amount of time spent on an activity tends to increase the amount of information per unit of time, thus placing potential stress on an already overloaded system. Although most organizations are guilty of reactive hibernation by wasting time with useless meetings, they can create the explosion of reactive stress by suddenly reducing their meeting time to an unrealistically small period of time. This may lead to a harried organizational game destined to produce collapse. For example, when involved in labor negotiations, there's no real way to speed them up because each side ritualistically has to state its position, followed by careful bargaining, compromises, and more bargaining. Reducing the amount of time for such meetings may signal to labor that management isn't taking labor seriously, or worse yet, that management is hurrying because of a weaker position.

Finally, time may be viewed from the sense of *timing*. What is the best time of day or week or year for sending particular messages? One manager announced a new salary schedule, including several cutbacks, only hours before the company picnic. If you feel the timing of messages can be ignored, try to call your boss at home at 11:30 P.M.!

Traditions

A final internal contingency is the traditions, norms, and values of the organization. Establishing an organizational identity helps employees maintain a sense of belonging. Our findings show that most workers are highly satisfied with their organizations as compared to others. Unfortunately, our findings also show that organizations typically do not encourage feedback, input, and criticism, perhaps mistaking disloyalty for valid negative reactions. The proactive organization learns to balance the influence of its traditions and norms against the need to encourage creativity and risk taking.

We have all joked about the key to the executive washroom, reserved parking zones, and dress codes, but the fact remains that these and other traditions are thriving today. In fact, John Molloy has established a new discipline, clothing engineering (along with a new career as a consultant), helping managers conform to the clothing norms of their organization. His general rule is to dress for the person you are trying to influence.

When norms or traditions are blindly followed, without contemporary purpose or rationale, reactive hibernation is the probable consequence.

Such is the case with the United States Congress. Here is a list of just some of the norms and customs permitted today:

1. Free use of the Library of Congress (for Congressmen's children to access for their term papers)
2. Two free potted plants every month
3. Free luggage
4. Tax-free cigarettes
5. Free combs and brushes
6. Subsidized haircuts, shoe shines, and meals
7. Hiring the children and wives of fellow congressmen
8. Free physicals, free lab service, and free funerals
9. Subsidized private hospital room at Walter Reed Hospital
10. Secretaries who shop for congressmen's groceries, clean their houses, and take their cars to be repaired
11. Free car washes, free parking
12. Free WATS lines

Anyone for politics?

As newer, younger members join an organization, its traditions and values tend to change. Even Congress is slowly changing and in 1977 underwent its first major reorganization in its history. Former Secretary of Labor James Hodgson described the youth who are entering today's organizations as better educated and reflecting many of the values of today's youth culture:

I don't mean the subculture of raffish styles and a predilection for pot, although I expect some of them will have these things too. What I do mean is less patience, greater expectations, a heightened interest in innovation and creativity, a desire for a voice in decisions. This group will be the first generation having had wide exposure to career counseling, and they have developed some independent concepts about careers. They will not be industrial hippies but industrial "hopies." *A wise business management will examine their hopes. A competitive edge will flow to those who best meet them.* (Hodgson, 1971)

Hodgson's last words could also have been "proactive coping will lead to greater information power." Tom Clary (1976) has offered us these questions to help a manager cope with the traditions of his or her organization:

1. Where do you want this organization to be ____ years from now?
2. What are the most important changes to be made?
3. What are the desirable directions for growth?

4. What changes in you or in the organization would bring renewed enthusiasm, excitement, and creativity?
5. What changes are you going to begin making?
6. When are you going to start making these changes?
7. Where do you start with the changes?
8. Who is going to be responsible for seeing that you keep on target in making these changes?
9. How will you know when you've made these changes?

EXTERNAL COMMUNICATION CONTINGENCIES

In addition to those factors within the control of the organization but typically beyond the control of the manager are *external contingencies*, typically outside the organizational system. Here we will see, usually more indirectly, the effect on intelligence of such external factors as the economy, current technology, laws, socio/political/cultural influences, and the environment itself.

The Economy

Many managers view the economy as the most critical contingency affecting their organization. Rates of inflation and unemployment affect the size and shape of their labor force, the availability and cost of capital needed for growth and expansion, and their ability to market their stocks and bonds to the investing public. Knowledge of your various financial publics —stockholders, suppliers, customers, financial exchanges, brokerage houses, security analysts, banks, insurance companies, financial publications—can help you cope with traditional economic cycles.

Witness the reactive stress state of most American universities facing the recession of 1974–75. For the first time in their history they were forced to consider wholesale retrenchment, firing of tenured faculty, and phasing out of entire academic programs. When the bottom fell out of New York State's borrowing market, sending credit and bond interest rates skyrocketing, the legislature was forced to cut back the State University of New York budget by several million dollars. Further, the lack of availability of bonds virtually closed down construction on one of the university's newer campuses.

Faced with retrenchment, the university made plans to eliminate programs, faculty, and staff. Thus, economic conditions were affecting goals, outputs, demographics, and even the structure and amount of space of the university. The impact on communication was that already overloaded faculty and administrators were forced to become involved in dozens of new meetings ("What criteria should be used to retrench the department?"), new memoranda ("Here are the reasons why we should survive"), and new lawsuits ("You can't break my contract").

Although the university could have done little to prevent the economic conditions causing their problems, it was guilty of ignoring the crisis until its only option was reactive stress. Contingency plans should have been drawn up in advance of the recession. Intelligence should have been gathered and people's reactions determined. As a result of this experience, most nonprivate universities are now more aware of the limited amount of money in "the pot" and now have lobbying efforts underway to persuade legislators and other donors to give them what they consider their rightful share.

Profit-making organizations have always viewed the economy with respect, probably because of its direct link to their survival, whereas private universities and hospitals, for example, have typically gone through intermediary parties for their major funding. As costs increase dramatically, hospitals must now become more aware of their potential clients (the public) and their competition (other hospitals). They must, as one far-sighted hospital in northern Wisconsin has been doing for three years, regularly survey the public to identify its needs, its preferred services, and its concern for costs versus patient care. Even banks, typically secure in shifting economic conditions, are now engaging in extensive media campaigns to attract new customers and provide new services (supermarket banking, plastic banking).

Technology

> The computer is the first machine that consumes and produces the same material—information. (Jovanovich, 1972)

> Computers can do better than ever what needn't be done at all. Making sense is still a human monopoly. (McLuhan and Nevitt, 1972)

We have already seen how organizations in England and Canada are using new technologies of telecommunications to reduce travel costs brought about by relocating away from metropolitan areas. Technology influences our behavior by creating uncertainty in our organizational lives. We establish Research and Development Departments (R&D) to monitor technology, to help us develop response mechanisms to process the impact of any changes in technologies affecting our organization. But even with sophisticated R&D units, we soon become overloaded because the pace of technological innovation, according to some estimates, is now on a 10–1 scale. This means that one year brings technological changes that would have taken ten years in the past.

A colleague of ours, Tom Porter, has commented on the rate of change in technology:

> Because the information in the scientific and non-scientific world has grown in the last 25 years more than the growth of information since the beginning of time, mankind has been forced to develop technology to understand all the data he has collected from his technology. (Porter, 1975)

A good example of this phenomenon is the computer technology developed to analyze computer networks. The programs which were written produced output of such a complex nature that a new program, using the first one's output as its input, had to be written to interpret the first.

Today's manager must be statistician, accountant, operations researcher, cost-benefit analyst, financial planner, computer programmer, and systems thinker—all in order to cope with the high uncertainty in his technological environment. Not only are computer technologies changing, but also communications and even filing systems are finding new methods of operation. Microfilm now allows organizations to save almost four times their present filing space and eight times the retrieval time, while practically eliminating lost document problems. Telex transmissions allow managers to send business correspondence by telephone, exchanging a small long-distance phone tab for the four-dollar-per-letter processing fee. Word-processing systems, conference calls, video-cartridge memos, and use of recorded telephone messages all contribute to this new communication environment.

How effective is the use of these new developments? The answer is that we don't know because they're too new and the research isn't in yet. However, we do know some things in general about communication channels and specifically about the telephone. Swedish researcher Bertil Thorngren (1977) has compared the telephone with face-to-face contacts, and among his findings are:

1. The telephone is used mostly for short events (under ten minutes) involving two people with almost no planning time preceding the event.
2. People are more likely to use the telephone *either* to give (usually) *or* to receive information, and to use face-to-face contacts for a mutual exchange of information.
3. The telephone contact is typically limited to one question, whereas face-to-face contacts are used for either one or several questions.
4. Telephones are used for more regular contacts (daily, weekly), whereas face-to-face contacts are used to establish new contacts.

Our own research has shown that most employees in organizations receive adequate information through impersonal channels (including the telephone), but there is a greater need for more information through face-to-face contact.

Although we cannot yet offer conclusions about the effectiveness of most newer technologies, we can raise some questions which should be answered before installing new devices:

1. Do you need it?
2. Can you afford it?
3. Will it cause more problems than benefits?
4. Will your people use it?
5. Will the technology create people problems?
6. Can you determine exactly what the net return on your investment will be with it? Is that return sufficient?

Failure to provide honest answers to the above questions may lead to the kind of reactive stress that plagued a manufacturing company whose new WATS lines cost more money in lost time ("After all, it's free, why not use the phone!"), whose new automatic typewriters failed to produce better results than the old form letter, and whose computer was inadequate to handle the company's information system.

One of our clients, a manufacturer of automobile radiators, recently installed a new computer system and hired a highly trained EDP (electronic data-processing) staff. Within their first month on the job, the EDP staff had scheduled workshops for potential computer users to explain the best strategies to minimize distortion and misunderstanding between them and EDP. Such proactive behavior, even in a relaxed condition, helped that company prepare for later heavy demands on EDP brought about by the last recession.

A final note on technology. After watching the lengthy silence, created by faulty equipment, during the first 1976 presidential debate, Marshall McLuhan stated, "the medium has revolted against the message."

Laws

While attempting to bring some computer cards across the Canadian border to a colleague's university, we were stopped by a Canadian customs agent who asked us if we had anything of value on the cards. We replied that it was just some information for a journal article and the agent insisted that we pay a duty on the cards. We protested that we had not purchased the cards, nor were we going to sell them in Canada, but the agent persisted. Finally, out of frustration, we asked the agent just how he was going to assess a duty and he smiled, "Why, by the pound, of course."

Just as we were harassed by a minor technicality in Canadian customs law, so are hundreds of organizations confronted with local, state, and federal laws and regulations, many of which have direct implications for their very survival. Ten years ago, OSHA, ERISA, ESOP, EEOC were unknown, but today they affect millions of people and account for billions of dollars in "compliance money."

No organization seems able to escape the long arm of the law. Pharmaceutical companies must clear all potential carcinogens with the FDA; utility companies must seek approval for rate increases from their Public Service Commission; automobile manufacturers must conform to EPA specifications for emission standards, while attempting to meet other guidelines governing fuel economy; and school systems must conform to HEW guidelines for desegregation. In Albuquerque, building heights are regulated by the City Council (to protect the view of the mountains), and in Virginia tobacco companies are forced by federal law to print warnings on all cigarette packages.

Jack Anderson has estimated that it costs $100 billion dollars annually to fill out the forms to comply with just the federal regulations, enough money to create 3 million permanent jobs in private industry. Businesses currently fill out 114 million forms every year just to communicate with the government (at a cost of $40 billion). Most large organizations now employ full-time public affairs specialists who monitor changing government regulations and large corporate legal staffs to protect their interests in the face of these regulations. Only recently did OSHA (Occupational Safety and Health Administration) drop its requirement that toilet seats have a gap in front!

Laws and Organizational Intelligence. Naturally, many laws and regulations are necessary to protect us as consumers and workers. For example ERISA (Employee Retirement Income Security Act) requires organizations *completely* and *clearly* to provide information about its benefits plans. Most of the OSHA regulations are designed to protect worker safety on the job. Affirmative action is intended to guarantee every person, regardless of race, creed or color, the opportunity to gain employment. Finally, with the recent revelations about illegal campaign contributions and bribery of foreign governments, more and more stockholders are demanding that their executives maintain a high ethical and moral posture, in addition to a legal one.

One of the best ways an organization can demonstrate conformity to a particular law is by written records (minutes, training records, reports, logs, posted instructions, memoranda). Some questions you may want to ask about your organization to determine the amount of proactive coping it is doing as the laws create more uncertainty are:

1. How much does your organization spend each year to comply with local, state, and federal regulations?
2. What are the potential effects on your organization of increased regulation in such areas as environmental standards? energy policies? antitrust laws? interstate commerce? airline rates? employee safety? employee hiring?
3. Has your organization developed a code of ethics for its personnel which bars illegal gifts at home and overseas?
4. Does your organization have adequate internal controls to prevent or detect illegal or questionable payments, fraud, inventory shortages, and accounting errors?

Socio/Political/Cultural Factors

The laws to which most organizations conform were brought about typically by social, cultural, or political influences from within the environment. For example, the EEOC (the Equal Employment Opportunity Commission) evolved after several turbulent years of black unrest. Environmental groups' lobbying and protest efforts preceded many of the EPA restrictions and pollution controls. Individual managers should be aware of these influences and how they specifically affect their daily jobs. This monitoring of such differences is particularly important for the large multinational corporation.

While we were probably shocked initially by the bribery scandals involving Lockheed Aircraft and the Japanese government, students of Japanese politics and culture were probably far less surprised. Influence peddling in Japan has been part of the accepted norm of doing business for years. Japanese workers qualify for the better jobs according to the amount of high-quality education they have and who they know. Friends are always rewarded during the gift-giving season immediately following the bonuses.

Another difference between Japanese and American organizations is the former's preoccupation with group involvement and consensus-seeking behavior in decision making. Japanese businessmen emphasize analysis of problems, whereas Americans emphasize the solution. Because of the frequent opportunities for input and because of the attempts to provide Japanese workers with almost lifetime security with one company, many Japanese workers, when asked who they work for, answer proudly, "I'm a _____ man!"

When we were studying a bilingual hospital in Canada, we discovered some significant differences between French- and English-speaking workers in their communication attitudes and preferences:

1. Francophones (F's) were more satisfied than Anglophones (A's) with information they received about their specific jobs.
2. F's were more satisfied than A's with their opportunity to send information upward to management; F's viewed this as more important than did A's.
3. F's were more satisfied with those channels of communication used to disseminate information to larger groups of people (newsletters, films).
4. F's were more satisfied than the A's with their job, particularly with the intrinsic and interpersonal factors and the overall communication efforts of the organization.
5. Overall, F's were more satisfied with the communication environment of their organization than the A's and viewed it as more important to them in the conduct of their daily jobs.

Roy Foltz (1973) tells us about the time that the General Electric Company began operations in Europe, and "it tried to run its French computer plant just as it ran its Phoenix plant. All was well until GE tried to lay off a few hundred French workers. The action caused a national labor crisis and a leading French newspaper ran a black-bordered editorial entitled, 'France is not Phoenix' on the front page." In Mexico, American workers soon learn not to conduct business in the afternoon during siesta period, and visiting Germany or Scandinavian countries reveals a very close relationship between labor unions and the respective governments.

Not only are organizations composed of networks of people who must adapt to foreign cultures and political systems, but when you consider that an organization like AT&T has more than one million employees, you are also dealing with a separate subculture, with its own norms, values, and attitudes.

Several organizations today recognize their social responsibility toward the community with which they interact. For example, IBM for years has been supporting two small schools in North Carolina and Texas. Mobil has been publishing a series of advocacy advertisements (discussing strong politically oriented issues), and Equitable Assurance Society more recently began this same strategy. In addition to the public relations benefits, the organization is also using the opportunity to get a closer reading on the pulse of its community, information it can readily use in predicting environmental trends.

Environment

Organizations today, in addition to attending to their social responsibility, are attending to the overall quality of life of their employees and their families and community. More and more attention is being spent on problems of pollution (air and water) and on the ecology of the land on which the organization exists. Another environmental concern today, perhaps among the most important, is the amount of energy available to fuel the machinery and heat the buildings of our organizations. One Senate study indicated that world energy supplies will fall below demand in 1981!

When discussing energy, the case of Amcord Cement Company presents a good example of proactive coping with the energy crisis. Roland Speers, president of Amcord, indicates how intelligence was carefully collected, evaluated, and made useful to the decision-making process:

> Remember when people called natural gas our cheapest, most abundant fuel? We gambled $9.5 million that they were wrong (converting from gas to coal). A railroad marshaling yard able to handle a 100-car unit train, unload it, and have it back on the main track in four hours flat; and storage bins, conveyer equipment, and grinding mills that prepare the coal to burn in the kilns were both purchased. When we made this decision, I spent a lot of sleepless nights. The cost was considerable and when I looked around, no one else was doing what we were doing. My God, I thought, am I out on a limb by myself?" In the fall of 1973 the Arabs made us look good. (Speers, 1977)

Other organizations considering conversion may want to ask:

1. How much energy does the plant use? What kind of fuel? At what cost?
2. How price-critical is the fuel? (Can the organization be hurt by a competitor with lower fuel costs?)
3. How close is the plant to a coal-producing region? (Transportation costs mount quickly.)

Another environmental element to be carefully considered is the weather. The winter snowstorm of 1977 was cause for several alterations in organizational communication systems. As schools and hospitals closed, they needed to inform parents and children. As the city of Buffalo, worst hit in the United States, was totally immobilized, snowmobiles became the primary means of transportation—which meant organizations with employees stranded at work would have to identify and borrow (or rent or buy) available equipment. Informal communication networks (social as well as rumor) were rapidly established to handle the overload associated with the sudden lack of stability in the weather.

ASSESSING COMMUNICATION CONTINGENCIES

Organizational intelligence is not easily obtained. It takes commitment and hard work on the part of managers serious about proactive coping. Although we explore ways to develop intelligence systems in Part Three of this book, we close this chapter with a test which will quickly and simply indicate the total impact of critical contingencies on a given organization.

For each of the following questions, select the one best choice that represents the organization today, then add up the values for all ten questions. The total score is the organization's current communication contingency score. The higher the score, the more the organization is currently being affected by critical internal and external communication

FIGURE 2-3. CONTINGENCY ANALYSIS TEST

None	To a very little extent	To a little extent	To some extent	To a great extent	To a very great extent
0	1	2	3	4	5

Internal Contingencies

1. To what extent is your organization currently undergoing any changes in its organizational structure?____
2. To what extent is your organization currently undergoing any changes in the diversity or quality of its products and/or services?____
3. To what extent does your organization's work force vary in its demographic composition?____
4. To what extent is your organization currently being affected by any spatiotemporal factors?____
5. To what extent is your organization currently undergoing any changes in its traditions?____

External Contingencies

6. To what extent do quarterly changes in the current economy affect your organization?____
7. To what extent do current technological changes (innovations or advances) affect your organization?____
8. To what extent do changes in local, state, or federal laws affect your organization?____
9. To what extent do current socio/political/cultural changes affect your organization.____
10. To what extent do changes in the environment affect your organization?____

contingencies—and consequently the greater the need to have a highly developed communication system so that the organization may enjoy proactive coping instead of reactive stress.

Guidelines for Interpreting Scores

    0–10 Almost no effect of contingencies upon your organization; a highly stable environment

  11–20 Little effect of contingencies upon your organization; moderately stable environment

  21–30 Some effect of contingencies upon your organization; somewhat uncertain environment

  31–40 Great effect of contingencies upon your organization; uncertain environment

  41–50 Very great effect of contingencies upon your organization; highly uncertain environment

The Next Step

The challenge awaiting those who appreciate the need to manage power in their organization has been succinctly expressed by Salancik and Pfeffer (1977):

> The real trick to managing power in organizations is to ensure somehow that leaders cannot be unaware of the realities of their environments and cannot avoid changing to deal with those realities.

Part Two (the next four chapters) is designed to remedy any "unawareness" the manager or future manager may have about the information and communication environments in his or her organization. We believe that if these "unawarenesses" can be identified and explained, then the probability of effective managerial proactive coping will be immensely increased.

part two

Information and Communication in Managerial Work

Personal Variables

INTRODUCTION

> In this "information economy," information itself is the chief lever of power. . . . Organizations are really information-processing systems, and the men who get power are the ones who learn how to filter the incredible flow of information into a meaningful pattern. (Bennis, 1976)

Most managers today would hardly disagree with Bennis's claim that (*a*) information is a chief power lever, (*b*) organizations are information-processing systems, and (*c*) the individuals who obtain power are those who are capable of sorting the incredible maze of information they deal with into a meaningful pattern.

Most managers today would also heartily subscribe to Harold Wilensky's view of the current knowledge explosion:

> The knowledge explosion intensifies an old problem: how to draw good intelligence from a highly compartmentalized body of knowledge and get it into a room where decisions are made. Sources of failure are legion: even if the initial message is accurate, clear, timely,

and relevant, it may be translated, condensed, or completely blocked by personnel standing between the sender and the intended receiver; it may go through in distorted form. If the receiver is in a position to use the message, he may screen it out because it does not fit his preconceptions; because it has come through a suspicious or poorly-regarded channel, because it is imbedded in piles of inaccurate or useless messages (excessive noise in the channel), or simply, because too many messages are transmitted to him (information overload). (Wilensky, 1967)

In spite of the fact that most managers today agree with these claims and warnings, because they experience them in one shape or form almost daily on their jobs, it is sadly true that information and communication in managerial work remain, at best, poorly understood subjects.

We propose to untangle some of the unnecessary complexity that continues to add confusion in the mind of the serious practitioner in connection with the means by which efficient and effective organizational information processing can be accomplished. We are reminded in this regard of a description given to us recently of organizational information/communication specialists: "If you took all these specialists in the world and laid them end to end, they would still be unable to reach a conclusion."

No doubt this is a valid charge. As Peter Drucker (1973) remarks about communication in particular: "In no other areas have intelligent men and women worked harder or with greater dedication than psychologists, human relations experts, managers, and management students have worked on improving communications in our major institutions." Drucker adds that while we have learned a lot, we have not yet learned enough because most organizations continue to be plagued by thorny communication problems.

OVERVIEW

The approach of this chapter and the three that follow is based upon four assumptions gleaned from previous research and our experience as consultants to business, educational, and governmental organizations:

1. *From an information viewpoint, today's organization has never been more complex.* Even small organizations are finding that they need more sophisticated information-processing techniques; toward this end they are hiring more highly educated managers and are relying more greatly on the use of computer hardware and software technology. This is occurring not only because business in general is becoming more complex, but also

because the environment within which business must thrive is demanding a more sophisticated response. (On the one end of the continuum you find the complicated machinery of governmental rules and regulations, and on the other end you find a more vociferous public expressing its demands through consumer interest groups and political lobbies.)

2. *The magnitude of the management problem in this era of accelerated information complexity continues to threaten the survival potential of the modern organization.* In 1964 John Diebold's book *Beyond Automation* caused considerable reaction in the business community. At a time when the industrial world was just becoming accustomed to the new technology, here was an expert who was claiming that their problems had just begun— and that the problems did not involve automation per se. With considerable insight and foresight, Diebold identified four emerging problems that an increasing rate of technological change would bring to management.

First, he pointed out that the *planning process* will emerge as a prominent activity linked with the success or failure of business, especially planning by management for constant change. He cited four reasons for this: (*a*) the shortening of product life as a result of technological innovation; (*b*) the shortening of management's reaction time because of new product developments as well as accelerated product obsolescence; (*c*) the shortened life of business and industrial processes due to innovations created by improved information-processing technology; and (*d*) the increased complexity of managing the necessary functional interrelationships within the organization and with other organizations to keep pace with rapid technological innovation.

Second, Diebold foresaw that the effective management of creative and service personnel (we would add: of staff in general) would become an important prerequisite for business success. In his words:

> The problems in this area are substantial and numerous. One is that the product, *an idea*, is so difficult to schedule; another is that scientists tend to direct their prime loyalty to their professions, rather than to their employees; a third is the magnitude of the task of integrating what must remain individualized effort; and a fourth, the *lack of standards* to measure performance. (Diebold, 1964; italics added)

In short, he recognized that the human integration side of the new technology was adding a new dimension to the concept of general management. Today, we do indeed find a greater reliance upon technicians, scientists, and staff specialists than ever before in our industrial history. While this tremendous shift in the employment structure is accepted as a necessity, there is scant evidence to suggest that management techniques have been correspondingly altered to resolve the problems that this new structure brings—one of which is the manufacture and consumption of a vast array of complex information.

Third, Diebold warned that many business concepts must change. He cites several examples, most of which have indeed since succumbed to the forces of change. For instance, due to the increasing unavailability of capital in conjunction with the massive capital investments needed by business to support technological change, a return-on-investment-and-asset-management yardstick is no longer just an interesting accounting calculation; it is vital to a firm's survival.

The 1960s witnessed the so-called go-go overnight growth of giant conglomerates whose assets in many instances represented little more than the value of the paper on which they were specified. Growth for growth's sake was the theme; as we know, however, this philosophy was short-lived. Now businesses are heeding Peter Drucker's (1973) warning that "you must define who you are first"—instead of afterwards. This exercise is causing the business of today to establish clearly defined strategies with very-long-term implications; to search out, assimilate, digest, and act upon information related to profitability, markets, competition, ecological trends, governmental mandates regarding products, distribution, manufacturing techniques, employment conditions and international trade regulations.

And as we witness the redefinition of many traditional concepts of private enterprise, we are also witnessing another change that Diebold accurately predicted: the composition and skill base of middle management is enlarging to meet the complicated information needs of the modern organization. With this enlargement, new problems have been created, but the challenge that looms above all is the need to equip this group with efficient and effective information-processing techniques that will enable them to continue to meet organizational goals and objectives.

The fourth problem Diebold anticipated was that the new technology would change the process of management. Information systems have already been developed which Diebold said would "transcend the compartmentalized structure of business organization." In large organizations, the use of management information systems is no longer a luxury; likewise, in the late 1970s there have been tremendous advances in word-processing technology, which allows management to produce, store, and retrieve needed information at a rate double that which was possible at the time Diebold wrote his book in 1964.

Finally, Diebold stresses throughout his book that the advent of the new technology will cause problems of human displacement in organizations. Former organization roles which were sanctified will give way to the formation of temporary management roles to confront the never-ending stream of contingencies demanding special expertise that the organization confronts. We see this happening now, and it is not just the large organization which has had to adapt. In the process, however, we also see evidence of continued management dissatisfaction; we also sense the emergence of a new organizational movement which many are terming "small is beautiful." In short, we find ample evidence which indicates that the human factor has not been managed as nearly successfully as has the advent of modern technology itself.

3. *Management's information environment will continue to become more complicated, and the real challenge facing management in the 1980s will be to control information, not be controlled by it.*

This assumption gets to the very heart of our concern. What can management do to increase the probability that it will control the vast amount of information the organization must use to survive and prevent that same information from controlling the organization to the point of the organization's extinction?

Many managers have complained to us that they expend unnecessary time and energy reacting or responding to organizational crises, many of which can be traced to communication and information breakdowns. These same managers add that they characterize effective management in terms of its ability to proact and anticipate organizational problems, opportunities, and challenges, rather than the reverse.

Finally, it has been our observation that the answer to these problems will not be found by simply adding more technologically sophisticated information hardware and software to the organization's existing library of automated machine technology.

The answer, we believe, will be found by alerting management to the human causes of the information problems it encounters. Once these human causes are understood, then management can take proactive steps to reduce and eliminate the threats which an uncontrolled organizational information environment produces. In this chapter and the succeeding three, we will outline the critical factors that are often the root causes of an uncontrolled organizational information environment.

4. *A preeminent, emerging condition to an uncontrolled organizational information explosion is the growing inability of management to cope with and tolerate the ravaging effects of information overload.*

The term *information overload* here refers to the total complex of information acquisition and dissemination activities that most organizations experience. While precise documentation does not exist, we estimate that better than 50 percent of an organization's information requirements do not bear directly on the chief output of the organization—whether it be in the form of goods or services. The record-keeping function alone of the average organization has reached staggering proportions. Compliance with government (state and federal) regulations adds an awesome quantity to this percentage. Besides record-keeping and governmental compliance, most organizations devote considerable information output to the maintenance of goodwill among suppliers, customers, and intermediaries, as well as the public at large.

Besides these functions, the use of information internally by the organization is the main artery by which it meets organizational goals and objectives, by which it meets the needs of its organization members; in short, the main artery by which it succeeds or flounders and fails.

The goal of information usage is accuracy. This is accomplished by insuring that messages reach the appropriate individuals or organizational units in a manner that they will be understood. Achieving this accuracy objective, however, usually entails the dissemination of more than one message. More messages—redundancy, as it is called—increases the probability that the message will be received by the target audience and understood. Paradoxically, more messages also increase the flooding of communication channels and increase the likelihood of information overload.

To cope with this paradoxical situation, managers are urged to keep their messages brief; to economize in their use of communication channels, and, following the well-known "exception principle," to report only significant variances from standard. And yet these very actions—respecting brevity and communicating only exceptions—increase the probability that accuracy and completeness will be lost, that misunderstandings will occur.

Complicating this picture—which most managers can testify to as continuing sources of frustration in their jobs—is the *serial transmission* phenomenon; that is, the content of a message will undergo alteration as it moves further away from its original source. This occurs both by omission and distortion of message detail and is closely associated with another message phenomenon termed by March and Simon (1958) "uncertainty absorption." This phenomenon represents a human defense against information overload—at the cost, unfortunately, of message accuracy. What happens is that the person closest to the facts relating to a message has the most knowledge of the nuances and uncertainties associated with the message. As the message progresses to others, however, this knowledge is inadvertently diminished in transmission.

The usual organizational response to information overload is not at all encouraging. Portions of the message are omitted; errors are made in deciphering the message; portions of the message are set aside to be used at a later time (which can be an effective tactic; all too often, however, that which is set aside for later use is forgotten or simply misplaced); portions of the message are psychologically filtered to conform with one's own expectations of what the message should be; the message is approximated because details are unknown; or the person simply "escapes"—refuses to acknowledge or act upon the message.

Information overload, we think, will be the major information challenge facing the organizations of tomorrow. We believe the case of too much information will severely aggravate other communication and information problems in organizations. We use the term *aggravate* selectively, because there is no empirical evidence or practical experience to conclude that the information overload problem will be the only cause of other communication and information difficulties that organizations will experience.

Prolific information that taxes the information-tolerance limits of organizations is *likely* to be related to:

a. more arbitrary decisions by managers about the relevance and utility of organizational information;
b. a greater incidence of misplacement of significant organizational information;
c. a greater inability by management to differentiate between information that needs to be stored for future use and information that is needed to meet a current organizational contingency;
d. a greater preponderance of distrust of message sources and message carriers, whether human or nonhuman; and
e. a greater variation in the meaning of organizational messages as intended by message originators and decoded by message receivers.

Any one or all of these conditions will undoubtedly diminish the ability of the organization to respond to the heavy information demands of its internal and external environments. We can now turn to a discussion of the prerequisites we believe are essential for insuring that an organization, regardless of its size, establish and maintain a *controlled* information environment.

INFORMATION AND COMMUNICATION

We will be using the terms *information, information processing*, and *communication* throughout our discussions of factors which bear on an organization's ability to control its information environment. Before we proceed, it is important that our usage of these terms be understood.

The Concept "Information"

We asked a random sample of twenty managers drawn from five medium-sized U.S. companies to tell us what the term *information* means to them. Here are some representative comments:

Information is a piece of knowledge.

Information is an idea, opinion, feeling, or fact.

Information is something that precedes action.

Information is something that has the quality of being true or false, correct or incorrect, timely or untimely, relevant or irrelevant, and vague or precise.

Information is something that helps to eliminate "second-guessing."

Information is a unit of something to which humans assign meaning.

Information is something that stands by itself.

Information is the means by which humans and machines exert control over themselves and their environment.

Not surprisingly, these descriptions are all basically accurate. Peter Drucker (1973), also speaking from the viewpoint of the manager, states that "information is logic. As such information is purely formal and has no meaning. It is impersonal rather than interpersonal." He goes on to point out that the more information can be freed of the human component that acts upon it—that is, freed of emotions and values—the more valid and reliable it becomes.

Unfortunately, everything we have said so far might lead one to believe that information is a "thing," consisting of several mysterious properties. More formally, the concept "information" has importance to the manager only if it is viewed as a total process. The following steps illustrate what we mean by *information process*:

Step 1. There can be no information unless there is some system (human, mechanical, electronic) to receive it. For several thousand years, it has been debated whether there is any sound if a tree falls in a forest and there is no one there to hear it. The correct answer, in terms of our definition of information, is no. In other words, without a receiving system, information is nothing more than a change in some energy pattern. So the minimum requirement for information is that (*a*) there exist a receiver for the information and (*b*) there be some use of energy to transfer the information to the receiver.

Step 2. After information has been received, it is processed in the *control system* of the receiver. The control system (brain in a human) extracts information and then uses or rejects that extracted information immediately. Using information that is extracted is accomplished through a short-term-memory system (in humans, our consciousness), which has a rather limited information-handling capacity. In fact, it has been determined that the average human being can process no more than ten bits of information at a time, or somewhere between five to ten words simultaneously. After short-term-memory processing has occurred, the information in some form is passed on into long-term memory or is rejected. What goes into long-term memory are not words per se, but ideas and meanings.

Step 3. Only after information has been extracted in the manner described can we talk about the *value* of the information to the receiving system. At this point, we can consider the information's meaning and the way that the receiving system intends to use the information. In terms of our total information-processing activities, many researchers believe that information obtains value for the receiver as a consequence of how a piece of information interfaces between short- and long-term memory. It is this interplay that allows us to put the information to use.

Step 4. Finally, the control system of the receiver constantly uses *feedback*—both from the control system itself and from the external environment—to regulate the information-processing activity. This feedback is critical to the control mechanism's ability to accomplish the entire information-processing event; without it, information processing would be impossible.

Wiio has developed a simple equation that summarizes our four steps:

$$1_P = f(C, 1_c, 1_v)$$

The equation states that the information process (1_p) is a function of three components. First, a receiving system, the human being, for instance, receives signals (C), which carry information. The brain (neurological mechanisms) undergoes changes as it responds to these signals which constitute the processing of raw information (1_c). When 1_c is processed further as short-term and long-term memory interface with one another, *information with value* (1_v) is produced. Throughout this activity, feedback is used by the control system to regulate the process. In other words, the entire information process involves (1) input information, (2) process information, (3) output information, and (4) feedback information.

Why is it important to understand how humans process information—especially from the manager's viewpoint? There are two reasons. First, when we typically envision information problems in organizations, common experience leads us to consider difficulties that occur *after* a message is communicated and *before* it is received. As Wilensky suggested earlier, the sources of failure are legion—and include information blockage, filtering, distortion, and overload.

In short, we tend to view information problems as a category of happenings in organizations that somehow are symptomatic of system shortcomings, not individual shortcomings. What our approach to information processing would tell the manager is this: *Information is always and inevitably generated by the receiver system itself.* To the extent that human receivers recognize this very important information-processing property, then the likelihood that information problems and breakdown will be avoided or circumvented is increased a hundredfold.

Why is this so? We have found that if managers exercise the same caution in generating information for consumption by others as they do in processing information received from others, then the effectiveness of their information systems is immensely enhanced.

A second reason for understanding how humans process information is that there is a remarkable similarity between human information processing in particular and the activity of complex organizations in general. For example, humans *input* information; so do organizations. Humans process information and assign a value to it; so do organizations. Humans act upon or output the information that has been processed; likewise, organizations act upon processed information in the form of decisions or choices. Finally, humans use feedback to regulate their information-processing activities; and organizations, too, use feedback to measure the results of their information application.

So to the extent that the manager can understand and appreciate the strengths and weaknesses associated with human information processing, we believe that this knowledge and experience will enable him to better grasp the reasons why his own organization's information-control systems are or are not functioning up to their full potential.

The Concept "Communication"

Consistent with our approach to information, Wiio (1975) believes that if we view information processing in a system sense (meaning there are inputs, throughputs, and outputs), then it seems plausible that the concept "communication *system*" would be parallel. Thus, we might say that a communication system includes the sender (information source, originator, or relay), some means of carrying the information (air waves, the five senses, wires, or any other conducting medium), and the receiver.

Both the sender and the receiver influence the information-processing activity of one another's control systems and do so primarily through self- and other-generated feedback. Inherent in the communication *system* concept is the presence of "noise." Noise manifests itself in many forms but always interferes with the information-processing activity of both the sender and the receiver.

Thus, when we ask the question, "How can we distinguish between information as a concept and communication as a concept?" our approach up to this point would be simply: *Anytime the information is initiated or commenced by another control system, we have an instance of communication.*

This means, then, that communication helps us to activate our information-processing activities; similarly, the activation of information processing in the human is usually associated with a concurrent or subsequent act of communication. There are obvious reasons why the total information-processing–communication system can break down or become inoperative. It is not especially important to be able to say that one causes the other per se; what is important is to understand that information processing and communication are truly interdependent, in that the dynamics of one always influences the dynamics of the other.

MAKING THE RECEIVER THE KEY

Our focus on the *receiver* of communication is not accidental. An example should make this clear. If I have a message which I wish to communicate, I must first engage in an information-processing activity to properly frame that message for the receiver; as is often the case, I may select the wrong frame for my receiver, but at this point have no knowledge of it.

Next, I select a channel to carry my message to the receiver. (We'll use the term *channel* loosely to mean face-to-face or physically removed from the immediate presence of the intended receiver—e.g., a memo, phone call, a letter, teletype, closed-circuit TV, a cassette recording.) Again, as is often the case, I may select the inappropriate channel for the message I wish to communicate.

Finally, the receiver comes into the picture. Up to this point, I have no information to use which will tell me whether my message got through—as intended—and was understood in the way that I intended. The only way I can obtain this information is by acquiring solicited or unsolicited feedback from the receiver. In short, it is the receiver who can tell me if (*a*) I framed my message correctly, (*b*) I used the right channel, and (*c*) my message was decoded (interpreted) as I intended it to be. Put slightly differently, it is the receiver—and only the receiver—who can tell me how closely matched our information-processing systems were for the message in question. This is why we firmly believe that the first step an organization must take in gaining control of its information environment is *to concentrate on the information recipient*—not on its exotic communication or information technology, and certainly not on the information itself. We believe this concentration will produce an entirely different perspective on managing the information crises, and especially the case of too much information, that the organization will continue to confront in the future.

For the remainder of this chapter, selected *personal variables* will be examined which tie directly into an individual's and organization's capacity to manage its information systems effectively—in light of the four assumptions we have made in the "Overview" section of this chapter. The next chapters will look at what we term *relational variables* in the same context. Finally, Chapter 6 will discuss several *organizational characteristics* which bear on an organization's *proactive capability* to manage its systems of information.

In each situation, our discussion will reflect what we perceive to be an educated and experienced-based bias: that the strangling realities of information overload are commanding and will continue to command the closest attention by organization managements; *that to exercise control over this information phenomenon is the first step toward resolving the information complexities and uncertainties that the future will bring.*

GAINING CONTROL OF INFORMATION IN THE ORGANIZATION: PERSONAL VARIABLES

By *personal variables*, we simply mean those important individual characteristics that are likely to vary considerably from one person to the next. The processing of information by individuals is an extremely private matter. Its occurrence can be substantiated only after the fact insofar as human diagnostic ability is concerned. Technology has advanced to the point where we can trace this processing activity in humans to some extent, under carefully controlled and medically supervised conditions, but in general we must rely upon the action taken by the individual in response to an information input to make any statement at all about the quality or capability of that private activity.

The personal variables which we believe especially germane to a discussion of the case of too much information include: (*a*) the individual's *cognitive complexity*; (*b*) the individual's *personality*; (*c*) the individual's *past experience* with the information stimulus; and (*d*) the individual's personal *motivation, need, and goal* configuration.

Cognitive Complexity

It is axiomatic that the less cognitively complex a person, the greater the probability that too much information at a relatively low input level will produce an *immobilized* reaction. The most visible sign of such an occurrence in a person who is cognitively "noncomplex" is a stoic—almost deadpan—expression when confronted by others in need of a decision by the individual. Defining the less cognitively complex person is difficult. Psychological assessments are helpful here but not infallible. Identifying someone who *may become* immobilized with the advent of too much information is somewhat easier and more reliable. Table 3-1 lists several

**TABLE 3-1. SYMPTOMS OF INFORMATION OVERLOAD IN RELATION
TO COGNITIVE COMPLEXITY**

Situation	Symptom*
1. Attention to inconsequential trivia which are not germane to issue/project or event under consideration.	Claims that an "important" aspect of the issue/project or event has been overlooked; refuses to accept the belief of others that the aspect is *unimportant*.
2. Obvious use of vague, imprecise, and general statements lacking in substantive content.	When asked to express an opinion or take a position and justify such, uses broad and abstract language that leaves others wondering what the individual's position or opinion really is.
3. Takes no action or makes no decision or fails to solve an assigned problem.	Observable lack of performance in action/decision or problem solving with no acceptable explanation for unsatisfactory performance.
4. Postponement of action or decision while allegedly waiting for more information that is relevant to the action or decision.	Unexplainable procrastination which others believe is *not* due to a lack of necessary information to resolve the situation.
5. Failure to discriminate positive and negative qualities, to see advantages and disadvantages, pros and cons, and strengths and weaknesses.	Tends to group things together in arriving at a judgment which others feel should not be grouped together; holds to one interpretation and refuses to see merit in other interpretations; declines to weigh opposite points of view.
6. Reluctance to explain or justify action taken or decisions made in writing.	Has difficulty crystallizing and synthesizing thoughts; tends to fragment important information rather than integrate into a cohesive whole; unable to summarize positions reached in no more than a few paragraphs or one or two pages.
7. Overattention to familiar detail and underattention to unfamiliar detail.	In both oral and written communication tends to report or stress information that fits comfortably within a perspective that closely matches personal past experience and knowledge.
8. Inability to meet assigned deadlines (projects, reports, actions, suggestions).	General personal disorganization: verbal complaints of insufficient time; long working hours with no results; unkempt personal office surroundings; devotes excessive time in search for information.

Table 3-1. Continued

Situation	Symptom*
9. Forgetfulness—forgets plans, policies, work procedures, and rules, as well as issues and actions for which previous agreement has been achieved by work group or decision unit.	Suffers lapses of memory with no plausible explanation, especially with respect to information inputs that should not have to be committed to memory deliberately for subsequent action recall.
10. Inability to separate cause from effect, antecedent event from consequent event, supporting arguments from major arguments.	Observable faults or breaks in reasoning style; use of non sequiturs; unusual adherence to feelings ("gut" emotions) as the primary vehicle by which information is diagnosed and acted upon.
11. Inability to work effectively on several projects or tasks simultaneously.	Tends to miscalculate priorities; seems grounded to the task itself for the sake of the task—not in terms of its prioritized importance.
12. Inability to immediately reconstruct oral directives, instructions, reports, or meeting content; perception of an information event differs from the common perception shared by other participants to that event.	Misrepresents ideas and information supplied by others immediately following exposure to idea and information sources. In spite of note taking or the use of other recording aids, this symptom may still be recognizable.

We are using the word symptom in a general sense; we could also use the term indicator to stress the point that these twelve situations are usually accompanied by some warning devices which indicate that a manager's information-processing system is being taxed to its cognitively capable limits.

symptoms which should alert the manager to the fact that the individual—himself or herself included—is, due to limitations in personal cognitive equipment, suffering from *overload*.

We could devote considerable space to the provision of detailed examples that would dramatize each one of the twelve situations identified in Table 3-1. Such an exercise, while helpful in some respects, would not do much, however, to underscore the point Table 3-1 makes: *A cognitively inferior manager is highly susceptible to overloading of his information-processing capability*. Once overloaded, his mental functioning and personal organizational effectiveness begin to rapidly deteriorate. The wrong decisions are made or no decisions are made at all. Important information becomes lost among the trivial. In short, the ability to react decisively within one's assigned area of management responsibility becomes severely impaired. For those who wish to further their understanding of general cognitive mechanisms affecting information-processing capabilities, Table 3-2 lists seven typical cognitively ascribed information errors, with each error's cause identified, in conjunction with an associated possible remedy.

TABLE 3-2. DIAGNOSING SYSTEMS OF COGNITION/PERCEPTION

Error	Probable cause	Possible remedy
1. Attributing cause-effect (problem/solution) explanation to events or occurrences because they are proximate in time or space.	Cognitive proximity mechanism	Seek alternative explanations in the form of verifiable data and evidence from the environment or from impartial sources. Assume multiple causes and multiple effects.
2. Attributing cause-effect explanations to events or occurrences that seem similar physically or psychologically.	Cognitive similarity mechanism	Search out dissimilar events and occurrences which might be explained by the same attributed phenomena; discount previous experience as the obvious explanation for concurrent phenomena.
3. Ignoring significant information and apprehending insignificant or irrelevant information.	Cognitive apprehension mechanism	Establish numeric or alphabetic codes for significant information and implement feedback systems to verify information apprehension. Apply the "exception" principle whereby insignificant information is preempted; position significant information with commonly known cognitions; limit the number of significant apprehension (whole-message) units to seven or less in written transmissions and three or less in oral (nonrecorded) transmissions.
4. Selecting those characteristics of an event or situation which are congruent with one's expectations or existing cognitive structure.	Selective or distorted perceptual mechanism	Confirm or disconfirm perception with other sources. Select more than one perspective as means for analyzing information. Use a simple mnemonic self-check: "Am I hearing what I want to hear, seeing what I want to see?"
5. Assuming that similar units of information appearing together necessarily form a composite that yields a homogeneous whole.	Cognitive assimilation mechanism	Segregate the information content of significant messages into mutually exclusive or overlapping categories, each of which is scrutinized for its relevance to any conclusions drawn from the original intact message.
6. Assuming that dissimilar units of information appearing together are necessarily incompatible to form a homogeneous whole.	Cognitive contrast mechanism	Follow the same procedure specified for the assimilation mechanism; additionally, make an effort to defuse contrasts whose bases are clearly attributable to differences that reflect polarized value assignments (e.g., good-bad, right-wrong).
7. Attaching more significance to the frame of reference for the information than to the objective quality of the information itself.	Cognitive context mechanism	Recognize that while information context is invaluable to the interpretation of message importance in most cases, context has little to do with the quality of information per se. Significant information should be evaluated "in the blind" (by detached sources) if its context is likely to distort the meaning assigned to the information.

Do organizations control the flow and availability of information to their managers to deliberately regulate information-overload levels? Our experience says no—and yet such a practice by any organization would unquestionably increase its responsiveness to the *real* information needs of its members. Earlier we pointed out that psychological assessments are helpful but not infallible. Psychological assessments of individual managerial intellectual aptitude combined with observation of performance in the job environment do provide management with a basis for regulating and controlling the amount of unnecessary information which filters through the organization environment (some intentional and some unintentional). Later we will provide a simplified format for establishing such a regulated mechanism to diminish the more nefarious effects of information overload.

Personality

The second personal factor affecting a manager's response to the case of too much information is individual personality. The scientific data accumulated to date on the effect of personality in general, much less its relationship to information-overload potential in particular, is sketchy at best. But there are some clear and undeniable trends.

First, let us remove some of the mystery surrounding the term *personality*. If it is any comfort, the 1976 edition of the prestigious *Annual Review of Psychology*, reporting on significant research in the study of personality, simply did not have much to report. The term has perhaps added more confusion than enlightenment for the psychological discipline. With these disclaimers, however, *personality* seems to mean the following:

1. The consistent way that a person acts in nonprivate circumstances.
2. The consistent way that a person acts in nonprivate circumstances as perceived (witnessed, interpreted, judged) by others.
3. The expectations that a person has for the way he or she will act in nonprivate circumstances.
4. The expectations that others have of the way a person will act in nonprivate circumstances.

Consider, as an example, "Mr. X:" (1) Mr. X always meets others with a polite, aggressive, confident enthusiasm that is matched with an equally confident expression of poise and gregarious shrewdness; (2) others also describe Mr. X as a person who meets others with a polite, aggressive, confident enthusiam, and so on.; (3) Mr. X states that this is the way he believes he appears to others—this is his expectation; and (4) others say this is the way they expect Mr. X to appear to them.

The key terms associated with our description of *personality*, then, include *consistent*, *nonprivate*, *perception of others*, *expectation of self*, and *expectation of others*.

The manager interested in understanding how personality relates to information overload must understand each of these key terms. Regardless of the personality involved, or the way we choose to describe that personality, unless a pattern of consistent behavior in nonprivate settings can be identified and expected—and then confirmed—it is highly unlikely that the term *personality* will have much more significance to a manager than the "personality" of the actors that most people identify with in a TV commercial.

Listed below are several stereotyped personalities; with each description we provide a characterization of the most probable reaction of that personality type to the case of too much information.

1. The dogmatic/authoritarian personality. * This personality type is easily spotted by the highly opinionated and unchangeable position he or she takes on controversial matters, especially issues involving social and ethnic beliefs. Furthermore, these opinions almost always reflect an exceedingly narrow viewpoint, one which contains obvious bias, and one which seems to categorize the subject of the opinion into clearly differentiated "either-or" or "black-white" categories. For the dogmatic personality, there are seldom any shades of gray, any exceptions to the rule, or any carefully expressed qualifications of opinions.

Here are a few sample utterances that a dogmatic personality would conceivably make; "Employees fall into two categories—for management or against management—and that's how we treat them here!" "If a manager puts in less than sixty hours a week, he's not worth his keep—I know, because I always put in sixty hours a week." "We haven't found one woman manager who can carry her weight around here; and we never will." "In spite of what they tell you, Jews only have one thing on their mind; we put them in accounting whenever possible." "We used one management consultant thirty years ago, and we will never use one again."

The dogmatic personality's response to the case of too much information is also predictable; whenever in doubt, the individual simply *ignores* confusing, uncertain, or multiple information inputs and relies upon prior experience with similar situations. Hence, information overload as we have described it is rarely perceived as a problem for the dogmatic individual.

---

*We are describing what Milton Rokeach (1960) terms *dogmatism* as a specific personality type. The authoritarian person (a person who tends to be a political conservative, who identifies with power figures, and who shows open hostility toward minority groups) responds to information overload in much the same manner as Rokeach's dogmatic personality.

He has constructed an impenetrable shield against any information input that would threaten the sanctity of his rigid "either-or" world.

Finally, in terms of our operational description of personality, the dogmatic individual is seen by others as behaving consistently, and in fact is expected to manifest the "either-or" or "black-white" type of communication behavior. Unfortunately, the dogmatic personality does not see himself that way; typically, he will adhere to the belief that he is open-minded, multifaceted, and so on—the exact opposite of what others know to be true.

2. The information-compulsive personality. This personality type poses a real threat to the effective information-processing capabilities of the modern organization. Like a vacuum cleaner, the information-compulsive manager does everything he can to gobble up any and all types of information, whether germane or irrelevant to his job responsibilities. He is a prime victim of information overload; when overloaded, he responds erratically. Detecting this type is sometimes difficult, but information-compulsive personalities have one characteristic in common: they seem to be always reacting to a problem or difficulty, never proacting or effectively planning for contingencies or deviations from everyday routine.

In supervisory-subordinate relationships, the information-compulsive supervisor may show his colors in several ways: constant memo writing to subordinates in quest of insignificant details; frequent meetings where the time invested has little bearing on the value returned; and unnecessary over-the-shoulder surveillance of subordinates' work. Further, the information-compulsive does not have many deep and trusting relationships with other managers and subordinates; and he is usually found to be active in the organization grapevine.

The overall response of the information-compulsive personality to the case of too much information is typically to seek out more information—thus aggravating the problem. This is the reason why this type of personality poses a real threat to the information-processing capability of an organization—especially an organization that is already deluged with too much information in relation to the organization work being accomplished.

Finally, while the information-compulsive personality behaves consistently in the sense that he is an information sponge, his consequent behavior and management performance may be erratic and unpredictable. His own behavioral expectations are frequently clouded with feelings of insecurity and inferiority. If not monitored, such an individual can severely disrupt important organization activities—not to mention the demoralizing influence he can have on those who must work with him.

3. The Machiavellian personality. In 1973, Robert McMurry wrote a provocative article for the *Harvard Business Review* entitled, "Power and the Ambitious Executive." In that article, he defined *power* "as the capacity to modify the conduct of other employees in a desired manner, together with the capacity to avoid having one's own behavior modified in undesired ways by other employees."

McMurry went on to argue that the position of a top executive is tenuous at best; and that to preserve and maintain that position certain power tactics (Machiavellian in character) must be employed. He then specified a number of strategies that a top executive can utilize to secure this power objective. While we disagree with many of McMurry's recommendations, his description of what it takes to perform as a Machiavellian is, in our judgment, well documented by actual practice.

Anyone familiar with Machiavelli's classic treatise *The Prince* will recall the icy description of a cold, calculating, and impeccably shrewd ruler carefully and deliberately executing his plans. Fairly recent research by Christie and Geiss (1970) indicates that many of the characteristics described by Machiavelli do, in fact, describe certain rather prevalent personality types.

The Machiavellian personality has chiefly these characteristics: (*a*) behavior which seems to allow the end to justify the means; (*b*) a recognition of the forces of influence that exist in human affairs; (*c*) an ability to manipulate these forces to achieve certain desired outcomes; and (*d*) a technique or modus operandi that is not readily apparent to others.

Interestingly, some Machiavellian managers can only meet their objectives by forcibly imposing their personal style in a manner that is clearly obtrusive to everyone—superiors, colleagues, and subordinates alike; other Machiavellian types achieve their aims quite subtly and unobtrusively. In other words, the style used—aggressive, dominant, boisterous, or low-key, cautiously inquisitive, and polite—while variable among Machiavellian managers (personalities), usually produces the same result—submission and acceptance, though no one can put their finger on the precise reason why!

In terms of the case of too much information, the Machiavellian seldom allows others to witness the confused and frustrated state that accompanies an overwhelming bombardment of information that cannot be sorted systematically and acted upon. In fact, the Machiavellian is probably the best equipped—in a cognitive sense—to satisfactorily deal with information overload. Recall that the Machiavellian has what we might term a "grand design"; nothing short of a literal organizational disaster is likely to shake the Machiavellian from this all-powerful image and conviction.

With respect to our operational description of personality, the Machiavellian typically meets all specifications: he or she behaves consistently, even calculatingly so; others do perceive this consistency and expect it; and the Machiavellian type knows very well that each behavior exhibited will indeed reinforce a predetermined image.

4. The yes man or submissive personality. Every organization has yes men employed, and most organizations we have been associated with are not sure about what they can do with them—short of discharge. One common trait they all share is an absolute repugnance to taking a stand or making a decision. President Harry Truman once said, "The buck stops here," and Alfred Laykey (1959) said, "I know a man only when he does not apologize about his personal convictions." Also, many organizations, governmental and private, encourage yes men.

The yes man's style is easily identified. Given a superior's opinion or the suggestion of a superior's opinion, he readily adopts his own views to conform. When under fire, he is mushy. Subordinates view him as being indecisive; colleagues view him as the guy who always sits on the bench with a dry brow; and as we implied, organizations tolerate him, but only to a point.

In the case of too much information, the yes man or submissive personality is, unfortunately, highly vulnerable. Given that a strong motive of this individual is simply to survive, excessive information only complicates this objective. The response to information overload then becomes entirely personal, and is evidenced in such thinking as "Shouldn't someone else deal with this?" "What does my superior expect from this?" "What can I do to minimize my responsibility for this?"

Again in terms of our operational personality model, the yes man behaves rather consistently before others; but he or she believes that the images communicated are nonrevealing of the basic insecurities and fears being experienced; others, however, tend to read these insecurities accurately—and are, in most cases, consequently demoralized (e.g., "If the boss can't do it, how can I?").

5. The neurotically anxious personality. In today's organization, managers are constantly confronted with a never-ending stream of stressful circumstances. Some managers learn how to manage stress as well as they manage people; others, however, fall victim to harmful physical or psychological side effects of stress which, among other things, include coronary disease, alcoholism, drug addiction, deep depression, and various nervous disorders.

Information overload is unquestionably a strong stress-producing stimulus. The personality most subject to its pernicious influence (physically and psychologically) is what we call the neurotically anxious personality. This individual tends to be a chronic worrier and never seems totally satisfied with his or her personal performance. Further, he or she may be a "workaholic"—consistently putting in long hours, even on weekends and holidays, and complaining to others that there is never enough time to get the job done. Every small problem that comes up is treated by the neurotically anxious type as a major crisis. Behaviorally, this person may smoke heavily, bite his nails, be overweight or anemic, and subject to frequent minor ailments (colds, flu, headaches).

Like any other neurosis, the anxious type can be rehabilitated; usually the most difficult task is convincing the individual that he is suffering from this form of neurosis by getting him to recognize and accept the symptoms of such. To repeat, for the case of too much information, a dangerous situation is created where overload can trigger a more damaging and permanent state of neurosis and/or harmful physical side effects.

As far as our personality model goes, the neurotically anxious personality does behave consistently to others; but the individual's self-perception is highly distorted or ignorant of these consistent impressions that others see. Thus, the challenge is to help the individual see him- or herself in the same way as others do.

To summarize our discussion of this second personal factor—personality—the following points can be made:

1. Information overload affects individuals differently; some can tolerate it and cope with it better than others.
2. To our knowledge, most organizations do little to regulate their information systems in such a way that insures effective adaptation by the individual to the information requirements of his job.
3. Information overload does diminish personal individual managerial effectiveness; and for the neurotically anxious personality, it can damage physical and psychological health.
4. There is no personality type that is absolutely insulated against information overload; and at least one personality type—the information-compulsive—thrives and feeds on it.

Past Experience With the Information Stimulus

The third personal factor affecting how a manager responds to the case of too much information is one's past experience with the information stimulus or situation. By *past experience*, we are referring to an accumulation of impressions which are usually thought to be stored in the long-term-memory component of the individual's information-processing apparatus. These impressions need not be stored in the form of words or images; they may be abbreviated impulses, or a collection of thoughts that are tied together in a logical or emotional sense.

Psychologists have known for some time that past experience with a stimulus is a strong influence on present and future behavior. Organizations know that what got them to where they are today is a good frame of reference for what it is they want to accomplish tomorrow. So the concept we are discussing here is not something new; however, its relation to information overload is something that is frequently overlooked.

Can past experience be used deliberately by a manager to improve his ability to cope with information overload? We think so, especially if the manager uses a tactic well known in the advertising trade: *positioning*.

Recognizing that most people are overwhelmed with the constant barrage of information originating from a multitude of media sources, the advertising specialist *positions* his client's product or service carefully. He positions his information in relation to information that already has a high probability of existing in the individual's information-processing system.

For example, during the early 1970s, Avis Rent-A-Car claimed in its ads that "Avis is only Number 2 in rent-a-cars, so why go with us? We try harder." Positioning in this ad was accomplished in two ways: by claiming they were "Number 2" in the rent-a-car business, an immediate association was made with their strongest competition—known throughout the world as Hertz; secondly, Americans have sided historically with the underdog in legitimate competitive rivalry. Thus, Avis's claim that "we try harder" psychologically positioned them with a second existing information unit, already firmly entrenched in the minds of the consumer.

Other advertising positioning examples include "7-Up—the 'Uncola'" (where an effort was made to position 7-Up with Coke); Henry Ford's "horseless carriage"; and one computer company calling themselves "the *other* computer company"—in relation to IBM.

Positioning, in other words, is deliberately designed to command attention to new information with the least amount of recognition energy expended by the individual. In short, positioning capitalizes upon past experience or old knowledge to insure the recognition and hopeful acceptance of new knowledge.

Information overload, we know, constitutes a situation where the individual is being subjected to multiple information inputs; as the inputs increase, the individual's ability to effectively process the information decreases at an even greater rate. To the extent that the individual can in effect use past experience as a psychological crutch to cope with information excess, then his or her ability to increase overload tolerance is enhanced.

What we are suggesting, then, is that the effects of information overload can be tolerated to a greater extent if the individual makes a conscious effort to position new information against other information units already accumulated from personal past experience. This can be done by following a simple exercise:

1. "What do I know that relates in time, space, or substance to this information?"
2. "How did I use what I knew at the time it was new information?"

3. "Is that use still appropriate with this new information?"
4. *If it is not still appropriate*:
    "Would it be if I altered the new information in some way?"
    "Would it be if I altered the way I used the old information in some way?"
    "Would it be if I altered both the old and the new information in some way?"

Finally, the effective manager seldom has to be reminded that his greatest information resource is his fellow organization members. In fact, the accumulation of past experience by his total management group is usually sufficient to cope with almost any unexpected organizational contingency. For the case of too much information, we have observed that managers who are experiencing overload resist drawing upon the past experiences of others to help them resolve their own personal information dilemmas. In most cases, unfortunately, managers do not even seem to be aware of this powerful antidote—the total organization's past experience resource pool—as a means of partially immunizing themselves against the more draining information-processing effects of excessive information inputs. If they are aware, we find that there is an overt reluctance to take advantage of this pool in an overload situation.

Motivation, Need, and Goal Configuration

The last personal variable bearing on a manager's ability to cope with the case of too much information is the character of one's motivation, need, and goal configuration. Highly motivated managers whose personal needs are being satisfied and whose goals represent strong commitments to difficult objectives seem to be able to cope with information overload most ably. These individuals are industrious, tend to be self-starting, and are not easily defeated. They have greater stamina than their colleagues, a much stronger desire to achieve in spite of obstacles, and in general exhibit a greater capacity to tolerate uncertainty and unpredictability in their job environments.

Much has been written on the subject of motivation, and it is not our purpose to reinvent the wheel on that subject. However, we would like to call the reader's attention to an important observation we have made in relation to the source of an individual's motivation and his ability to tolerate information overload.

It is generally agreed that sources of human motivation can be classified into two categories—extrinsic and intrinsic sources. Extrinsic sources typically found in organizational environments include pay and benefits, working conditions (including appurtenances), organizational policies, status, supervision, security, and interpersonal relations. These extrinsic sources will be recognized as Frederick Herzberg's (1968) "hygiene" factors.

The intrinsic sources of motivation are believed to include achievement, recognition for job accomplishment, challenging work, increased responsibility, and personal growth and development—termed "motivators" by Herzberg. The intrinsic sources, Herzberg and others have found, produce enduring motivated behavior, as well as higher levels of personal productivity.

We have observed, and have verified from the accounts of others, that intrinsically motivated managers have a greater propensity to withstand information overload than do extrinsically motivated managers. Insufficient research has been accomplished to explain precisely why this is so, but several reasons seem plausible. For one, the intrinsically motivated manager has been found to be more highly motivated toward accomplishing organizational objectives than the extrinsically motivated individual. Thus, in line with our earlier comments, this manager may simply be more strongly compelled to accept information overload as a characteristic of the job, and consequently he manages to work around it. The extrinsically motivated manager, on the other hand, is less dedicated to what we might term "job content" and more dedicated to personal conveniences (pleasant working environment, adequate pay, incentives, vacations). Hence, his or her drive to overcome obstacles to the successful accomplishment of job content may be less. And information overload, as most managers testify, is a major job-content obstacle.

Second, while the information is sketchy at best, there is some evidence which suggests that persons who respond well to sources of intrinsic motivation have a more sophisticated information-processing capability than do individuals who seem incapable of being intrinsically motivated. Job enrichment,* for example, a concept that relies heavily on intrinsic motivation sources and which has been found to be extremely successful in some job settings, has been documented as a miserable failure in others. Some people simply have no need for enrichment of their work opportunities—and in fact may resist it.

Finally, the opportunities in most organizations to benefit from intrinsic motivation sources increase as one rises in the organization; similarly, the complexity of information overload increases at higher organizational levels, as well as the overload potential. Thus, it is conceivable that this coincidence accounts for the fact that the intrinsically motivated manager is better equipped to deal with the case of too much information.

---

*Job enrichment is a procedure originally developed by Herzberg to design jobs that include more work content variety and which demand a higher knowledge and skill level. For a critical discussion of the concept, see Luthans and Reif (1974).

Closely associated with sources of motivation for the individual manager is the character of his personal need systems. In fact, the association reduces to the fact that an individual's needs, especially the strength of these needs, will determine how highly motivated he or she is to seek need satisfaction. Abraham Maslow is given credit for explaining how human needs tend to be organized. As Figure 3-1 indicates, these needs form a hierarchy, with physiological needs toward the left and self-actualization needs at the right.

Physiological needs are the basic needs that must be satisfied if human life is to be maintained: hunger, thirst, shelter, and sex. In Figure 3-1, we depict these needs first in the hierarchy because their relative need strength is by far the strongest of all human needs. If they are not satisfied, then man in effect is frozen at this need level—because these needs are critical to human survival.

Once physiological needs are satisfied, Maslow argues, *safety* or *security needs* become a top priority for satisfaction. After these needs are satisfied, then *social needs* (for belonging and companionship) become important. Next, the need for *self-esteem*, which involves obtaining recognition from others as well as experiencing feelings of personal accomplishment, social usefulness, and personal prestige, emerges as a strong motivational influence. Finally, *self-actualization*—the most controversial part of Maslow's need hierarchy—governs behavior. Self-actualization is difficult to describe, but it refers in general to the maximization of human potential, the exemplary performance by a human being in some difficult human endeavor. In short, it is a drive toward full realization of one's potential.

In most organizations, the opportunity to satisfy the social, self-esteem, and self-actualization needs increases as one reaches higher organizational

FIGURE 3-1. MASLOW'S NEED HIERARCHY

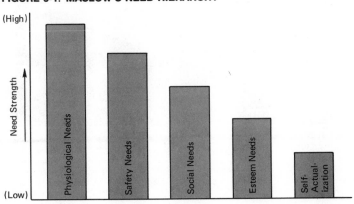

levels; this corresponds to the opportunity for intrinsic sources of motivation to become more readily available as one rises in the organization. Consequently, as was the case with managers who are motivated by intrinsic motivational sources, so also managers whose needs and drives are at least at the self-esteem level of the hierarchy manifest a greater tolerance to the deleterious effects of information overload.

Again, the reasons for this are debatable, but we suspect they are similar to those discussed above under sources of intrinsic motivation. The implication, however, is more intriguing. To the extent that organizations encourage managers to seek higher levels of need satisfaction, it is conceivable that some greater progress toward insulating the organization against the damaging effects of overload will be made.

Closely linked to sources of managerial motivation and human need satisfactions are the personal goal systems which the individual manager establishes for him- or herself. A few years ago, Katz and Kahn (1966) discussed the notion of the *psychological contract*. Briefly, this concept entails an unspoken agreement that an employee makes with the organization. This agreement represents a commitment by the individual to perform certain duties and meet certain obligations for the organization in return for compensation, job opportunities, and other privileges which the organization agrees to provide.

Also implicit in the psychological contract is a commitment by the individual to organizational goals and objectives. Ideally, the individual's

FIGURE 3-2. HOW GOALS RELATE TO MOTIVATION SOURCES AND NEED SYSTEMS, IN RELATION TO THE MANAGER'S ABILITY TO COPE WITH INFORMATION OVERLOAD.

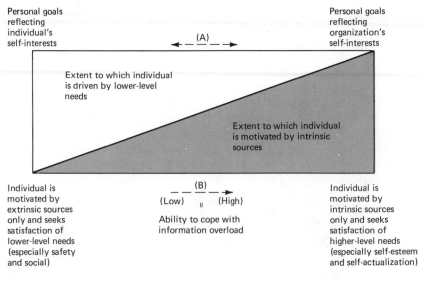

personal goals and objectives match those of the organization; practically, this match-up seldom occurs—for a multitude of reasons.

Important to our discussion of the case of too much information is recognition of the fact that a manager's personal goals reflect his or her underlying motivation sources as well as dominant need systems. Figure 3-2 illustrates how a manager's goals can be related to motivation and need systems. Of special significance are lines (A) and (B). These lines indicate that the closer the manager's personal goals approximate the goals of his organization, the greater should be his capacity to tolerate information overload; likewise, as personal goals approximate organizational goals, we find that the individual is obtaining satisfaction from the higher-level needs on Maslow's need hierarchy and is being motivated by intrinsic sources which correspond to these higher-level needs (recognition, challenging work, achievement). Figure 3-2, in short, shows the complementary relationship of motivation, need, and goal systems as they relate to the case of too much information.

SUMMARY OF PERSONAL VARIABLES

We began this chapter with some remarks by Warren Bennis that indicated that we are now experiencing the age of the "information economy." We provided illustrations to show that the knowledge explosion has not only intensified but has brought with it a need to examine four assumptions that will weigh heavily on an organization's ability to control information needed to secure and sustain organizational goals and objectives; we earmarked these assumptions for the future while recognizing that for many organizations, they do, in fact, characterize the present.

The assumptions pointed to the observation that the management of tomorrow must find ways to control its information resources and avoid being controlled in a reactive sense. Chief among our concerns is the problem and paradox that information overload presents for the modern organization. The capacity to cope with overload will be the distinguishing competitive and survival advantage characterizing the successful organization of the future.

A distinction between *information, information processing,* and *communication* was made. We maintained that management must be aware of the dynamics that affect the manner in which people working in organizations respond to oftentimes competing and multiple information demands. We stressed that this awareness must begin with a concentrated effort to examine the information predicament of the receiver or recipient of organizational information, not with an organization's exotic information or communication technology.

Next, we examined four personal variables which impinge upon an individual's tolerance for information overload: (*a*) cognitive complexity; (*b*) personality; (*c*) personal past experience with the information stimulus; and (*d*) personal motivation, need, and goal configurations. Table 3-3 summarizes our discussion of these variables.

As Table 3-3 shows, for two of the variables we have discussed, management of an organization can take action to increase the tolerance or capacity of the individual to cope with information overload. For example, the job environment can be structured to provide opportunities for sources of intrinsic motivation to become available for the manager; the organization can improve the means by which higher-level needs can be satisfied (by providing more individual recognition, by encouraging delegation so that subordinate responsibilities are increased); and a greater effort can always be made to bring an individual's personal goals more in line with organizational goals (through incentives, open discussion, effective job evaluation, and management training/development programs). Elsewhere we talk about organization development, and this, too, can be used effectively by management to strengthen individual motivation, need, and goal configurations.

The past-experience variable is also subject to influence. We discussed in some detail the conscious use of psychological positioning, and also presented a simple exercise that the individual can perform to enable the past-experience variable to increase his or her ability to cope with information overload.

Table 3-3 also indicates that the cognitive complexity and personality variables are personal components that cannot be modified by management to increase the organization's information overload tolerance. However, psychological testing in conjunction with management observation of individual job performance enables the organization (*a*) to screen candidates for a particular job where the information overload exposure is likely to be high, and (*b*) to detect people who are already in these positions who should perhaps be reassigned if the job content itself cannot be altered to reduce overload.

To conclude this chapter on personal variables, we quote a senior vice-president of a mail-order insurance company whose situation puts the overload problem into a perspective that every manager can appreciate:

> No, I'm not overextended . . . I coordinate the job assignments for seven different departments, requiring me to complete seven job summaries daily, attend a minimum of two scheduling meetings daily, . . . have an in-basket where the bottom never meets the top, have a phone that rings incessantly, have memos that don't get answered and letters that get lost, . . . a secretary who can't take dictation, . . . and a "john" that is exactly 323 paces and eleven staircases away from my office.

TABLE 3-3. SUMMARY OF PERSONAL VARIABLES

Personal variable	Information overload tolerance Low	High	Can tolerance be increased? Yes	No
Cognitive Complexity				X
Noncomplex person	X			
Complex person		X		
Personality				X
Dogmatic/authoritarian		X		
Information-compulsive	X			
Machiavellian		X		
Yes man or submissive	X			
Neurotically anxious	X			
Personal Past Experience With Information Stimulus			X	
Through the use of positioning		X		
Through the conscious pooling of past experience of the organization's human resources		X		
Personal Motivation, Need, and Goal Configurations			X	
Extrinsically motivated individuals	X			
Intrinsically motivated individuals		X		
Individuals seeking satisfaction of lower-level needs	X			
Individuals seeking satisfaction of higher-level needs		X		
Personal goals not coinciding with organization goals	X			
Personal goals coinciding with organizational goals		X		

4

Relational Variables I

INTRODUCTION

> I will pay more for the ability to deal with people than any other ability under the sun. (Quoted in Bergen and Haney, 1966)

The man who uttered these words needs little introduction. He was the famous entrepreneur John D. Rockefeller, and his brief remarks on the subject aptly capture the driving force of this chapter: gaining control of information uncertainty in organizations requires that people understand how to deal with people.

Expanding on this thought, it is insufficient that organization members understand the personal information-processing capabilities of one another; it is also necessary that organization members, and especially organization management, comprehend the impact that human organizational relationships have on both individual and total organizational information-processing capabilities. Clearly, it is at the relationship level where most of the work of the organization is accomplished, where most of the communication difficulties are primarily encountered, and where the survival potential of the organization is qualitatively judged.

In this chapter, we will introduce a concept to which we are indebted to Chris Argyris. Argyris (1976) has articulated a theory of action that is based upon valid information, informed choice, and internal commitment by organization members; central to his argument is a concern for the quality of the relationships that people have in organizations. It is his interpretation—and ours, too—that these bases for a theory of action in organizations demand a revolutionary, not evolutionary, changeover on the part of organization managements.

As in Chapter 3, we have structured our discussion of relationship variables to reflect the experienced-based expectations of many organizational specialists that the growing inability of management to cope with and tolerate an overload of its information-processing systems looms as a major threat on the horizon for the industrial, educational, and governmental organization. Our views on this matter coincide with the position described by Galbraith.

It will be recalled that Galbraith (1973) has observed that uncertainty increases the amount of information that must be processed during task execution—where *uncertainty* is a condition reflecting the amount of information possessed by an organization in contrast to the amount of information required. He then describes four organizational design strategies for coping with uncertainty—strategies which either reduce the amount of information overload or increase the capacity of the organization to process more information. While Galbraith chose to concentrate his attention on variations in organization structure as strategic coping mechanisms, in this chapter and the next we shift the focus of his important observations to selected characteristics of human organizational relationships.

THE MODEL I VERSUS MODEL II ORGANIZATION

As organizations grow more complex, it is becoming increasingly necessary for the manager to become comfortable with alternative mechanisms for making significant organization decisions and choices. The concept of the omniscient manager in command of all the necessary data needed to make unilateral decisions is, with the exception of the small, entrepreneurial organizations, irreversibly obsolete; also obsolete is the short-lived concept "management by committee."

Emergent, however, is a new concept in management termed *consensus decision making*, which first entails power sharing by managers at an organization's apex. In practice, consensus decision making simply means that all of those with valid data play a role in reaching a decision, and that these same individuals—even if not unanimously supporting the decision —agree to implement it.

Also central to the consensus-decision-making concept is the belief that the quality of the decisions made cannot be greater than the quality of the information available for making them—regardless of where this information might be situated in the organization's formal hierarchy. An informed source with reliable information in consensus management, then, is attributed a greater decision-input opportunity than an uninformed source with greater hierarchical status. Finally, consensus management does not mean that individual organizational responsibilities are abdicated in favor of group decision making. To the contrary, the locus of responsibility becomes much more visible, and the individual much more accountable, in a consensus-decision-making environment.

The consensus-decision-making concept will undoubtedly become the preferred management alternative for controlling the complex information environments that organizations will most certainly encounter in the twenty-first century. Whereas the concept of decentralization has become the most popular alternative in the latter half of this century, it will be shown to be obsolete as organizations continue to become more complex and fragmented in their respective business definitions.

Unquestionably, at the heart of the consensus management concept is the ability of organizations to structure human relationships in such a manner that power sharing among managers will be viewed as a desired outcome—so that power will no longer be treated as a closely held, carefully guarded commodity that is only shared and dispersed, selectively, among a few individuals or organizational units. This brings us to the important differences between what Argyris (1976) has termed the *Model I* and *Model II organization.*

Argyris has determined from many years of research and work as a distinguished organizational consultant that there are two contrary theories of action which influence the behavior patterns of people in organization settings. The following example dramatizes these theories:

> *Senior financial manager to a new junior financial executive*: "In this department, we value individuality and individual achievement; we want you to question and challenge systems and procedures and design better ones that improve our ability to meet our department's objectives; you will find the door to my mind always open to the thoughts and suggestions you have on these matters; it is this attitude which makes our department shine in XYZ Company."
>
> *Another executive in the department to the new executive*: "The best way to gain instant but temporary prominence in this department is to challenge or find something wrong with one of the boss's pets. You'll learn what those pets are in due time and will quickly understand what I mean when I say that if you question them, your prominence will be instant and temporary."

We deliberately carried this example to an extreme (although some of our managerial colleagues tell us that the example is not extreme at all) to illustrate Argyris's theories. Simply stated, he has observed that people hold one kind of theory which they can verbally articulate to others—their *espoused theory* of action. People also hold another kind of theory which others come to realize by observing one's behavior—what Argyris terms one's *theory-in-use*. Typically, a wide gap is found between what people—managers—state (their espoused theory) and their observed theory-in-use. It is, of course, the theory-in-use which has the greatest impact on human organizational relationships.

Argyris has also observed that while most managers think they are guided by a Model II theory of action, in practice 95 percent of them are governed by a Model I theory. Values associated with a Model I theory include the following: (*a*) to achieve the purpose—whatever purpose—as the *individual* has defined it; (*b*) to always win, never lose; (*c*) to suppress and discourage negative feelings and dissent; and (*d*) to stress "rationality" in all human intercourse. The net effect of these values is expressed in a behavior pattern that is characterized by a high need to exert control over others.

Others who are exposed to a Model I manager behave accordingly: they tend to react defensively; they screen their ideas to insure that they conform with the theory-in-use expressed by the Model I manager; and they make certain that any feedback they give to the Model I manager is void of a contradictory personal value system. Coincidentally, on the surface, such individuals will deny that they respond to the Model I manager in the way we have described—just as the Model I manager will typically deny that there is a wide gap between his espoused theory of action and his theory-in-use.

The governing values of a Model II organization are quite different and are ones which lend themselves to expression in a consensus-decision-making organization environment: (*a*) *valid information*—the unanimous recognition for such to make effective organization decisions; (*b*) *informed choice*, meaning that decisions are based on information shared by anyone who participates in the decision-making event; and (*c*) *internal commitment*, which represents a private and public subscription to the organization's consensus-based, decision-making apparatus.

The governing values of a Model II organization, in short, are contingent upon the development of a carefully cultivated human relationship environment in the organization—an environment where feelings are not ignored because they lack "rationality"; where ideas are not expressed for fear of retaliation; and where the concept of power is defined as a contingent of information, not as a contingent of hierarchical position or status. We believe that a Model II organization offers the manager a unique opportunity to gain positive control of his information environment and to do so by capitalizing on those features of relationships in organizations that make such control possible. We also agree with Argyris and others who claim that the revolutionary changeover from a Model I to a Model II is not accomplished overnight. It is a painstaking process that requires a tremendous organizational commitment. But it can be done, and has been done.

The Model II Organization In Action

William Dowling (1977) describes an application of Argyris's Model II concept at Graphic Controls Corporation, headquartered in Buffalo, New York. The company manufactures recording charts and other expendable products that are used in combination with electronic equipment to present visual information—the industrial, research, and medical applications of Graphic's technology are virtually unlimited. Graphic is a medium-sized, public corporation,* employing thirteen hundred persons, with operating facilities in the United States, Canada, Mexico, Brazil, England, Spain, France, Belgium, India, and Australia.

Dowling points out that consensus decision making is the most distinctive characteristic of Graphic's management process. That is, decisions are made based upon an agreement to implement by those managers who have valid information, an informed choice, and a commitment to carry decisions into appropriate action.

The president of Graphic, according to Dowling, does not believe that consensus management entails an abdication of responsibility by the chief executive officer; to the contrary, it allows him to practice his ultimate accountability to shareholders even more effectively. As is true in most organizations, the advent of circumstances which led to Graphic's acceptance and practice of Model II management was inspired by its president, who recognized during a turbulent period in the company's history that the key to survival would be the successful harnessing of the top management group (about ten people) toward the accomplishment of a much-needed turnaround strategy.

The president of Graphic was unusual in one sense: he subscribed to a personal philosophy that Dowling describes as "humanistic" and "egalitarian." He was impressed and moved by the writings of such behavioral science authorities as Douglas McGregor, Alfred Marrow, Rensis Likert, Warren Bennis, and, most notably, Chris Argyris. Further, this president had a first-hand opportunity to learn what Argyris meant about one's "espoused theory" and "theory-in-use"—he discovered that while he saw himself as open, receptive, and inviting of criticism, others saw him as autocratically inclined.

---

*At the time of this writing, Graphic Controls was being acquired by the Times Mirror Corporation.

This combination of circumstances—a deteriorating business situation and the commitment of a chief executive to elevate the synergistic capability of his top management team vis-à-vis a conceptual vehicle supplied by the behavioral sciences—resulted in the adaptation and commitment to Model II consensus management by Graphic Controls. We should mention in passing that ever since Graphic's inception in 1957, the company has been known for its management openness and for its pledged support of theories whose origins can be found in the behavioral sciences. Thus, when the current president assumed his position in 1970, the greatest hurdle to Model II that he had to overcome was in himself—the organization was primed from its prior experience to accept the changes that Model II would bring.

Some of these changes were relatively uneventful, and others turned out to be contradictory and were abandoned. At the time Dowling wrote his article, Graphic had formed three responsibility-distinct management groups: the *Executive Management Group*, composed of five key people who had formerly made up the "Office of the President" and whose task it now was to concentrate on the "management needs of tomorrow"; the *Operating Management Group*, eleven people charged with the management of the corporation "today"; and the *Innovation Group*, three key people who apparently are responsible for determining new business opportunities.

How does consensus management work in practice at Graphic? One example is cited in the regular meetings of the Executive Management Group. The president presides in one sense (he holds the title, and his family owns 20 percent of Graphic's stock), but not in another (he takes a back seat during the meeting). Usually, he will express his opinion on a subject early in the meeting, so that the other participants will not feel after a lengthy discussion that their opinions have been ultimately preempted by those of the "boss."

These meetings are conducted informally, and the amount of influence any one individual is able to exert will vary from one meeting to the next depending upon the quality and extent of information possessed in relation to the issue under inquiry. The meetings are taped for a twofold purpose: first, to permit the group to review a particularly important interaction about an issue that occurred during the meeting; and, second, to permit post hoc participation by a member who was absent at a meeting. Graphic has also employed an outside consultant at these meetings from time to time, who functions as a facilitator and diagnostician of how well the group is performing together to meet its consensus objectives.

We should mention that the Executive Management Group (EMG) has held meetings to discuss its own effectiveness as an entity—members' satisfaction, the degree to which they believe they are relating to one another effectively, and so on.

Another example of consensus management at work is in the area of compensation. While it appears to be not entirely uniform throughout the company, top management at both the corporate and division levels use peer evaluations to distribute incentive rewards and establish compensation ranges. A special four-person group (the president and three others) serves as the final screening body of all compensation recommendations (which must ultimately be approved by the board of directors). Two restrictions on this group, at the insistence of the board, are (*a*) no incentive compensation will be given unless the company reaches a minimum profit objective, and (*b*) no individual incentive can exceed 50 percent of base salary. In spite of these restrictions, the amount of freedom top-level executives and division managers have in arriving at fair and equitable compensation decisions far surpasses that found in most companies—where one's adjusted compensation is usually a one-on-one matter between the subordinate manager and his or her superior.

Still another area where consensus management is used at Graphic is in the executive selection process. Depending upon the position opening, a group of managers will constitute the screening body, relying on both one-on-one and group interviews with the candidate to arrive at the selection decision.

Finally, Graphic is a strong supporter of MBO (Management By Objectives), and uses the MBO goal-setting process to arrive at its three-year strategy, as well as to determine the personal and business objectives of its individual key managers. The planning process and the setting of personal objectives is "bottoms-up" in the truest sense. That is, consistent with an inherent tenet of the Model II organization, planning initiative and planning input originate from those individuals or operating units who possess the information required for effective decisions; plans, in short, are produced by those people who must implement them.

Has Graphic's subscription to a Model II approach produced bottom-line results? According to Dowling, from 1971 to 1975 Graphic had four consecutive record-breaking sales and profits years. At the time of the article, 1976 continued to show the same upward trend (with sales doubling and profits eight times higher than they were in 1971). Recalling the devastating effects of the 1974 recession—which lagged for many companies well into 1976—this performance is laudable.

Of course, there have been problems with consensus management, and Graphic readily admits to them. The president, for example, admits that his management group has difficulty giving and receiving *negative* feedback. Also, during the early experimentation with consensus management, in the spirit of achieving delegation a number of task groups were formed —with sometimes as many as fifteen operating in the company at one time. This proved to be unmanageable, and task groups are now used sparingly. Third, at the division level there is, according to Dowling, a lack of standardization in the implementation of procedures. As a result, divisions progress at different rates and with different results that can perhaps be attributed to the absence of uniformity existing among the divisions. Fourth, and finally, at the time Dowling wrote his report, consensus management at Graphic had not been extended below the division management level. Such penetration of the underlying philosophy, skills, and knowledge required to practice the consensus management concept at all levels of organizational functioning may take years.

We would be remiss if we neglected to add that Graphic's desire and attempt to become a Model II organization would probably never have succeeded to its present point without the planned and what we interpret as "aggressive," intervention at Graphic by outside consultants (James Gillespie was involved from the beginning, and Chris Argyris made periodic visits during the course of Graphic's experience with consensus management).

What, then, are the steps an organization can take to develop the management philosophies necessary to move closer to a Model II organization? In the next section, we discuss four major relationship dynamics that must be understood to get the process under way.

ACHIEVING EFFECTIVENESS IN ORGANIZATIONAL RELATIONSHIPS

Becoming a Model II organization, as we emphasized and illustrated above, is no easy chore, especially at the relationship level. Not only do old attitudes and behaviors have to be overhauled, but new insight and appreciation of what affects how people relate to one another needs to be grasped. In this section, we describe some essential relationship dynamics that the manager must understand if he or she wishes to achieve a higher level of effectiveness in human organizational relationships. As one specialist put it:

> The underlying assumption...is that the managerial response will be
> appropriate when it solves the problem situation, at the same time
> *strengthening the human resources and the process of interfacing,* and
> when it contributes to the growth of the organization while responding realistically to the external environment. (Lippitt, 1969; italics
> added)

Gordon Lippitt is perhaps best known for his writings on the subject of organization renewal. At the core of his renewal concept is the belief that organizations can make planned responses to the situations and problems they confront; but to do so, organizations must strengthen their human resources and improve their human interfacing capabilities.

When Lippitt uses the term *human resources*, he is referring to four organization subsystems: the individual, the dyad, the small group, and the relationship existing between groups (departments). His term *interfacing* refers to a relationship process that involves (*a*) dialogue, (*b*) confrontation, (*c*) the search for meaning and understanding, and (*d*) human coping with the weaknesses and mistakes that almost always accompany the human interfacing process in organizations.

Given these considerations, what can we say specifically about human relationships in organizations that will enable the manager to understand the dynamics of his relationships with others—dynamics which strongly influence whether a response to a problem or situation is planned and controlled or unplanned and uncontrolled? There are four relationship dynamics which we believe must be understood.

Reasons For Human Organizational Relationships

George Homans (1950) pioneered our understanding about why human relationships are necessary in organizations. He introduced three elements to explain this viewpoint which remain viable today: *activity, interaction,* and *sentiments*.*

First, Homans maintained, people form relationships because they have things (work) to accomplish which they cannot do on their own, but which they can accomplish with the help and assistance of others; this he labeled *activity*. Second, he observed that an instance of activity by one person can stimulate an instance of activity by another person; this he termed *interaction*. Third, he found that as people engage in activities and as they interact with each other, they develop *sentiments* or feelings toward one another.

Homans made another interesting observation about the formation and continuance of human relationships. He noted that these three general properties of relationships are systematically linked with one another. For example, individuals who frequently and positively interact with each other tend to develop favorable sentiments (feelings of liking) toward one another; likewise, as individuals begin to like each other more, they tend to interact more frequently. Also the reverse was found to be true. Finally, Homans observed a mutual dependence between sentiment and activity. If two people like each other very much, they may arrange their activities to bring themselves closer together; similarly, if their work brings them

---

*We briefly discussed these concepts in Chapter 1 when we described Whyte's interaction analysis model.

together regularly, they increase their sentiments respectively. And again, the reverse was also noted.

What Homans's work tells us, then, is that these three reasons for human relationships—activity, interaction, and sentiments—are mutually dependent on one another for the relationship to thrive. If one component is neglected or negatively influenced, the other two will also be. So in our discussion of relationship characteristics, we must develop a model that deals adequately with all three elements.

The Concept Of Relational Control

Once a relationship is established between two or more individuals, the opportunity to control both the content (what is done) and the process (how it is done) of the interaction presents itself. By *control*, we mean nothing more than the influence one person has over another, which may be either overt and quite direct or subtle and, in many cases, deceptively indirect. This opportunity is utilized in one of three ways in a relationship, according to Watzlawick and his associates (1967).

The first way that relational control is utilized can be seen in what is termed a *complementary* interaction, an example of which follows:

> *President to his marketing vice-president*: "When do you plan on having the results of the recent market survey analyzed by our fourteen market segments?"
> *Marketing vice-president*: "I'll try to have the preliminary findings to you by Monday morning, if that's okay."

Note that in this example, the first utterance by the president was, in effect, *accepted* by the vice-president. If we use the terminology *moving up*, *moving down*, and *holding position*, we can dramatize the distinction being made for relational control. The president in the previous example was "moving up," and thereby exerting control; the vice-president was "moving down," and thereby conceding control. The next example illustrates a *symmetrical* interaction:

> *President to his financial vice-president*: "How can you assure me that sufficient precautions have been taken in our new inventory control computer program to prevent inventory values from being overstated?"
> *Financial vice-president*: "You authorized the ranges we inserted in the program feedback modules yourself, to insure that overstating of inventory would be absolutely minimized for major items . . . don't you remember?"

In this example, the financial vice-president rejected the control definition offered by the president and offered his own; in other words, in response to the moving-up attempt by the president, the vice-president reciprocated by moving up himself. If we carried the example further, the president could choose to adopt either a moving-up or moving-down tactic for his next response. Common sense would argue that he graciously move down.

The third possibility is characterized by the fact that neither interactant deliberately tries to exert control over what is said or how it is said. In effect, each interactant, or one interactant at a given moment in time, simply assumes a holding position:

One manager to a colleague: "I guess we'll have to come this weekend to finish refining some of the budget calculations that the head office rejected at the quarterly budget meeting this morning."
Colleague response: "Yes, and while we are at it, it probably wouldn't hurt to go over those new capital expenditure items, too."

In this illustration, the manager's initial comment could have constituted an effort to exert relational control; however, the colleague's response indicates that the exchange was equal. If, however, the colleague had responded, "Well, you can come in if you want, but I have an important golf game and don't get paid to work weekends," then the relational characteristics of this exchange would shift from a holding position to a moving-up position.

Before leaving this brief but important discussion of relational control, let us stress a point that bears repeating in spite of the fact that its implication is perhaps obvious from the preceding remarks. Many times in organizations, individuals find themselves expressing viewpoints that are divergent from the opinions of others. This divergence can ordinarily be a healthy competitive sign in the organization that has learned to live with its uncertain information environment.

On the other hand, in the Model I organization that we described earlier, the expression of divergent viewpoints is typically discouraged if not altogether forbidden. When such viewpoint differences do occur, the argument may not be indicative of true and valid differences, but may very well be indicative of a more unhealthy disagreement basis—the question of who has immediate command of the situation, of who has *relational control*. This is especially true in the Model I organization where power is viewed as a sacred resource, because, clearly, relational control is one manifestation of an attempt to display power (or to submit to it). Neither alternative facilitates effective organizational information processing.

Communication Roadmaps About What Is Said
And How It Is Said

A map of any kind identifies a number of points, geographical or otherwise, and then indicates how they are connected to one another. A roadmap, for example, gives us access routings between metropolitan centers and outlying rural areas; we, in turn, rely on this description to get us to our destinations. The roadmap, in short, specifies where we can go as well as how we must travel to get there. In the organization context, we have maps, too. Some are explicit and leave little doubt or confusion in anyone's mind as to what is expected; others are implicit and are learned from experience or from watching others. There are several important organizational roadmaps which have profound effects on human organizational relationships; these roadmaps, in turn, influence an organization's ability to control its information environment and especially its susceptibility to information overload.

Most organizations and most individual managers operate with two distinct sets of roadmaps. One is reflected in the formal policy of the organization or the manager and is articulated in employee handbooks, published management directives, and other (mostly printed) organization material, including, as we are increasingly finding, organization planning documents. The second set of roadmaps are not published, and may, in fact, be at variance with the first set. This set of roadmaps tells us, for example, how much of a gap there is between top management's espoused theory and its theory-in-use; whether there is a place for sentiments in organizational interactions; and whether a subordinate has the freedom to take a moving-up position in a conversation with a superior.

In short, these roadmaps tell us about what we should communicate as well as how our "what" should be communicated. For example, in a particular superior-subordinate communication relationship, we might ask the following questions to help define the communication roadmaps being utilized by both the superior and the subordinate:

Regarding what is said:

Are task problems freely discussed, and with what degree of openness?

Are certain subjects avoided (salary raises, promotion opportunities, achievements made in other departments, politics, personal management style)?

Is a special code to increase conversational or communicative efficiency utilized ("R & D" as opposed to "research and development," "P & L" as opposed to "profit and loss statement")?

Does semantic compatibility exist in terms of the words (symbols) that are chosen to express thoughts? (If the subordinate expresses concern about efficiencies in production, does the superior assign the same meaning to the word *efficiencies* as the subordinate does?)

Can what is said be assumed to be important in the mind of the listener, if the subject is worthy of discussion by the communicator?

Are personal problems freely discussed, and with what degree of openness and candor?

Is bad news as worthy a subject as good news?

Are new ideas assigned the same careful consideration given to existing ideas?

Are mistakes freely admitted and distinguished from abject failures?

Is criticism viewed constructively and not defensively?

Regarding how it is said:

Is relational control (moving up and moving down) important to the interaction?

Does it matter who communicates first?

Does it matter how long the communication lasts?

Does it matter if the information is presented by oral or written means (face to face, by memo, by phone)?

Does it matter where the communication occurs (the superior's office, the subordinate's office, or on "neutral" ground)?

Is the tone of the communication important (urgent, matter-of-fact)?

Does it matter who is given the perogative to terminate the exchange?

Just as we have given this example of some questions that might be asked in terms of communication roadmaps that exist in superior-subordinate communication, we could also ask similar questions about communication relationship in organizational meetings, with peers or colleagues, with customers or clients, with suppliers, with regulatory officials, and with stockholders.

The message we have here needs little elaboration: Rules are valid and essential if they produce an increase in the organization's ability to process information effectively and if they enable an organization to cope with information overload more efficiently. Rules are invalid and nonessential if they undermine human relationships and cause people to govern their behavior only to satisfy or conform with rules that bear no relationship to organizational effectiveness and achievement. Who would follow a roadmap that led you to the wrong destination?

Coorientation in Human Organizational Relationships

The final factor that affects the underlying dynamics of a relationship between two or more people is termed *coorientation*. Central to this concept are the notions of agreement and accuracy, both of which are closely related to our discussion above about communication roadmaps.

In simple terms, coorientation refers to nothing more than the way that relationship partners are oriented to the information that is the subject of the interaction. This orientation is a direct function of the perceptual inclination of the parties involved. For example, in a superior-subordinate relationship, two issues which always seem to prevail are (*a*) the techniques, skills, and methods the subordinate employs to accomplish his or her job and (*b*) how effectively the job is accomplished. It is not uncommon to find discrepancies between the "means-end" orientations of the superior and subordinate toward the subordinate's work.

Thus, in coorientation terms, we identify *agreement* as a condition where the superior and subordinate, in the example above, describe the means-end aspect of the subordinate's work *similarly*. We identify *accuracy* as a condition where either the superior or the subordinate, in the example above, is able to predict the position held by the other individual. To round out our example, then, a superior might predict that his subordinate believes he performs his job effectively; the subordinate confirms this prediction—an instance of *accuracy*. However, the superior may add that he does not feel the subordinate accomplishes his job effectively—an instance of *disagreement*.

What makes coorientation especially important in human organizational relationships is the fact that agreement and accuracy in a relational exchange are based upon *perceptual* understanding about the communication roadmaps governing the relationship. It is generally uncomfortable to learn that one's own perception is at variance with those of others. Psychological research on the subjects tells us that this discomfort can produce tension in the human that is not always easily resolved. Sometimes, when a perceptual disparity is found to exist, the individual may simply adopt the orientation held by the other (or others); or the individual may simply deny the validity of the perception held by the other—in spite of the fact that it might be true; finally, the individual may convince the other person that his or her perception is the most valid—whether or not, in fact, such is the true case. In each of these instances, because of the underlying psychological discomfort of holding a discrepant orientation, the possibility that erroneous information will be introduced to accomplish balance in the relationship is increased. For this reason, the underlying processes of coorientation deserve particular attention from the manager seeking to understand what contributes to a "troubled" information environment in his organization.

Scheff (1967) has produced an interesting matrix to illustrate the possible agreement-accuracy combinations that can characterize a relationship. This matrix is reproduced in Figure 4-1.

Here is a description of the concepts identified in each cell:

1. *Pluralistic ignorance.* This is a condition where agreement is high but accuracy is low. How many times has it been said, "We really don't disagree, we have a semantic problem"? In other words, the parties to an exchange really agree on something, but they think they disagree. For example, both my subordinate and myself may pride ourselves in our ability to thoroughly research a job problem before initiating corrective action. However, because my subordinate has the habit of not keeping me informed of his progress on this problem until he has arrived at a solution, I may believe that he is engaging in an avoidance tactic. He, in turn, may feel that I am putting unnecessary pressure in the form of surveillance over his work. As a result, the relationship is strained because we both think the other person holds a different orientation toward the problem and its urgency.

2. *Monolithic consensus.* This occurs when there is both high agreement and high accuracy. On the surface this condition would seem to reflect the ideal situation for most relationships. However, it has its shortcomings. A superior and subordinate may both agree and accept the fact that the only way to get ahead in organization X is not to rock the boat; do as you are told and don't question why. Similarly, each may accurately predict that the other deliberately practices this philosophy. While the relationship is harmonious, such consensus is certainly not in the organization's best interest.

FIGURE 4-1. ACCURACY/AGREEMENT LEVELS IN A RELATIONSHIP

		Accuracy	
		Low	High
Agreement:	High	Pluralistic Ignorance	Monolithic Consensus
	Low	False Consensus	Dissensus

SOURCE: Based on Scheff, 1967.

3. *False consensus*. This happens when there is low agreement accompanied by low accuracy. Unfortunately, this condition has led many managers to mistakenly assume that organizational conflict is an unhealthy state of affairs. Labor-management negotiations, in particular, produce innumerable instances of low agreement and low accuracy where the net outcome is sometimes prolonged strikes and walkouts. A common complaint we hear from managers is, "I did what I *thought* he wanted and got chewed out for it." In other words, when people disagree about the communication roadmap itself as well as falsely perceiving what the other person thinks about the roadmap, we have a case of false consensus. It is termed *false consensus* because, typically, it is not until one of the two parties takes action that what was assumed to be true consensus is disproven.

4. *Dissensus*. This is a condition where agreement is low but accuracy is high; it is a constructive coorientation situation in most instances. It is a condition where each party disagrees with the other but understands the basis for the disagreement. Quite clearly, dissensus is a healthy antidote for false consensus.

A special application: the management of agreement. Jerry Harvey, an organization development consultant from George Washington University, tells an interesting story, the moral of which has tremendous implications for coorientation in human organizational relationships. He calls his story "The Abilene Paradox" (Harvey, 1974).

Some years ago, Jerry and his family were visiting his in-laws in Coleman, Texas, a small town located about seventy miles from Abilene. It was a hot, humid Sunday afternoon, and as Jerry explains, "Because Coleman is 'dry,' about the only thing you can do for relief and entertainment is to sit on the front porch and play checkers and sip lemonade." This they did, and by late afternoon boredom began to set in. One of Jerry's in-laws casually suggested that the group break the monotony by driving to Abilene for supper at a local cafeteria. There was a brief discussion, and the family piled into a 1957 Chevrolet station wagon (no air conditioning) and headed for Abilene.

Little was said en route; the heat combined with dust, however, was unbearable. At the cafeteria, they managed to swallow a bland supper, and someone remarked that it tasted somewhat like army "K rations." The trip home to Coleman was equally uneventful except for the heat and dust.

Back on Jerry's in-laws' front porch, lemonade was again served and the checker game was resumed. A long period of silence was broken by someone who inquired, "Why did we go to Abilene?" Silence again prevailed, and someone else interjected, "I didn't want to go in the first place." At this point, a heated argument commenced and tears began to fall, as Jerry tells it, *because it became apparent that the entire group had done something it did not want to do in the first place.* This is the "Abilene Paradox"—agreeing to do something that no one really wants to do, but doing it anyway. Jerry's research and consulting experience has shown that this paradox is symptomatic—yet prevalent, too—of management groups in modern organizations.

Our discussion of coorientation shows that the "Abilene Paradox" is a clear instance of *pluralistic ignorance*—agreement appears high, but accuracy is low. At one time, the phrase "You led me down the primrose path" was a popular expression denoting pluralistic ignorance. The implication of this to the processing of information in organizations should be clear. Whether the phenomenon in question is pluralistic ignorance, false consensus, or monolithic consensus, the fact remains that these coorientation characteristics can significantly diminish management's ability to control its information environment effectively. They do not constitute, however, insurmountable obstacles: careful communication behaviors and skills—questioning, confirming the perceptions of others and not assuming that these perceptions match one's own, and listening with "one foot in the other person's shoe"—can overcome many of the coorientational difficulties that we have pointed out above. One manager told us recently that he has a note taped to the back of his in-basket: "Hear not what you want to hear, but what they want to hear you hear, and then decide." We think this manager is on the right track. He is making a conscientious effort to integrate the communication roadmaps of others with the communication roadmaps he, himself, understands.

Bringing Relationship Dynamics Together

Reasons for organizational relationships—namely, *activity*, *interaction*, and *sentiments*; the concept of *relational control* (moving up, moving down, or holding position in terms of what is said and how it is said); *communication roadmaps* (rules about the content of an interaction and about the way the interaction will be initiated, sustained, and terminated); and *coorientation* toward the subject of the interaction as well as the rules governing the interaction—these four relationship dynamics will inevitably influence the manager's ability to engage in effective social intercourse with others. They do not constitute causes of information overload or communication breakdown; but they certainly contribute—in fact, quite substantially. Figure 4-2 shows how these four relationship dynamics interrelate to influence the extent to which management's information environment is controlled or uncontrolled and is subject to decay under the umbrella of a high incidence of information overload.

FIGURE 4-2. CONTROLLING ORGANIZATIONAL INFORMATION ENVIRONMENTS AND IMPROVING INFORMATION OVERLOAD CAPACITY

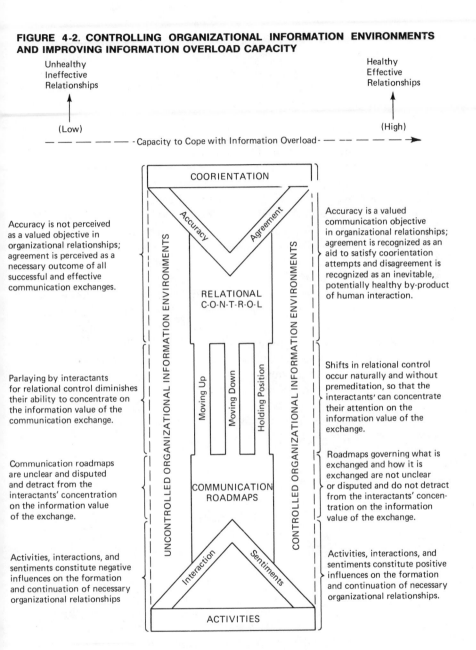

Unhealthy
Ineffective
Relationships

↑

(Low)

Healthy
Effective
Relationships

↑

(High)

— — — — — — Capacity to Cope with Information Overload — — — — — — — →

COORIENTATION

Accuracy

Agreement

RELATIONAL
C-O-N-T-R-O-L

Moving Up   Moving Down   Holding Position

COMMUNICATION
ROADMAPS

Interaction   Sentiments

ACTIVITIES

UNCONTROLLED ORGANIZATIONAL INFORMATION ENVIRONMENTS

CONTROLLED ORGANIZATIONAL INFORMATION ENVIRONMENTS

Accuracy is not perceived as a valued objective in organizational relationships; agreement is perceived as a necessary outcome of all successful and effective communication exchanges.

Parlaying by interactants for relational control diminishes their ability to concentrate on the information value of the communication exchange.

Communication roadmaps are unclear and disputed and detract from the interactants' concentration on the information value of the exchange.

Activities, interactions, and sentiments constitute negative influences on the formation and continuation of necessary organizational relationships

Accuracy is a valued communication objective in organizational relationships; agreement is recognized as an aid to satisfy coorientation attempts and disagreement is recognized as an inevitable, potentially healthy by-product of human interaction.

Shifts in relational control occur naturally and without premeditation, so that the interactants' can concentrate their attention on the information value of the exchange.

Roadmaps governing what is exchanged and how it is exchanged are not unclear or disputed and do not detract from the interactants' concentration on the information value of the exchange.

Activities, interactions, and sentiments constitute positive influences on the formation and continuation of necessary organizational relationships.

121

On the left side of Figure 4-2, a set of conditions are described for each dynamic characteristic of uncontrolled information environments; on the right side, corresponding conditions are listed which are characteristic of controlled information environments. Note that the capacity to cope with information overload diminishes in uncontrolled information environments.

Finally, Figure 4-2 is drawn in such a way that the relationship dynamics are interconnected. This was deliberate on our part and represents an attempt to show that these concepts are truly interdependent. You cannot begin taking action on one dynamic while not recognizing the effect of such action on the other dynamic. For instance, suppose that in organization X a genuine effort is made to install an "open-door" policy among supervisors. (We know of one manufacturing company with a thousand employees where the president sets aside one-half hour daily at a published time to meet with employees in his office for the purposes of "listening" to their points of view.)

If the open door is truly *open*, such a policy will have a definite impact on the sentiments and interaction side of our interaction-sentiments-activities triangle (the bases of Figure 4-2); this, in turn, will to some extent restructure the communication roadmaps used by the organization—a restructuring produced as a consequence of expressed dissatisfaction with the present rules. Again assuming a genuine open door, the restructuring of roadmaps governing what is said and how it is said would probably affect the "moving up," "moving down," and "holding position" traits of supervisors with their subordinates. With these influences, coorientation would also be affected; especially communication accuracy—knowing how the other person thinks and acts and believes—and communication understanding. By the way, for the skeptics, we continue to witness some very successful open-door programs; our emphasis on the word *genuine* above, however, was not fortuitous.

Before leaving this important discussion of achieving effectiveness in organizational relationships, we wish to stress that becoming a Model II manager or organization, as Chris Argyris has described them, is no easy task; further, as Gordon Lippitt has shown, the notion of the planned response is absolutely essential—but only possible if the concepts of "human resources" and "interfacing" (dialogue, confrontation, searching, and coping) are appreciated. We have just provided four inherent relationship dynamics that organization members must rate themselves against if they wish to control their information environments, improve their capacity to cope with the ravaging effects of information overload, and meet the challenge that Argyris and Lippitt have so thoughtfully identified.

FIVE PROMINENT STRESS POINTS
IN MANAGEMENT RELATIONSHIPS

Perceptual uniqueness/disparity, physical proximity, the need for task interdependence, the degree of shared knowledge about organizational information functions, and the authentication of the organization's information environment constitute five major stress points in management relationships. These stress points present a number of interlocking challenges for the manager who sees the need to improve the quality of management relationships in his or her organization.

Stress Point One:
Perceptual Uniqueness/Disparity

In the discussion concerning coorientation, reference was made to the idea of perceptual disparity. Adding to our comments there, we will assert here that the most singularly responsible agent for miscommunication in human relationships is a confusion that arises when what one perceives to be true is not perceived by others to be true. I see black, you see white, and somebody else sees a shade of grey. Among the three of us, we have great difficulty understanding why our perceptions differ so.

There are a number of reasons for perceptual differences, many of which we referred to in the preceding chapter. Here is a summary of the most common reasons:

"I see what I want to see, hear what I want to hear—because my wants dictate everything that is important in my life."
"I know more than the other individual(s) does about this perceptual event, so my perception must be right."
"When I perceive something, I tend to look at the whole—and especially the background, which is most revealing—to make my judgment."
"When I perceive something, I tend to look at the detail—and from the detail look out upon the whole, which is most revealing—to make my judgment."
"I tend to perceive things that I can recognize from past experience, as a means by which I can judge my present perception."
"I tend to perceive things that I can explain to myself—everything else is in the world of fantasy and I don't deal with that."

Perception—sensing through one or more of the five senses and interpreting what is sensed—is a strictly private matter; yet it must be shared if we are to understand the bases of one another's perceptions. Consider Figure 4-3—what does it communicate? We list several responses we have obtained beneath the figure.

FIGURE 4-3. AN ILLUSTRATION OF PERCEPTUAL VARIATION

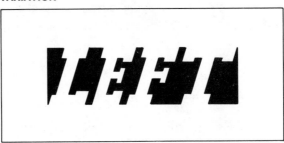

"I see a series of nonsense symbols that don't have any meaning to me."
"I see a series of designs that have geometric meaning."
"I see some abstract art representing a series of houses."
"I see several jagged pieces of rock."
"I see the word L-E-F-T."

Your perception of Figure 4-3 depends upon the figure-ground orientation you select: if you select the familiar one—black on a white background—which you are utilizing as you read this book, you might see one of the first four descriptions listed under the figure; if you select the unfamiliar one—white on a black background—you will see the last description mentioned above—the word *LEFT*.

In general, perceptual disparity aggravates an information overload condition in managerial work. The greater the disparity between what you and others perceive to be true and accurate, as was pointed out earlier, the greater the psychological stress and discomfort experienced by either one or both parties subject to the disparity. And typically, instances of perceptual disparity run rampant in supervisory-subordinate relationships: the superior views a problem one way based upon his or her sources of information, and the subordinate views the problem differently—many times because he or she is not privy to the same information sources the superior has; or the superior holds an expectation that the subordinate believes such and such, when, in fact, the subordinate does not hold the belief at all. Better than twenty years of research with industrial organizations has confirmed to the authors the widespread presence of substantial perceptual disparity in superior-subordinate relationships.

To solve this problem, first one must confirm that a disparity does exist. The manager can simply list a series of problems or situations that he knows his subordinate(s) confront. Then, he briefly describes how he thinks his subordinate(s) will say that he or she is managing the problem. Next, the manager simply asks his subordinate(s) to supply a description of their approach to the problems he has identified. Comparing answers, he can determine the extent to which perceptual disparity exists in his relationships with his subordinates.

Second, the manager should make it a habit to always inquire and confirm the perceptions of his subordinates of any problem he has communicated to them or of any problem that has been communicated to them from another organizational source. He should not make judgments about subordinates' perceptions until he fully understands their bases. The manager should ask himself the following questions:

1. Does their perception reflect the fact that I have different information than they have? Can my information be shared with them?
2. Is their perception influenced by a bias they have which I do not have? For example, is it simply because they hold a position of lower status and less responsibility than myself? Is their bias attributable to the way we have reacted previously to problems or situations of this nature?
3. Is their perception influenced by the fact that they have less experience, less education, less technical training, less skill accomplishment, or less overall professional experience than I have?
4. Is their perception based upon the fact that their professional competencies are inadequate to deal with the problem or situation at hand? Am I, in short, expecting the impossible from them in response to this problem or situation?
5. Is their perception influenced by the feelings they have in response to the problem or situation? (For example, can the problem or situation affect them emotionally in some way that I am immune to?)
6. Is their perception influenced by my observation that they have strong mobility aspirations, and that these aspirations for future advancement cause them to couch a response to a problem or situation in such a way that these mobility aspirations will not be jeopardized?
7. Is their perception influenced by the fact that they do not trust certain sources (perhaps myself included) who are responsible or

connected with the problem or situation at hand? Are there legitimate reasons which would make my subordinates submit a guarded response to a problem or situation that I would not submit?

Naturally, a perceptual disparity requires, at minimum, two parties. The seven questions we recommend the manager ask about his subordinates he can also ask about himself. If he has the courage, he can ask his subordinates to answer these seven questions about him. We have tried this with several of our consulting clients, and the exercise has proven extremely effective in reducing fears about holding perceptions and beliefs that differ from those held by a superordinate authority.

Once again we remind the reader that we have concentrated our discussion of perceptual uniqueness/disparity primarily on the superior-subordinate relationship. What we have said, however, applies to more complex information-sharing events in organizations—for example, staff meetings or task force assemblies where a number of people are involved, management communication to employees, the communication of information to managers who are geographically separated from one another as well as the source of the information, information supplied by governmental regulatory agencies, suppliers, customers, clients, and consultants, and communication shared in labor-management negotiations.

We also wish to emphasize this: It is foolhardy to believe that two or more perceptions will ever perfectly coincide. It is sensible and prudent to always confirm the perceptions that others hold; without this vitally important data, it is simply impossible to gain control of the organization's information environment, much less increase the organization's capacity to cope with information overload. True, a manager counters perceptual disparity with the acquisition and sharing of more information (superficially adding to the overload); but he or she simultaneously increases overload capacity by reducing the psychological pressure and discomfort that one experiences in connection with perceptual disparity.

Stress Point Two:
Physical Proximity

Physical proximity refers to how physically close the participants of a relationship are to one another when they interact.* With geographical distance, the need arises for communication and the sharing of information to be mediated (letter, phone, Telex, TV). There are two features of

*See our discussion of physical space as an internal communication contingency in Chapter 2.

physical proximity which an organization must take cognizance of, because these features weigh significantly in efforts to reduce uncertainty and doubt about one's information environment.

Error potential. As the distance between communicators increases, the probability is very high that errors in transmission, errors in the channel carrier, and errors in reception of the message will double, perhaps triple. Unfortunately, unlike face-to-face communication, there is less opportunity in distance-based communication to obtain immediate feedback which would provide the data necessary to correct these errors. In short, as the distance between communicators increases, so does the time it takes to correct—on both ends—transmission, channel, and reception errors. And many times such correction is too late. Figure 4-4 expresses this potential, and also points out that as the distance is increased between the communicator and the communicatee, the potential for frequent communication is diminished.

The human value of physical proximity. Earlier we discussed Homans's description of why people agree to form relationships in the first place. In his triangle of factors, it was noted that activity and interaction result in the formation of sentiments among those who are participating in a relationship. Later research has shown that physical proximity—regardless of sex—is associated with the sentiments that are developed, especially the "liking" that the participants of a relationship have toward one another. Positive sentiments, in turn, influence the quality of the interaction in an enhancing way.

Thus, physical proximity, besides its obvious value in helping to overcome some of the errors that are inherent in distance communication, has the advantage of giving interactants an opportunity to develop positive sentiments, develop cohesion, and thereby improve the quality of their communication relationships with one another.

Only recently have organizations made a serious effort to study office architecture, to learn what impact modular workplace arrangements have on efficient work accomplishment as well as on personal job productivity. In the future, management can expect greater attention to be given to office design *as it increases the information-handling capabilities of the organization.* In particular, it is highly probable that organizations will structure management work groups close to information libraries. These

FIGURE 4-4. EFFECT OF DISTANCE ON ERROR POTENTIAL

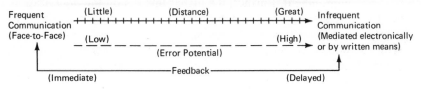

libraries will have the capability of cataloging, storing, and retrieving information at a heretofore unheard-of high processing speed, for almost instantaneous use by the work group. Multinational corporations will be using satellite information centers to accomplish the same function for their globally dispersed operating divisions.

In spite of these technological innovations, many of which are already well beyond the developmental stages, we want to stress that the human value of physical proximity will continue to represent an important factor in determining how organizations tolerate information overload and exercise control of their information environments. We doubt that there will ever be an adequate technological substitute for face-to-face communication.

Stress Point Three:
Need for Task Interdependence

There is an interesting relationship between the need for task interdependence—that is, the need for people in organizations to coordinate their work performance with others—and the presence of what Galbraith and others have termed *uncertainty*. *Uncertainty*, it will be recalled, refers to the amount of information possessed in relation to the amount of information required. Specifically, as the gap between the amount of information possessed versus the amount of information required widens, the need for task interdependence increases. In short, it becomes more difficult to accomplish one's managerial work without the assistance or collaboration provided by others—other individuals, other departments, and other organizations. Figure 4-5 demonstrates how this phenomenon increases the probability of information overload in the organization.

At point (A) on the figure, for a given task the amount of information uncertainty is relatively low; hence, the need for task interdependence is not as great and, correspondingly, the probability of information overload occurring is not too high. The situation changes considerably, however, as we move to points (B) and (C), where the gap between the information possessed and the information required increases considerably.

Obviously, we can expect to find a greater need for task interdependence as the organization becomes more complex, whether such complexity is due to the technological and/or knowledge requirements of the organization or to the complex interface the organization must sustain with its external environment. Further, the higher one sits on the organizational hierarchy, the greater the potential that information uncertainty will routinely characterize task requirements.

While solutions to the problems presented by an increasing need for task interdependence are not easy, management can rely upon several

FIGURE 4-5. EFFECTS OF INFORMATION UNCERTAINTY AND THE NEED FOR TASK INTERDEPENDENCE

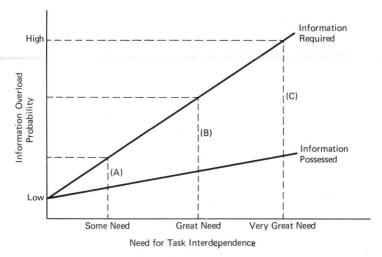

decades of social science research findings that shed light on one very important task-interdependent role: the role of liaison. Liaisons, or message "linkers," exist in the formal and informal hierarchy of most every, if not all, organizations.

Figure 4-6 shows how a liaison is structurally connected to other members of a communication network. The figure shows two hypothetical organization work groups, one containing two subordinates and one superior, the other three subordinates and one superior. The dashed line indicates that the work groups are *task-interdependent* through the relationship their superiors have with one another. In a manufacturing organization, for example, the two work groups could represent sales/marketing and production, where clearly a task-interdependent relationship is essential to coordinate sales forecasting with production capabilities and scheduling. The liaison, illustrated by a shaded circle, does not belong to either group, but he or she shares a contact with one group member on the left and two group members on the right. Using our manufacturing example, this individual could very well be an "expediter."

There is some evidence which suggests that liaisons in general have a greater capacity to withstand information overload than other organization members (with the exception of literal isolates who are either excluded from this information network by organization design or by personal desire). And from Figure 4-6, it should be apparent that liaisons can serve a vitally important function in task-interdependent relationships: Because of their structural position in the communication network, they can link

FIGURE 4-6. ILLUSTRATION OF A LIAISON ROLE

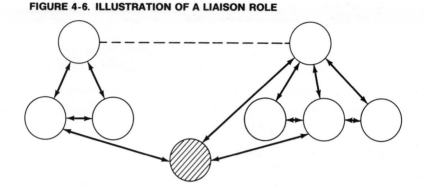

individuals in different work groups and thereby share information of value to these work groups simultaneously. Hence, the potential distortion of information that normally accompanies the transmission of a message along a chain of contacts—say, from a subordinate in one work group through his superior to a superior in another work group, who in turn communicates the information to his subordinates—is measurably reduced.

If organizations can successfully spot their true liaisons, then two things can happen: (*a*) because liaisons have more information contacts that nonliaisons, the uncertainty problem shown in Figure 4-5 can better be brought under control; and (*b*) the information overload probability which increases with a greater need for task interdependence can be reduced because of the liaison's (supposed) superior ability to absorb and process task-relevant information.

Farace, Monge, and Russell (1977) have summarized the research conducted on the liaison. Among other findings, they report that (*a*) the liaison has a greater probability of being the first source of organizational information; (*b*) he or she tends to enjoy higher status in the organization than nonliaisons; (*c*) both the liaison and others perceive that the liaison has greater influence in the organization; (*d*) both the liaison and others perceive that the liaison has more task-relevant information in connection with their liaison role; and (*e*) others attribute to the liaison more control over organizational information than nonliaisons.

Finally, let us conclude this discussion by reassuring the reader that "liaisons" are not mystical supermen and superwomen. They can be identified in most organizations by simple observation; later we describe a specific diagnostic technique, network analysis, that can be used to identify organization liaisons more scientifically.

Stress Point Four:
Degree of Shared Knowledge About Information Functions

There are four organization levels where knowledge about information functions affects a manager's ability to understand and exercise control over his or her information environment. First, at the *individual* level, knowledge about information functions in the organization is largely the result of (*a*) the manager's personal skills and competencies, (*b*) his or her experience in the organization, and (*c*) the extent to which the manager is integrated into the organization's existing information-sharing networks.

Second, at the *dyadic* or two-person level, knowledge about organization information functions is traditionally viewed as the supervisor's responsibility in keeping his or her subordinates well informed and vice versa. However, also at the two-person level, colleagues and coworkers perform a similar role with one another.

Third, at the *group* level, formal meetings and informal gatherings offer an opportunity to share knowledge about information functions in the organization.

And fourth, at the *organizational* level, formal policies, rules, and work directives provide written guidelines to existing organization information functions.

What are the information functions to which we refer? While there is a wide assortment of nomenclatures, Farace and colleagues (1977) have offered one of the most precise delineations of these functions to date. They term them *production, innovation,* and *maintenance.*

Production messages contain information that relate specifically to the accomplishment of organization objectives or the achievement of organization output. These messages are designed to coordinate human resources and utilize material resources in such a way that the organization meets its targets, profit or otherwise, efficiently and effectively. Production information also concerns itself with variances and deviations from plans and budgets, as well as from approved work procedures and techniques. It is probably safe to say that the sharing of knowledge concerning the production information function is the first prerequisite to organization success.

Innovation messages deal with the generation of new ideas for improving almost any aspect of organizational activity. In manufacturing organizations, for example, the research and development function is charged with the responsibility of introducing innovation to the organization in the form of new or modified products or improved work technology. The need for innovation messages is dictated in most organizations by the need to respond effectively to the rapidly changing demands of the external environment. Sometimes these demands may be so great that a preponderance of organization energy is devoted to the successful accomplishment of innovation.

For example, one of our clients is a manufacturer of soft drinks with a fairly well-known product image in the dietary soft drink market. Recently, a Canadian research team reported that dosages of the sugar substitute saccharin had produced cancer in rats. The U.S. Food and Drug Administration has responded by considering the banning of the saccharin additive to dietary soft drinks; similarly, a number of state legislatures are receiving testimony from industrial and scientific sources about the effect of the additive as a cancer-producing agent in human beings.

If, in fact, saccharin is banned, it will mean an abrupt 20 percent loss of this soft drink firm's sales. As a consequence, the president of the company has taken two measures: he has formed an internal task force that is devoting a tremendous amount of time to collecting evidence in favor of using saccharin, which he then intends to present to the regulatory authorities; he is also hard at work seeking alternatives to saccharin in the form of new products, new substitutes, new marketing, and so on. In short, the organization is dominated now by a need to innovate—and to do so quickly.

Before leaving the subject of innovation messages, we wish to make an important distinction: It is one thing to generate new knowledge or ideas in an organization; it is a quite different thing to implement these ideas. In fact, for many organizations, it is in the adoption and implementation stage of the innovation information function that the process breaks down and becomes dormant. This is due principally to the fact that the creative idea generators in most organizations are poor idea enactors. We make this distinction because it has been our experience that unless a crisis arises, an organization is reluctant to innovate; then, when it finds that it must innovate, there is a gross misunderstanding concerning the fact that innovation is a two-step process: idea generation followed by idea implementation.

Maintenance messages are always the most troublesome for organizations to recognize—in terms of their inherent value—much less appreciate as a viable information function. An analogy may help to peg the importance of this function.

In manufacturing organizations, routine machine maintenance is scheduled: bearings and belts are replaced, sensors are replaced, oil is applied to metal subject to friction, and gauges are checked for their accuracy. This periodic maintenance is essential to keep factory machinery running at an efficient operating level. Besides routine maintenance, the unpredictable inevitably occurs: a machine breaks down and corrective—as opposed to preventive—maintenance springs into action.

Just like machine maintenance, human beings in organizations need periodic and emergency "tuning." Without such tuning, the activities of the organization would come to a grinding halt—much like a machine that was trying to operate with pulverized bearings. Berlo (1969) assigns three categories to encompass this important organization function: (*a*) the sustaining of the individual's self-image—his or her sense of self-importance to the organization and, specifically, to the job; (*b*) the sustaining of satisfying relationships with others in the organization— working with people with whom one can get along, even in the presence of disagreement; and (*c*) the instilling of a desire and determination by people in the organization to actively support the organization's production and innovation functions.

Thus, coffee room chatter about poor morale constitutes evidence that the maintenance information function is perhaps being ignored. Unexplained organization turnover is symptomatic of the same. Excessive waste, tardiness, inferior product or service quality, job dissatisfaction—these are also symptoms that should alert management to suspect that the maintenance function is not being well maintained.

Relating organization levels to information functions. We began this section by citing four organization levels where knowledge about information functions affects a manager's ability to control the information environment. At the *individual* level, information about production, innovation, and maintenance concerns is typically processed on a contingency basis—reflecting both the needs of the individual at a given point in time and the needs of the organization. The individual will consistently prioritize production information, which is in the organization's best interest, if he or she does not feel deprived of *maintenance* inputs. Prioritizing innovation information is somewhat more difficult simply because—and in spite of popular management seminars preaching the contrary—not everyone can respond to a problem or challenge heuristically, applying a "Eureka, I have it" type of insight.

At the *dyadic* level, the capacity to prioritize maintenance-type information is increased, especially in superior-subordinate relationships where the superior can express support, satisfaction, and encouragement in his or her interactions with subordinates. We talked earlier about the fact there is no substitute today for one-on-one, face-to-face communication in managerial relationships. The maintenance function is unequivocally exercised most effectively in this interpersonal setting. Prioritizing production and innovation information is made somewhat easier at the dyadic level because of the added input that one individual can supply to the judgments made and opinions held by another.

At the *group* level, the concept of "cohesiveness" can become a powerful force that reinforces the maintenance and production functions. Especially as the members of the group begin to identify with one another and sense a common purpose in their being together, there emerges a tightening in interpersonal solidarity, accompanied by the formation of an internal maintenance dynamic within the group. Sometimes, in fact, this dynamic becomes so forceful that the group sees itself competing with other organizations groups toward we win/they lose outcomes. Other times, the development of a group maintenance dynamic can lead to undesirable pressures to conform, which are as pernicious to group effectiveness as win/lose attitudes. Unless allowed to brainstorm, moreover, the group has not proven to be an effective organization vehicle for generating innovation information. In problem solving, decision making, consensus seeking —here the group can excel in quality of output as well as acceptance by the group and others of that output.

At the *organization* level, it is perhaps most difficult to enforce the maintenance function—simply because information of this type is largely concerned with internal feelings and states of mind; matters are not that readily observable, except after the fact (as in the case of high turnover, high absenteeism, or in the extreme—organization sabotage). It is considerably less difficult to concentrate on production information since most organization feedback and control systems are tuned to production or organization output types of traffic. As for innovation information, the organization can and does certainly demand it, but aside from personnel replacement has little opportunity to enforce it—except for conducive policies which go so far as to reward innovation at the expense of production.

Finally, we can ask: How does the degree of shared knowledge about information functions in organizations relate to the concept of an uncertain information environment? Figure 4-7 presents our hypothesis. The amount of uncertainty between possessed and required information will vary from one organization level to the next depending upon the contingencies that are being faced (see "Internal and External Contingencies," Chapter 2). The extent to which information overload achieves prominence for one or more of the information functions will depend upon the need that is expressed for task interdependence (see Figure 4-6) in connection with the information demands placed on the particular organizational level —individual, dyad, group, or total organization. Here is a brief list of questions managers can ask themselves to evaluate shared knowledge about information functions in their organizations:

1. *When information problems involving uncertainty and/or information overload surface, where do they occur?*
Using the matrix in Figure 4-8, the manager can use checkmarks or, alternatively, assign subjective probabilities (percentages) to each cell in an

FIGURE 4-7. INFORMATION UNCERTAINTY AND INFORMATION FUNCTIONS

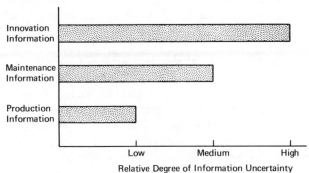

Relative Degree of Information Uncertainty

effort to isolate the location of suspected information problems. The exercise can be completed once for problems associated with information uncertainty (where there is a suspected difference between possessed and required information) and once for suspected problems with information overload.

2. *What percentage of time does a given organization subunit (for example, the Engineering Department) devote to each of the information functions over a typical work week* (for example, 70 percent to production, 25 percent to maintenance, and 5 percent to innovation)? Do these percentages reflect the current information needs of the subunit under study?

3. *How does the organization (through its supervisors) reward individuals, dyads, and groups for prioritizing the information function in greatest need of attention at a given point of time?* Are these rewards evenly distributed across the organization's management population?

4. *For task-interdependent activities (where two or more people must pool their managerial resources for a given period of time to meet some organizational demand), is an appropriate emphasis given to the information function holding the most immediate organization priority?* Do managers who are

FIGURE 4-8. SAMPLE MATRIX

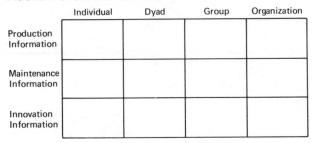

involved interdependently demonstrate, by their actions, knowledge of the parallel requirement existing between a particular task demand and a corresponding information function? (In short, are the two synchronized?)

Stress Point Five:
Authentication of the Organization's Information Environment

We turn now from the subject of degree of shared knowledge about information functions to the way that information is authenticated in human organizational relationships. Our use of the term *information authentication* will mean that individuals in the organization view either the information source or the information itself as reliable and true. Authentication means, further, that we need to recognize *source factors* that enhance authentication, specific *message factors*, and *context factors*, in addition to *receiver* factors. Figure 4-9 presents a composite of information authentication. The figure indicates that as distance is increased from the information source, the perception of information authenticity tends to decrease—a decrease typically associated with greater uncertainty. In Chapter 3 we discussed the principle of *uncertainty absorption*, referring to the fact that as a message moves further away from its source, more details are left out. When the receiver of information is near the information source, the overall opportunity is great to correct confusing, ambiguous, or questionable message aspects. When the receiver of the information is far from the source—even when message transmission is timely and speedy— typically the message is shortened to economize in distant transmission.

FIGURE 4-9. THE CONCEPT OF DISTANCE AND INFORMATION AUTHENTICITY

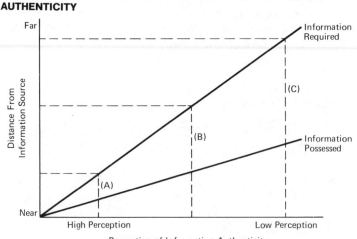

This economy and subsequent delay in reporting feedback and asking for clarification leads to information uncertainty.

Furthermore, we use the word *distance* with two meanings: *physical* (perhaps separated in space as well as time) and *psychological*. The former meaning does not need an explanation, but the latter meaning does. By *psychological distance* we are referring to a distance that evolves for a number of reasons, but chiefly:

1. *The information receiver refuses to accept information from a particular information source* (because of personal dislike, personality conflict, or because previous information from that source has proven to be unreliable).
2. *The information itself cannot be cognitively assembled by the receiver because it goes against the receiver's past experience or personal value systems or it presents a psychological conflict that the receiver is unwilling to confront.* (Consider, for instance, cigarette smokers who ignore data published by the surgeon general and the American Cancer Society.)
3. *The receiver is preoccupied with other information of an emotional or rational basis that makes him or her unable to concentrate upon the information provided by the current information source.*

Most managers provide adequate compensation for distance difficulties but give inadequate attention to psychological dispositions that increase distance from the information source—even in the source's presence. Many times this distance can be diminished by simply ascertaining that the information receiver is framed into the source's message. If such framing is not apparent, then the source should take the time to make it possible—by listening to the receiver and recasting the information accordingly.

Source factors that affect information authentication. If we attempted to establish a list of ideal source characteristics that would lead to the greatest acceptance by the receiver of a message's authenticity, the list would minimally include the following:

1. Possessing extensive knowledge (special expertise) about the message subject matter.
2. Exhibiting good intentions toward the message receiver.
3. Putting the interests of others above personal interests.
4. Being perceived by the receiver as somewhat similar to the receiver in terms of personal values and beliefs.
5. Presenting information with a passionate belief in its authenticity and appearing dynamic and genuinely interested in the information's significance.

6. Being sociable in the eyes of the message receiver.
7. Being trusted and respected in the eyes of the message receiver.
8. Having a means-end rationale that is compatible with the receiver's means-end rationale.

These eight source characteristics, then, have been shown to be associated with the greatest acceptance of message authenticity. Note that we did not include status (hierarchical position) in the list. We find that many managers view status as "an assumption by some that whatever they say is always the gospel." In other words, the stamp of perceived information authenticity does not necessarily correlate with a manager's position.

Message factors that affect information authentication. Messages containing important organizational information can be communicated in a variety of ways: by word of mouth (face-to-face or relayed) from the source, or by vicarious substitution of word of mouth (the memo, the letter, the computer printout, the notice on the bulletin board, the tape cassette, and the sound or video tape recorder—as well as the electronic digital sign). The message itself can be presented at an official occasion, one that is ceremonial, one that is routine, one that is formal, or one that is informal. It can be presented by a person of authority or a person with little authority. It can be said once or it can be said many times. It can be short or it can be long. It can use words of two syllables or less, or five syllables and more. It can be presented in color or black and white. It can also be presented by a shrug of the shoulders, a raising of the eyebrow, a forward lean of the torso, a crossing of the legs, a fidgeting of the hands, or a sweaty palm. Organizational messages, in other words, are affected by both content and presentation factors.

Content factors which enhance the perception of a message's authentic value can be controlled by the message sender and include such things as:

1. The presentation of familiar information, preferably before, but always in conjunction with, the presentation of new or unfamiliar information. This helps to create a favorable mind-set for the message receiver toward the new or the unfamiliar.
2. Assumptions stated as assumptions, and not confused with fact.
3. Inferences made by the message sender or originator supported by appropriate evidence (in the form of *verifiable* data or experiences).
4. A thesis point or key message statement stated early in the message.
5. If there are two sides to an argument that is presented, mentioning both sides in the message, although the message sender clearly takes a convincing position for only one side.
6. For both oral and written messages, summaries to enhance receiver comprehension.

7. If the message receiver is likely to subsequently receive a message from another source that contradicts the first message, acknowledging this likelihood (in a sense, the message sender is inoculating his or her receiver against subsequent attempts to discredit the first message).

8. Using threats or warnings judiciously, avoiding the specific use of strong or offensive threats to support the message.

9. Avoiding the tendency to "massify" the English language. Edwin S. Newman (1976) supplies this example:

> I happened to be in Madison, Wisconsin, when a local paper carried an interview with the new dean of the University's Department of Home Economics—only it isn't called Home Economics anymore, but Family Resources and Consumer Sciences. The dean was discussing her last job, in the Office of Education in Washington, and she said that much of her recent work was in "conceptualizing new thrusts in programming." Beware the conceptualized thrust. I saw one that had gone berserk and it took six strong men to hold it down.

As if that is not enough, try this one, which was reported in the *Milwaukee Journal*. The first quotation is from a Houston, Texas, high school principal to a parent concerning a new educational program; the parent's response follows.

> Our school's cross-graded, multi-ethnic, individualized learning program is designed to enhance the concept of an open-ended learning program with emphasis on a continuum of multi-ethnic, academically enriched learning using the identified intellectually gifted child as the agent or director of his own learning.

> I have a college degree, speak two foreign languages and four Indian dialects, have been to a number of county fairs and three goat ropings, but I haven't the faintest idea as to what the hell you are talking about. Do you? (*Milwaukee Journal*, 1977)

10. A message that invites and welcomes *feedback* from the receiver concerning information contained in the message that the receiver does not understand or does not accept.

11. A message that provides some opportunity for the receiver to confirm the message's accuracy—from a source or reference other than the message sender, including, incidentally, the receiver's own past experience with the message topic.

12. As a general statement, a message that is clearly communicated for its audience, meaning that it acknowledges listener goals and anticipations; this adjustment to receiver expectations is not accidental, but is carefully planned to guarantee that the receiver will not respond to the message as

another instance of "we/they" interests. We are convinced that such an approach will prevent (*a*) active antagonism and opposition, and (*b*) disbelief in or doubt about the message's authenticity—and therefore rejection of the message by the receiver.

Presentation factors that increase the chance a message will be accepted as authentic by the receiver include:

1. The careful weighing of message length against message complexity. For example, in a thirty-minute oral presentation, the most attentive audience will only recall about ten minutes of content, and that estimate may be high. In a written message, there exists an inverse relationship between the length of the message and the span of concentrated attention devoted to the message. In short, a message sender's goal is to present information meaningfully without unduly taxing the concentration or comprehension skills of his audience.

2. The careful selection of an appropriate form of organization for the message. Essentially, there are three: spatial, topical, and chronological. If the message is organized *spatially*, it simply means that the message sender provides for the receiver a "top-down, left-right, north-south, opening-closing, in-out" type of organization—in other words, one that the receiver can visually identify with because of his knowledge of the way that space is organized in the world.

Or the message may be organized *topically*. For example one client delivered a stern lecture to his managers concerning unexplained budget variances. He organized his message topically, segmenting his discussion into an analysis of both fixed and variable costs, and then demonstrated how each affected predetermined cost targets. Thus, he isolated significant topics and then demonstrated how these topics related in a logical sense to support his major argument that budget variances in the firm were excessive.

Finally, a *chronological* message may be organized "past-present-future," or any other combination thereof, the point being that the receiver can identify with the message organization through some time sequence that the message sender adopts.

3. Also bearing on a message's perceived authenticity is the form in which the message is presented. A memo sent to a subordinate tends to be viewed more authentically by managers than a memo received from colleagues or subordinates—simply because in the former case there is a stronger authority base for the memo. A message which is presented both in *oral* and *written* form seems to be more effective than the singular usage of either form. Likewise, the use of a combination video-oral presentation seems to produce better results than either alone. Bulletin boards, a frequently used communication device in most organizations, can be

effective if they are not cluttered with trivia and/or if they are not permitted to become bastions of obsolete information. Finally, computer printouts, in spite of the "garbage in, garbage out" phenomenon, tend to be perceived by managers as incontrovertible carriers of authentic information.

Some other message presentation forms that we should mention in passing because they are all too prevalent in most organizations include (*a*) messages transmitted through the grapevine; (*b*) overheard messages— for example, a manager who overhears his superior carrying on a telephone conversation with a higher organizational authority; and (*c*) messages that originate from outside the organization, usually received in written form, that use a confusing and complex jargon to describe legal, tax, and other governmentally regulated matters.

In short, messages can be presented formally or informally, personally or impersonally, and directly and indirectly. *Maximum perceived message authenticity occurs with a formal message that is communicated personally (and supplemented in writing) and directly.* However, one critically important factor affecting the receiver's response to the presentation of a message is the *message context*.

Context factors that affect information authentication. *Message context* refers to the environment surrounding the receiver of an organizational message: *This environment has a strong influence on the perceived authenticity and importance of the message.* During organizational crises, for instance, where information uncertainty is high (the information possessed falls significantly short of the information required), information that would not ordinarily be prominent is critically evaluated. Every effort is made to seek out and act upon information that will help subdue the crisis. In this situation, the normal authentication process is short-circuited in an effort to respond quickly and effectively to the crisis. Overload potential, not surprisingly, is also correspondingly quite high during these periods.

In Chapter 2, our discussion of internal and external contingencies also illustrated how context can influence information authentication as the organization attempts to adapt to the changing challenges and requirements of its internal and external environment. In other words, when the organization confronts a contingency (such as the recent natural gas crisis that shut down many United States factories in the winter of 1976–1977), any information related to that contingency achieves almost instantaneous authentication by the receiver.

Besides an organizational crisis, the line-staff dichotomy in most organizations offers a message context that influences the authenticity that receivers assign to various messages. Specifically, in a historical context, line messages have enjoyed greater *sender* or originator authenticity than have staff messages. More recently, the concept of staff as an authoritative if not definitive decision center in the modern organization is gaining increasing acceptance—even in smaller organizations. For one thing, the organization as an entity must be much more knowledgeable about its environment, especially as the variety of governmentally sponsored compliant regulations mushroom: EEOC, EPA, OSHA, and most recently ERISA. For another thing, many of the organizational functions that were once the proprietary domain of the line manager are now shared with staff specialists. In fact, implicit to Argyris's Model II organization discussed earlier is the need to replace the traditionally sharp line-staff dichotomy with a merging of functions that will facilitate consensus problem solving and decision making.

The line-staff concept influences the context for perceiving the authenticity of information when either the line or the staff engage in "empire building" and other disruptive practices that increase the prominence or supposed importance of one group at the expense of the other. In this type of "we win/you lose" atmosphere, the inherent authentic value of information disseminated between the line and the staff tends to be diminished. In short, old notions about line-staff are typically conducive to unnecessary rivalry and disruptive intergroup conflict; new notions stress the pursuit of common goals and objectives and a "we win/you win" attitude. Cooperation is no longer a luxury relationship descriptor for the line and staff elements of a modern organization; it is vital to organizational survival in an increasingly complex and confusing information environment.

The third important organizational influence that affects the context by which receivers are predisposed to authenticate information is the organization's implicit system for administering *rewards* and *punishments* to individuals as well as organizations groups (departments, divisions, subsidiaries). By *rewards*, we mean the recognition, encouragement, and reinforcement that is given by organization management for the exchange of authentic information by organization members. By *punishments*, we are referring to the failure of management to recognize the need to administer these rewards. We all know that people are driven to seek out rewarding experiences and avoid those that are punishing. This drive is much greater than we might expect.

We know one president of a medium-sized insurance company who makes it a habit at his weekly staff meeting to spend a few minutes verbally rewarding (complimenting) individuals on his staff who spearheaded the resolution of organization problems during that preceding week. In his words:

> My group must work closely together to keep our company profitable. Claims must keep underwriting informed and marketing must

coordinate with both of them. Then, the EDP manager must produce information from claims, underwriting, and marketing inputs that the financial v.p. can use in evaluating our overall operating performance. Our business by definition demands that constant effort is applied to the securing of accurate information—which cannot be assumed on the basis of an industry actuarial table. This is why I place such a strong premium on their ability to keep one another informed on a very timely basis. In our weekly staff meetings, in particular, I give a lot of "atta boys" to these boys because I know it must be pretty frustrating at times when you are working in a world where risk is part of your daily diet, not an exception to it.

The fourth and final important organizational influence that can "color" the context of authentication has been termed *climate*—specifically, organizational climate and communication climate. An analogy may help to explain what is meant by *climate*.

Ned Winkless and Iben Browning point out in their unique and interesting book *Climate and the Affairs of Men* (1975) that climate—the kind associated with the weather—has a more pervasive influence on our lives than we are ready to admit. Their research has shown that the geophysical and universal forces that affect climate also affect earthquake and volcanic activity on the earth's surface. Volcanic eruptions, in particular, in conjunction with the amount of sunspot activity (which is currently diminishing) and the configuration of the earth's magnetic field result in a *decrease* —historically, up to 25 percent—of the amount of sunlight that reaches the earth's surface. This decrease makes it more difficult to grow crops, which in turn affects the economic productivity of regions so affected. These same phenomena, Winkless and Browning add, are responsible for the unusual weather that many countries in the world seem to be experiencing today. Finally, that climate directly affects man is evidenced by the fact that presently throughout the world mass migrations (and starvation) are driving men and women from formerly fertile areas no longer able to sustain life to new regions where rainfall is still sufficient to sustain crop growth.

Climate, in short, influences the behavior of man, likewise, *climate* in the organizational context influences the behavior of organization members. The analogy stops, however, with the issue of *control*. Man is virtually powerless to control physical climate, but he can significantly influence climate in the organization. Climate in the organization—*meaning the perceived evaluation by organization members about how they can act and behave and about what is responsible for the way that others act and behave* —has the direct effect of influencing how people relate to one another in particular, especially in their intact work subunits, and to the organization in general.

Organizational climate, according to Taylor and Bowers (1972), who draw their work from the well-respected research conducted by Rensis Likert (1961, 1967), has six major components: (a) *human resources primacy*—whether the climate indicates that people, their talents, skills, and motivations are considered to be one of the organization's most valued resources; (b) *communication flow*—whether information is perceived to flow effectively upward, downward, and side to side in the organization; (c) *motivation climate*—whether conditions and relationships in the work setting are generally encouraging to effective work; (d) *decision-making practices*—whether decisions are made at the right organization levels, based upon access and use of needed decision-making information; (e) *technological readiness*—whether the technology and work resources are up-to-date and well maintained; and (f) *lower-level influence*—whether lower-level supervisors and employees perceive they have influence on what goes on in their departments.

Communication climate, Dennis (1974) has found, is composed of at least five important components: (a) *supportive communication*—whether subordinates perceive that their superiors are truly responsive to them—for example, subordinates believe their superiors understand the problems subordinates confront, subordinates feel that they can talk to their superiors freely, and subordinates believe that their superiors really do listen to subordinates' concerns; (b) *quality and accuracy of downward communication*—whether people are kept informed and information is freely exchanged, whether information is received from preferred sources, and whether people feel they are notified sufficiently in advance about important changes that affect their jobs; (c) *communication relationships with subordinates*—whether superiors believe their subordinates are frank with them, and whether superiors believe they really understand their subordinates' problems; (d) *upward communication and upward influence*—whether people feel their opinions make a difference with respect to decisions that are made, whether people feel that recommendations they make are ever seriously considered, and whether people feel they are given the opportunity to establish their own goals and objectives; and (e) *information reliability*—specifically, in two areas—the perceived reliability of information received from subordinates and colleagues or coworkers.

If an organization has an organization climate that is perceived by its members to be weak, then it will follow that the communication climate will also be perceived poorly. In fact, there is some evidence which shows that the quality and accuracy of downward communication in the organization may strongly influence managers' perceptions about the total organizational climate. Our point here, however, is that both organizational and communication climate influence how receivers are predisposed to authenticate organizational information. Furthermore, in every organization two kinds of climate seem to prevail: one is characteristic of member perceptions about climate in the *entire* organization; a second is characteristic of individual perceptions about climate in one's work group (one's office area or department). Unfortunately, at this point, we do not know which kind of climate affects the authenticating activities of receivers more strongly; we suspect the second, however. Figure 4-10 summarizes our discussion of this fourth context influence. (*Note*: in Chapter 7 measuring instruments to evaluate organizational and communication climate are presented.)

Receiver factors that affect information authentication. So far we have identified source, message, and context factors that influence the human authentication of information that is communicated in organizations. In one sense, we have been discussing the receiver all along; however, we also need to isolate several specific factors which are unique to information receivers—factors that directly influence how much psychological distance the receiver is likely to evoke in relation to the received information. The greater the distance (either physical or psychological), the lower the receiver's perception of the information's authentic value. We also identified

FIGURE 4-10. ORGANIZATIONAL AND COMMUNICATION CLIMATES' INFLUENCE OVER THE CONTEXT OF INFORMATION AUTHENTICATION IN ORGANIZATIONS

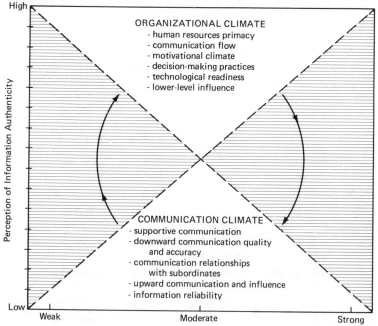

in our discussion of distance three reasons for it: (*a*) a flat refusal by the receiver to accept the information from a particular source; (*b*) a failure by the receiver to internalize information received because it conflicts with personal past experience or personal value systems; and (*c*) the preoccupation by the receiver with competing information that makes it difficult to concentrate upon the information being supplied by the present information source.

The first receiver factor is the receiver's response to the information source's *status*. We normally think of status as a condition where one individual is stationed by some criteria in a superior position to another (designation in the organization hierarchy accomplishes this—as well as the use of some form of power to control the rewards and punishments given another). Some receivers, furthermore, accept the assignation of status dutifully; others do not.

Some managers make it a habit of removing so-called status barriers that come between themselves and their employees; others ignore these status differences in spite of the fact that their employees may be very much aware of them; and still others pretend that there are no status differences. The receiver's response to status will be governed by (*a*) how he or she perceives that the information source uses status, and (*b*) the extent to which the use of status in some form is a condition to the relationship. If status is perceived to be misused and/or if the use of status is the only condition for engaging in the relationship with a given information source, then most assuredly one of the three reasons listed above for establishing distance from the source will obtain.

Listed below are a common set of guidelines for managers when attempting to understand the influences occurring in an interaction involving a person of higher status with a person of lower status:

1. Persons of higher status tend to approach persons of lower status readily and spontaneously; the reverse is seldom true. Hence, higher-status persons need to structure approach opportunities and occasions for lower-status individuals.
2. Persons of higher status tend to conceal their true feelings from persons of lower status when the persons of lower status are distrusted. Given the same situation, but one where lower-status persons distrust higher-status persons, the lower-status persons will not conceal their feelings—instead, they will behave evasively, compliantly, or aggressively.
3. Mobility or promotion desires affect how accurately persons of lower status communicate information to persons of higher status. The stronger the mobility aspirations persons of lower status have, the greater the probability that they will transmit information of questionable accuracy, especially to their superiors. Under condi-

tions of low trust, the chances that inaccurate information will be transmittted are increased.

4. It is more difficult to achieve a condition of reciprocal openness and candor in status relationships than in nonstatus relationships. Here we are referring to openness or "leveling" with one another about ideas as well as about feelings.

5. In an interaction between persons of unequal status, the persons with lower status tend to attach more significance to the interaction than do persons with higher status.

6. When higher-status persons initiate contact with lower-status persons, the higher-status persons tend to rate the ensuing interaction more favorably than those interactions which are initiated by lower-status persons.

7. When higher-status persons perceive that their status is threatened during interactions with lower-status persons or when lower-status persons perceive that higher status persons are using status to control the interaction, communication defensiveness is likely to occur.

Communication defensiveness, found in all communication relationships from time to time but in unequal-status communication relationships quite frequently, deserves some elaboration. A person who is responding to a communication relationship defensively exhibits one or more of the following characteristics: (a) tends to be evaluative and judgmental as opposed to descriptive; (b) tends to worry about relational control as opposed to a problem or content orientation; (c) tends to wonder if the correct communication strategy is being pursued as opposed to responding freely and spontaneously; (d) tends to listen almost neutrally as opposed to empathetically—the latter in an effort to really see things from the other person's point of view; (e) displays a feeling of superiority over the other person as opposed to a feeling of equality; and (f) holds firmly and definitively to positions taken on issues with no evidence of flexibility or provisionalism toward the other person's viewpoint. (These characteristics of the defensive communicator are derived from Jack Gibb's 1961 work.)

Defensive communication breeds in the receiver a skepticism toward the source's information authenticity—in spite of the fact that the information may very well be authentic. Note also that our description of defensiveness is almost the direct opposite of what we have described as *supportive communication*.

The effect of status on a receiver's response to information that originates from a higher-status source is complicated by the seven problems that we have outlined above. Managers, however, must operate in status environments, whether they personally wish to admit to such or not. As a feature of organizations, status cannot be assumed to be a small influence. But like most other things managers confront, status can be managed so that it does not interfere with effective information-processing activities; so that it does not lead to an increase in the psychological distance that receivers—subordinates in particular—place between information and their judgment of its authentic value.

The sound receiver factor we wish to mention here was anticipated by an earlier student of executive performance, Chester Barnard, in 1938. In fact, Barnard remains preeminently correct, in our estimation, concerning the remaining four receiver factors that we believe bear directly upon the receiver's willingness or capacity to judge information as authentic—"correct" in that he believed these factors essential to the acceptance of a communication as *authoritative* (his word for what we term *authentic*). The second factor is simply that the receiver *can* and *does* understand the information contained in the communication.

Understanding can be evaluated in two ways. First, before action on the information is initiated by the receiver, the source of the information can confirm that understanding exists. Redding (1972) describes two techniques that sources can use to accomplish this: feedback receptiveness and feedback responsiveness. *Feedback receptiveness* means that others perceive the information source to be open to feedback about information just communicated; *feedback responsiveness* means that the source of the information not only welcomes information from receivers which will tell him or her about the degree of understanding reached, but also is committed to responding to this feedback given by the information receivers. We will say more about this important understanding concept later.

The second way to evaluate understanding by the receiver is after the fact: Was the correct or anticipated action taken by the receiver? The difference between this way and the former is that all too often it is too late to take corrective action—when a misunderstanding has occurred. Needless to say, the perception that the information is authentic enhances understanding and the ability to understand information increases the perception of the information's authenticity. Barnard said "can" and "does"; what we have said above should doubly emphasize this.

The third receiver factor that Barnard mentions stipulates that *at the time* the receiver makes a decision in response to information supplied him, he believes that the information is consistent with the goals, objectives, or mission of the organization. Information which is thought to be inconsistent will usually produce some receiver challenge to the information's authenticity.

Barnard's fourth receiver factor specifies that again—at the time a decision is reached in response to an information input—the information will be accepted as authentic only if the receiver believes it is compatible with his personal interests. Personal interests include many of the things we have discussed earlier, including: (a) personal mobility aspirations, (b) the nature of the individual manager's psychological contract with the organization, and (c) the character of the individual's underlying need and motivation systems.

Barnard's fifth and final factor is perhaps obvious, but we find that many times it is simply overlooked. It is that the receiver be able physically and mentally to comply with the information received. Limitations in cognitive complexity (discussed in Chapter 3) and physical handicaps such as faulty hearing can contribute significantly to a receiver's inability to process otherwise authentic information.

We are now in the position to summarize the source, message, context, and receiver factors that influence the authentication of organizational information. From our discussion above, it should be apparent that authentication is a more complicated management stress point than simply stating that a unit of information received is either true or false. The concept of authentication is married to the concept of information uncertainty; the notion of uncertainty in the manager's information environment, in turn, determines the extent to which the information environment is controlled or uncontrolled; and the degree to which the environment is systematically controlled indicates how well the organization can cope with what we have stated will be increasing exposure to information overload as organizations continue to become more complex and the demands of their internal and external environments equally so. Table 4-1 summarizes our approach to information authentication.

TABLE 4-1. AUTHENTICATION OF ORGANIZATION INFORMATION ENVIRONMENTS

Distance from the information source	Information uncertainty
1. Physical Distance	In face-to-face message exchange, there are many verbal and nonverbal cues available to senders and receivers for determining if the information required matches the information possessed. With increasing physical distance from the source, the quality and quantity of these cues diminish, thus increasing the likelihood of information uncertainty.
2. Psychological Distance	Also increasing the probability of information uncertainty is a receiver who creates distance from the information source by (a) refusing to accept information from a particular source, (b) not accepting information because it causes conflict with other information the receiver possesses, or (c) not accepting information because the receiver is preoccupied with other infor- other information.
Impact	A lower perception by the receiver of the information's authentic value (its meaningfulness and its reliability).

Table 4.1. Continued.

Relational factors affecting information authentication	Factor components
1. Source Factors	Source's knowledge and expertise, good intentions, interests of others, value and belief similarity to receiver, enthusiasm toward message, sociability, trust and respect assigned by receiver, and compatible means-end approach to information.
2. Message Factors Content Factors	The presentation of familiar information in conjunction with unfamiliar or new information; assumptions clarified as such; inferences supported by evidence; messages containing key thesis statements; summaries used to enhance comprehension and retention; if a contradicting message from another source will follow, acknowledgment of this by the first source; avoidance of strong threats; the English language not "massified"; feedback welcomed by the message source; message content capable of verification by another source; and the message itself carefully planned from a receiver, not a sender, viewpoint.
Presentation Factors	Message length carefully weighed against message complexity; appropriate form of message organization—spatial, topical, or chronological; form of message presentation considered prior to message transmission; where the source's intent is to increase the likelihood of message understanding and acceptance as well as perceived authenticity, a personal message (supplemented in writing) that is directly communicated seems to produce the best results.
3. Context Factors (the message environment surrounding the receiver)	The presence of an organizational crisis—the presence of a particular organizational contingency or internal or external demand and need; the traditional line-staff differentiation; the organization's system for administering rewards and punishments; and the organization and communication climate.

5

Relational Variables II

INTRODUCTION

As a management population increases, many of the problems and opportunities we discussed in the preceding chapter become even more complicated. As most managers can easily testify, organizational growth is a painful process that requires some displacement of people and of financial and material resources. The growth itself may be planned or accidental, or as one senior vice-president of a national leasing company remarked, "It inevitably ruins your attempts to keep your operations predictable and simple."

In this chapter, we will examine the effect of *management growth* in particular (that is, an increase in the number of people involved in management relationships) on seven important dimensions of human organizational relationships. These seven dimensions all experience disturbance and will indeed require management attention if the management growth process is to be successfully negotiated. Our primary goal is to enable the manager to preserve the integrity and quality of organizational intelligence during a period of planned or accidental management growth.

We begin by showing the rather subtle but permanent effects of size increases on small work units in the organization (see Table 5-1).

TABLE 5-1. SIGNIFICANT UNITS OF ORGANIZATIONAL SIZE

Number of participants	Salient characteristic of each unit
1–2	This constitutes the fundamental unit of social interaction; if one person rejects the relationship, the unit is dissolved.
2–3	With three people composing the relationship unit, it is possible for a coalition to be formed.
3–4	With four people composing the relationship unit, evenly split divisions about relationship issues can occur.
4–7	A coalition of four persons is possible; minority rule is also possible if a triad gains relationship control.
7–9	Coalitions at several levels are possible, involving both dyads and triads; and, in general, all of the characteristics described for the preceding four units can be obtained.

SOURCE: Adapted from Weick, *The Social Psychology of Organizing,* © 1969, Addison-Wesley, Reading, Ma. Reprinted with permission.

Weick (1969) maintains that the units described in Table 5-1 constitute the critical transition points concerning the number of participants in an organizational relationship. But as the number of relationships increases further—as a department, for example, grows from nine employees to thirty—other changes occur. It is these changes to which the remainder of this chapter is addressed.

RELATIONSHIP DIMENSIONS AFFECTED BY MANAGEMENT GROWTH

Power

As an organization grows, the concept of power becomes more important in the group members' relationships to one another; especially, as coalitions develop, there is a vying for power which may reflect the interest of the coalition, but not the interest of the total group. Exercising power for power's sake in any organizational group usually constitutes a digression from its purpose as a group. Thus, with increasing group size, the challenge to the group's appointed, emergent, or elected leader becomes great. He or she must manage the group's resources, organize the group's productive effort, and satisfy the variant needs that are expressed by the differing coalitions making up the group. The underlying dynamics remain as we have described them earlier: group activity, interaction, and sentiment are interrelated—but they are much more complex.

For example, as the number of participants in a relationship increases, group activities must be functionalized within the group—larger tasks are broken down into smaller tasks and people are assigned to these subdivision activities on the basis of competence or personal influence. Some of the group subunits will have more power per se than others; the sentiments developed in some subunits of a larger group will be stronger than those developed by other subunits; and the interaction frequency will vary from one subunit to the next.

In other words, any organization represents a collection of groups, varying in size from two participants to perhaps fifty or more. Power, regardless of its base—raw or institutional (see Chapter 1)—becomes a more prominent feature of organizational relationships as the size of the group in question increases. Furthermore, as group size increases, power properly exercised—to achieve group objectives—becomes even more effective to insure the group's success. But the group suffers when power is sought as an object in and of itself by various group coalitions wishing to establish their own particular prominence; rather, positive results are achieved only when power is applied and utilized by the group's leadership to achieve true consensus in pursuit of group goals. This is the power usage we described earlier during the discussion of Argyris's Model II organization; a power usage that is multilateral rather than unilateral in application; a power usage that is defined by the group leadership *as a contingent of meaningful information* that leads to (*a*) the recognition of valid information, (*b*) informed choice, and (*c*) internal commitment by the group members to accomplish the group's purpose.

To illustrate our contention that as the group's size increases, power becomes a more visible and influential dynamic of group functioning, consider this description of a manufacturing company's president who personally felt the unanticipated effects of increasing his planning staff's size:

In our company we have what we term a Staff I and a Staff II. Staff I is composed of the president, the executive vice-president, the vice-president of sales and marketing, the vice-president of finance, and the vice-president of manufacturing. Staff II includes all other senior management, namely, the department heads. Normally, Staff I and Staff II meet separately, except for occasional informational meetings. I made the decision to combine these groups for the purposes of obtaining the greatest input possible on the development of a new three-year corporate plan. This resulted in a total of fifteen persons attending our first planning session. The meeting was largely uneventful, with the exception of the fact that my normally gregarious staff members on both staffs seemed subdued; and I clearly sensed that the communication atmosphere had changed. As our meetings progressed, two things happened. First; the respective members of Staff II began aligning their opinions with their respective superiors on Staff I; second, the members of Staff I began taking potshots at some of the comments made by those members of Staff II who did not report to these superiors. It became increasingly difficult for me to obtain spontaneous comments about the planning exercise, especially that portion of the exercise relating to planning assumptions (economic, political, energy, competitive). Then, unexpectedly, three members of Staff I and five members of Staff II formed an out-of-meeting alliance and developed their own version of the three-year plan. Apparently, they influenced the remaining members to endorse their version before presenting it at one of our sessions. When it was presented, I was baffled because not only did this new proposal deviate from our original planning assumptions, but it also altogether ignored our current efforts to bring in a new product line. When I asked if this plan really represented the thinking of the entire group, I got fifteen lowered heads and no discussion. Well, we abandoned our meetings, and Staff I is currently revamping the so-called alternative plan; and, we're making much better progress.

It should be clear from this example that with an increase in group size, power is subtly displaced within the group. Obviously, the displacement that occurred in these planning sessions can be attributed principally to the fact that two independent groups with unequal status in the company were required to function as a single entity in a temporary, almost arbitrary relationship. The president had assumed that he could simply convene fifteen people and that the governing climate of this new, enlarged group would be identical to the governing climates of the two smaller entities. Interviews with staff members of both groups revealed that throughout the planning sessions participants experienced apprehension and anxiety about the roles expected of them by the president. On the one hand, they felt they were expected to maintain a subordinate position in relation to their superiors in the group, the president included; on the other hand, they felt the need to express their opinions, constructively, since the final plan would influence the direction of their future work and progress in the company. As one member put it, "Our alliance was a welcome relief to the frustration we had been experiencing because it gave us a larger voice that reflected the sentiment of the majority." The net result, as the example indicates, was a power coalition that substituted expediency for decision effectiveness. We might add that the damage produced as a result of this planning experience included the eventual resignation of three members of Staff II and a lowering of morale and loss of cohesion among the members of Staff I—a problem which one of the authors is still attempting to help rectify today.

Intragroup Conflict

The management of intragroup conflict will become a greater organizational priority as the size of the group increases. With increasing group size, as Table 5-1 indicates, the number of coalitions similarly increases. Pressures are exerted upon minorities to conform and give way to majority rule. The individual group member is confronted with a perplexing problem. He is expected to identify with the goals of the total organization, while obeying the implicit roadmaps that pertain to the functioning of his smaller work unit. Further, he is forced to take sides with either group majorities or minorities, even though neither may reflect his true position. Loyalties become confused as well. Is it to the total organization? Is it to the smaller coalition of which the individual is a part? Or is it to a personal position that is viewed as untenable and unacceptable to other members of the coalition and/or the total organization? Most managers do, indeed, follow a survival instinct when placed in a situation involving organizational conflict. Following the survival instinct, however, does not diminish the frustration of not knowing clearly where one's personal allegiances should lie.

We are not suggesting that the presence of organizational conflict is necessarily detrimental to the organization. To the contrary, much research has shown that conflict and disagreements can lead to more creative and energetic solutions to nagging organizational problems. Conflict, in some form, will always be a fact of modern organizational life; it will also become accentuated as the size of the primary group in the organization with which the individual identifies increases. Current writing on the subject stresses that the net result of organizational conflict can fall into one of three categories: *lose-lose*, where both sides gain nothing and lose something; *win-lose*, where one side gains at the expense of the other; or *win-win*, where achieving a consensus (in the spirit of Argyris's Model II organization) allows both parties to the conflict to recognize some intangible or tangible gain.

With increasing group size, several specific methods are typically used to cope with conflict—only one of which produces a win-win situation. Most organizations we have worked with have experienced these conflict-resolution strategies at one time or another. We have summarized them in Table 5-2.

Identification of Information Networks

The identification and management of production, innovation, and maintenance information networks become increasingly difficult as the number of people participating in organizational relationships increases. We stated

155

TABLE 5-2. CONFLICT-RESOLUTION STRATEGIES

Strategy	Description
1. The "We Don't Have It" Strategy	Individuals and/or groups simply deny that conflict exists; this strategy gives the appearance of being effective but it does not prevent the conflict from escalating to the point where denial is impossible.
2. The "Conflict-Stroking" Strategy	Conflict, especially between individuals or groups that enjoy warm, interpersonal relationships is perceived as a destructive force; hence, differences are smoothed over and minimized and are not confronted openly by the dissenting parties. In effect, conflict is suppressed.
3. The "We Must Be Obedient" Strategy	Sources with power or influence may simply combine and/or deploy obedience-producing resources to superficially settle conflict. Usually, when power is publicly exercised for this purpose the losers experience a feeling of defeat and ineffectualness in their ability to override the power sources. The resulting attitude toward conflict is negative.
4. The "Give and Take" Strategy	Common to conflict situations where bargaining is involved, this compromise strategy is often accompanied by the plea, "Let's meet halfway." Parties to the conflict, however, knowing that they must give up something, tend to initially overstate their demands so that what they get is what they really wanted in the first place. One side inevitably leaves the negotiation feeling that they gave too much or received too little.
5. The "New Alternative" Strategy	This is the only true win-win conflict-resolution strategy. The conflicting parties accept their differences as a legitimate consequence of opposing perceptions of the conflict object. Through collaboration and open communication, an effort is made to establish a mutually acceptable alternative that will maximize the integrative capabilities of both parties toward a common organizational objective. In short, the aim of the strategy is true consensus on a solution, usually a new one, that will ultimately lead to individual satisfaction and increased organizational effectiveness.

earlier in our discussion about "Degree of Shared Knowledge About Information Functions" (Chapter 4) that *production* messages deal specifically with work processes and organizational output; *innovation* messages deal with the generation of new ideas for improving organizational functioning; and *maintenance* messages principally deal with the interpersonal needs of organization members.

When messages relating to production are communicated, a network is formed involving a cluster of individuals who attend to the output requirements of the network. For instance, in a manufacturing operation the need for a third shift could be signaled by the inability of the firm to meet rising sales demand. The addition of a third shift requires the close coordination of production, sales, and finance to negotiate the operating transition needed to insure a continued, efficient, and profitable overall operation. Until the transition is successfully completed, a multiplicity of messages relating to planning, scheduling, and control will be exchanged among a network of organization personnel that reaches from the top to the bottom of the organization.

Within the network just described, liaisons or "linkers" will play a crucial role as message coordinators between the various organizational groups who must collaborate and sequence their activities to make the transition successful. Besides liaisons, there are three other types of organization members who hold identifiable positions in the network: group members, bridges, and isolates.

Group members are individuals whose communication with one another is greater than to persons outside the group; groups exist both as temporary and permanent entities in most complex organizations. In some groups, all three information functions will be communicated; in others, one or more of the functions may be most prominent (for example, a product development team whose single mission is to explore the feasibility of product innovations). Finally, most managers belong to more than one organization group, which reflects their varying role participation in a multitude of organizational activity.

Bridges are group members who also have communication contacts with a member or members of another group. For example, we know of one organization where the manufacturing vice-president and the sales vice-president have a strong personality conflict; the two men seem unable to work together or collaborate satisfactorily. Within the sales group, however, the general sales manager has a close relationship with a senior production manager who reports to the vice-president of manufacturing. These two men effectively bridge their two respective groups and share information from planning meetings that is likely to have a consequence on the activities of the other group. The president of this company recognizes the problem he has with the manufacturing and sales vice-presidents, but he is also cognizant of the informal relationship between the senior production manager and the general sales manager. In fact, at present, he is considering an early retirement for the sales v.p. and a promotion for the general sales manager to that position.

Isolates are individuals in the organization who for one reason or another do not communicate with anyone else in the network; if communication does occur, it is so infrequent that it is largely inconsequential. Isolation *may* indicate the presence of serious relationship difficulties for some individuals in the organization and if detected in any organization deserves careful examination.

As organizational groups grow larger, not only is it more difficult to manage—as well as identify—the production, innovation, and maintenance networks, but also the task of managing group member roles becomes more complicated. Many organizations, for example, simply assume that superiors who are given authority and responsibility commensurate with their position will perform an effective liaison or linker role between their subordinate work group and the work group to which the superior—as a subordinate himself or herself—belongs. Such, however, is frequently not the case, and other individuals, managers with lesser authority and responsibility, emerge to occupy this important organization role. With increasing network complexity, the number of group "bridges" similarly increases. This introduces the probability that messages passed by bridges from one group to the next, due to uncertainty absorption, will become distorted and inaccurate. The controlling mechanism that should prevent this from occurring—the group's designated leadership—may be ineffectual in countering the distortion if the group bridges have not been deliberately identified by the organization. Finally, with increasing network complexity, the emergence of isolates poses the problem of how to insure that all members of the organization are provided adequate opportunity to participate in group membership.

In short, as the size of the organization increases, so do the problems of managing a larger work force. Our purpose, however, is not to belabor the obvious, but to describe how these problems can be analyzed in terms of the organization's significant information networks. Such an analysis can help the organization search for means to reduce information overload, cope with information uncertainty, improve its ability to evaluate conditions which threaten information authenticity, and, in general, move deliberately toward what Argyris calls a Model II organization.

System Formality

The tendency to formalize systems of communication and information exchange increases as the number of people participating in organizational relationships increases. Insisting upon the use of formal channels to communicate ideas, requiring heavy documentation to provide visible and preserved testimonials for actions taken, establishing intricate rules to govern who may have access and dissemination rights to certain specified types of organizational information, and implementing tedious information-control systems are all characteristics that accompany the enlargement of the organization's membership. A small entrepreneurial operation, by way of illustration, tends in practice to abhor formality; a bureaucracy, such as the U.S. federal government, seems to feed on it. What distinguishes these two organizational entities, besides time and maturity and staying power, is the extent to which problems or situations to which these organization types must respond can be reduced to a genuine problem of the organization's membership or to an extant problem that is beyond the immediate grasp and comprehension of any single individual or small group in the organization. Formalization, in short, is seen by many as an answer to organizational efficiency. Not too many are willing to look similarly at the impact of formalization on human effectiveness—defined simply as the ability to exercise prudent judgment in seeking to achieve the organization's mission or objectives.

There are innumerable examples from which we could extrapolate specific instances of the unproductive aftermath of excessive formalization of the organization's information and communication systems. As one executive put it, "We are strangled by top management's incessant need to have weekly reports—with visuals—about 'blips' in our management accomplishments." Another stated, "In our company, we are waiting for a directive to put the grapevine on the organization chart."

How much formalization is really necessary to effectively manage an organization? The answer is not simple, as every manager knows. However, there is a delicate balancing point between the informality that characterizes exchanges made within a small group and the formality that must accompany the exchange of information among and between large organizational groupings. As organizations grow larger in terms of their membership, it is critical that a modicum of "smallness"—and with smallness, informality—be provided for in organizational relationships. Weick (Table 5-1) hypothesized boundary problems that occur as the group increases from two to nine; his last category (7–9) fits comfortably within our range of smallness; we would even extend it to twelve, but no more. Formalization of rules regarding communication and information exchange are productive only if the manager is given sufficient opportunity —within the small group context as we have defined it—to accomplish his immediate work informally and in the company of his immediate superior and coworkers. Such an environment, in a bureaucracy or otherwise, gives the manager a sense of identification and a sense of impact. It allows him to become personal and significant, not depersonalized and robotized by a "third-person" system that has little place for the individual.

Grapevine Activity

As the number of participants in an organization relationship increases, so does the activity of the grapevine. During the 1950s and early '60s, a good deal of applied organizational research concentrated on the grapevine.

From this early research we learned that (a) the grapevine is fast compared to other methods of message diffusion; (b) in spite of the opposing odds, the grapevine can be highly accurate; (c) it can start and end anywhere in the organization; and (d) the grapevine message travels within a cluster (group) most typically, and then is passed on to another cluster by a bridge.

A number of explanations have been offered to suggest why the grapevine periodically makes an unpredicted debut in the organization. These include (a) the inability of the formal systems of organizational communication to satisfy the communication and information needs of organization members; (b) the belief that the grapevine mysteriously uncovers "juicy" organizational gossip; (c) the belief that the grapevine is more flexible than formal organizational communication in that it can travel in jigsaw fashion throughout the organization, while formal communication is restricted to up-down, side-to-side, or diagonal routings; and (d) the inherent nature of the human being to seek the "inside story" before it is publicly communicated through official organizational channels.

Given these conclusions and explanations about grapevine activity, modern management still remains reluctant to incorporate the grapevine into its overall information intelligence system—especially in a sensing capacity as described in Chapter 1. Why is this so? Among other reasons, the following were most frequently cited in a survey we conducted with four manufacturing companies, three service agencies, and five retailing firms:

1. "In our experience, the grapevine is not issue-oriented; it is people-oriented, and in many instances maliciously so."
2. "When you hear something from the grapevine, you are seldom able to document the source beyond 'They.' "
3. "We know that the union is responsible for planting grapevine material in our company, and it is usually antimanagement material."
4. "The grapevine is a carrier of rumor, and rumor is no good."
5. "We don't have a grapevine."
6. "The presence of the grapevine means that management is doing a poor job with its other means of communicating to employees."

If these reasons are indeed representative of most organizations, it is clear that the grapevine as a means of message diffusion and as a means of message access is not held in any esteem. In short, it is perceived to be lacking in general credibility. However, at least one manager we interviewed had this to say:

In our company, we have campaigned deliberately, and I believe effectively, to make the grapevine public. We have a "Heard from the Grapevine" section of our employee newsletter. We have a "Grapevine Square" on our bulletin boards, upon which any employee can place and/or correct grapevine information. And all managers are encouraged to incorporate and discuss grapevine information in their regular department meetings. Our president, in fact, sets the example by including grapevine items, if there are any, on the agenda of his weekly planning meetings. Our experience with the grapevine has as a consequence of this "gone public" approach been a good one; we can keep an up-to-date pulse on what our people are thinking, feeling, and doing.

The grapevine is an inevitable byproduct of the formation of human relationships in the organization; as organizations grow in size and complexity, so does the grapevine. Efforts by management to prevent, erase, or disparage the grapevine—as well as to ignore it—will have little effect on its viability as an organizational communication device. Hence, it would seem to be in management's best interest to implement systems or procedures—perhaps nothing more than a public philosophy—that acknowledge the grapevine as a legitimate source of organizational intelligence.

Organizational Feedback Systems

The effective management of organizational feedback systems becomes increasingly difficult as the number of participants in an organizational relationship increases. Every manager would heartily agree that the development of effective feedback systems in the organization is absolutely fundamental to organizational success. Feedback is needed to exert control and to take corrective action when some organizational activity has deviated from the charted course.

Feedback systems can be relatively simple—such as is seen in the give and take that occurs between two managers who are collaborating on a work project; these systems can also be complex—a computerized management-information-system, for example, that processes the work activities of hundreds of management units and determines the extent to which these units are performing according to plan.

Effective management of organization feedback systems becomes more difficult as the organization grows larger because of the timeliness variable. By definition, the concept of feedback for the manager implies that information is supplied *at the time it is needed* to take corrective action. The boards of directors of Mobil Oil, Lockheed, Oscar Meyer, and others claimed they learned too late of the payout schemes being negotiated with their foreign subsidiaries. Of course, one can maintain that the board members and top management learned too late as a matter of public convenience; however, a number of credible reports indicate that these directors were just as surprised as the American public to learn that these huge payouts were occurring.

A more frequent example of feedback timeliness that affects virtually every organization with a sales force is the annual need to obtain accurate sales forecasts. And most organizations revise sales forecast data many times a year as additional feedback is obtained about customer, supplier, and competitor behavior—as well as when additional information is provided about the firm's ability to meet production quotas or supply the capital needed to support the anticipated sales volume.

Redding (1972) identifies two critical aspects of effective feedback systems which sometimes tend to be ignored by managers who otherwise wholly subscribe to the importance of timely feedback. He points out that those individuals wishing feedback must be personally *receptive* to feedback in order for others to feel motivated to provide it. In Chapter 1, we discussed the tendency in most organizations to avoid supplying one's superior with bad news. In fact, in some organizations it is a well-known fact that the office of the chief executive can become relatively insulated and literally out of touch with the rest of the business simply because the information received is a severely distorted representation of reality (our discussion of Nixon in Chapter 1 exemplifies this phenomenon). Receptivity thus means that management welcomes the opportunity for both good and bad news on the assumption that timely input will lead to immediate corrective action. As most of us know, this is more easily said than done with some managers.

The second aspect of an effective feedback system is what Redding terms *responsiveness*. If management is supplied timely and accurate feedback, but then fails to act upon it, in due time the provision of that feedback will cease to occur. One of the principal reasons why management by committee has failed dismally is the inability of a typical management committee to respond decisively and unanimously to feedback input.

Feedback receptivity and responsiveness play key roles in the whole notion of feedback timeliness. In a superior-subordinate relationship where there is daily face-to-face contact, the opportunity for timely feedback is almost unlimited. Feedback to a small group is complicated by the fact that the feedback needs of individual group members are not uniform. Feedback between two or more organization groups is complicated for the same reason. Greater distance between sender and receiver results in delayed feedback. Achieving feedback receptivity and feedback responsiveness is considerably more complex between the corporate headquarters of a giant multinational company located in the United States and one of its subsidiaries located in Sydney, Australia, for example.

No question that electronic advances—including Telex, satellite transmission, and word-generative computer technology—have diminished the time it takes to complete the feedback loop. But these systems are not being used to accomplish timeliness through the effective vehicles of feedback receptivity and feedback responsiveness, according to the underlying dynamics described above. Feedback receptivity is clearly a perception, a belief on the part of the message receiver that the message sender is truly receptive to feedback about the matter in question. Feedback responsiveness is a deliberate action—and one that must be repeated as a matter of habit—which reinforces the feedback-initiating activity of the message receiver. This pattern, described from the receiver viewpoint, partially explains why numerous American foreign subsidiaries chose not to inform their parent companies in the United States about their bribery activities. It also explains the remark made by one chief executive officer who was querying his staff about the sudden flurry of prounion activity in one of his nonunion plants when he lamented, "Why didn't someone tell me that our employees haven't adjusted to our new seven-day work week schedule?" To which one of his subordinates replied, "You've always made it clear that you don't want to be bothered with detail."

Solidifying Human Relationships

The solidifying of human relationships becomes increasingly difficult as rapid management turnover accompanies accelerated organizational growth. As organizations grow larger in terms of both their overall populations and their key management groups, turnover of management personnel occurs at an undeniably increased rate. It is not so much the actual turnover events themselves that create the problem we are alluding to here; it is the turnover *attitude*—especially among those managers who expect interorganizational mobility to be a regular requirement or happenstance associated with personal career progression. The perception that one's placement is temporary or transient makes it somewhat unrealistic to develop deep and dedicated ties with one's relevant organizational group. The net result of this attitude is that other members of the manager's work group—who are probably experiencing the same perception—treat the group's relationship as conditional, transient, or temporary at best.

The Spring 1978 issue of *Industry Week* compared the movement of executives—and their salaries—to the movement of professional football, baseball, and basketball players from league to league. It was pointed out that the similarities between the business and sports worlds in this regard reflect the same underlying attitude—that talent, whatever its cost and depending upon its market value, is subject to caprice when it comes to permanent dedication and commitment. Why shouldn't business managers negotiate for the same financial rewards that their colleagues or equivalents in the sports world are obtaining? Regardless of the ethical considerations involved, one must ask: What about the team that was left behind?

Human relationships in organizations, and all that we have said about them, are indeed central to the concept of a team—a dedicated group of individuals who combine their energies to reach a unanimously agreed-upon objective. It is hard to accomplish this in an organization where the team is constantly acquiring and retiring players. Relationship building, relationship understanding, and relationship commitments take time, on the playing field as well as in the office.

This important point can be appreciated by citing a recent group development model reported by David Smith in the 1977 *Annual Handbook for Group Facilitators*. The vertical axis of Figure 5-1 represents the frequency of communication in a group, ranging from low to high; the horizontal axis depicts the stage of group life, from early to late. In terms of the directionality of communication, three different types of communication can be identified from Figure 5-1: (*a*) self-to-self or *intrapersonal* communication, which has a high frequency early in group life and a relatively low frequency late in group life; (*b*) self-to-other or *interpersonal* communication which replaces self-to-self communication at a relatively early stage of the group's life, increases to a plateau point, and then falls off as the group continues to mature; and (*c*) self-to-group communication, which occurs at a low frequency early in the group's life but advances rather steeply as the group matures and finally becomes the most frequent type of intragroup communication.

In practical terms, self-to-self communication is essentially silent "thinking" communication with one's self ("Where do I belong in this group," "What am I expected to say," "How am I expected to behave"); self-to-other communication is one-on-one communication with other group members to test each other's perception of group norms and standards and expectations; and self-to-group communication consists of comments directed toward the group as a whole as opposed to specific individuals in the group.

Stated somewhat differently, communication early in a group's life is directed toward concerns of the self and communication in a matured group is directed toward concerns of the group. William Schutz (1958) postulates that these underlying dynamics of group development follow a sequence that he terms *inclusion, control, and affection.*

Inclusion is a need expressed early in group life and is characterized by individuals attempting to establish and determine their identity as group members; *control* is characterized by interpersonal disagreements about rules and group norms, as well as acceptance of leadership moves, by different group members; and *affection* refers to the depth of intimacy that group members have with one another which typically increases as the

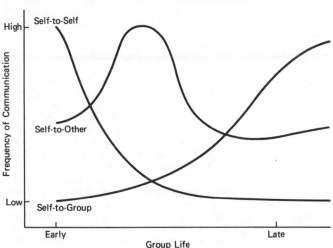

SOURCE: Smith, 1977. Reprinted from: John E. Jones and J. William (Eds.), *The 1977 Annual Handbook for Group Facilitators.* La Jolla, CA: University Associates 1977. Used with permission.

group members have increased contact with one another. In short, *inclusion* needs occupy group members early in group life; followed by *control* or *power* needs; and then *affection* needs.

Jack Gibb, mentioned earlier, is the author of the TORI concept— Trust, Openness, Realization, Interdependence (see Gibb, 1972). The TORI concept applied to group effectiveness has two significant components which correspond to our discussion above: "How I see myself in the group"—in terms of trust, openness, realization, and interdependence; and "How I see the group"—in terms of the same TORI concepts.

We have introduced the TORI concept here because obviously a group's evaluation of these concepts early in group life will be in contrast to an evaluation of the concepts in a mature group—if the group has truly increased its effectiveness.

We can return now to the turnover question we raised earlier in conjunction with increased organization population growth. As managers move in and out of organizations, so do they move in and out of groups. With group memberships changing, the developmental phase of group operation is also subject to change and, in many cases, unfortunately, regression. Managers must consciously acknowledge that this "musical chairs" phenomenon, which seems to typify the modern organization, will indeed influence organizational effectiveness precisely at the small-group level where most of the significant activities of the organization occur, as our explanation above indicated.

TABLE 5-3. SUMMARY OF RELATIONSHIP DIMENSIONS ESPECIALLY AFFECTED BY MANAGEMENT GROWTH

Dimension	Impact
1. The Power Concept	With increasing group size, power allocation becomes a more prominent part of group members' relationships with one another, and is expressed in the formation of coalitions that jockey for control over significant organization issues and concerns
2. Intragroup Conflict	As the size of the management population increases, pressures are exerted on individual members to adopt the positions held by the group majority or a powerful coalition of minority individuals within the group; while conflict can enable a group to become even more productive, typically, the resolution of conflict is the selection of a strategy which further aggravates the conflict-producing condition.
3. Production, Innovation, and Maintenance Communication Networks	In a small group, it is relatively easy to trace the networks that emerge, to isolate significant information functions, and to evaluate the effectiveness of the different roles that are assumed by or granted to group members. As groups grow larger and multiply, these three key organizational networks persist but they are considerably more difficult to identify, analyze, and evaluate—and therefore manage.
4. System Formality	As group size increases and as organization groups multiply, a "bureaucratic" effect becomes infused with organization structure. System formality is assumed to solve the problem of system efficiencies as organizations continue to increase in size. While some efficiencies are gained, management must weigh the question of whether such gains are in excess of losses in organizational effectiveness.
5. The Grapevine	The deliberate use of the grapevine by management as a management information tool has not taken hold as a viable concept in most modern organizations. Yet the grapevine is an inevitable byproduct of the formation and multiplication of human relationships in complex organizations, and it has been shown to be a fast and accurate carrier of organizational messages outside formal organization channels.
6. Organizational Feedback Systems	As organizations grow larger, it becomes increasingly difficult to obtain timely feedback which can be used to correct deviations from plans. A portion of an organization feedback system must encourage the expression of feedback receptivity and the practice of feedback responsiveness; without such expression and practice, the complexities associated with attaining timely and meaningful feedback from large and disperse management populations render management feedback systems ineffectual.
7. Solidification of Human Relationships	As organizations grow larger, turnover of management personnel occurs at an increasing rate; as a result, the composition of management groups is constantly changing. This "musical chairs" phenomenon interferes with the evolution of group dynamics that must occur if the group is to establish a level of group maturity that will permit it to effectively capitalize on its membership resources and accomplish its group objective.

Table 5-3 highlights the seven relationship dimensions discussed in this section. While our discussion is somewhat abbreviated, if a manager can diagnose his own organization against these seven dimensions, he will gain a better understanding of those circumstances that can vitally influence his ability to manage his organization's information environment.

SUMMARY OF RELATIONSHIP VARIABLES

In Chapters 4 and 5, we have introduced an original diagnostic approach that can enable the accomplishment of a single objective—*to gain effective control of the organization's information environment.* Throughout, we have endeavored to keep in focus the major concerns expressed in Chapters 1 and 3: modern organizations are complex and are increasing in complexity with each passing decade; with increasing complexity, information uncertainty, or the disparity between the information possessed and the information required by the manager, looms as an omnipresent threat to organization effectiveness; and, with increasing complexity, the cancerous spread of potential information overload situations makes the task of managing effectively more difficult and frustrating.

Given these circumstances, it is critical that the factors affecting the quality and underlying dynamics of human organizational relationships be given high and immediate priority. Throughout this book, we stress the singular importance of an effective system of organizational intelligence. This system simply cannot evolve unless managers concentrate on fine-tuning human organizational relationships at both aggregate and individualized organization levels.

To this end in Chapter 4 we introduced Argyris's concept of a Model II organization. Argyris maintains that power sharing among managers is possible, practical, and necessary; and that it can be accomplished through the vehicle of consensus decision making. What distinguishes a Model II from a Model I organization is the subscription by management at all levels to three governing values: (*a*) valid information, (*b*) informed choice, and (*c*) internal commitment to the organization's consensus-based decision-making apparatus.

There is nothing particularly mystical about Argyris's Model II concept; it reflects both an underlying philosophical commitment as well as actual organizational practice. It is measured quite clearly by the quality of human relationships that exist in the organization. It is likewise made evident by the extent to which management has succeeded in developing a superior system of organization intelligence. Unfortunately, the concept is all too often undermined because the espoused theories that managers articulate to their subordinates fail to correspond with the theories that others perceive these same managers to actually use.

To build on the foundation of a Model II organization, we isolated the important implications of organizational relationships, and then described four relationship dynamics that determine the level of effectiveness of human relationships: one pertains to the essential features of any relationship—activities, interactions, and sentiments; a second relates to the control of the content and process of human interaction; a third involves the implicit and explicit communication rules that characterize how people relate to one another; and a fourth pertains to the search for agreement and accuracy during an interaction by the relationship participants.

We concluded this discussion by showing how these four relationship dynamics combine to produce either a controlled or uncontrolled information environment for the manager, which in turn is associated with healthy or unhealthy communication relationships in the organization.

The remainder of Chapter 4 presented five prominent stress points in management relationships. The first stress point deals with how human psychological perception can lead to a disparity in the meanings that people attach to identical or nearly identical information events; the second, with how physical proximity in a communication relationship is vital to supplying the relationship with the necessary data needed to reduce uncertainty encountered in information environments; the third, with how the need for task interdependence places stringent demands upon human organizational relationships in the quest for achieving certainty and solving overload problems in relation to the organization's information requirements (and how the need for task interdependence emphasizes the important role played by organization liaisons); the fourth, with how the degree of shared knowledge about information functions relates to individual, dyadic, group, and organization levels as a consequence of the processing of three types of organizational messages—production, innovation, and maintenance; and the fifth, with how critical it is that management make every effort to provide information-authentication opportunities for members of the organization.

Chapter 5 examined the effect of management growth on seven important dimensions of human organizational relationships. Power, conflict, more complicated information networks, greater system formality, increased grapevine activity, more cumbersome organization feedback systems, and more transient or temporary organizational memberships were cited in this regard.

What we have said in these two chapters about human relationships in organizations may come as no surprise to the effective manager. We are talking about attitudes, underlying beliefs, and behaviors toward others that for some managers is accepted and practiced almost intuitively. Not surprisingly, some managers are able to consistently organize and control their information environments, and others are not. The relationship question is, as Zaleznik (1977) notes, central to the work of the manager:

Managers tend to view work as an enabling process involving some combination of people and ideas interacting to establish strategies and make decisions. Managers help the process along by a range of skills, including calculating the interest in opposition, staging and timing the surfacing of controversial issues, and reducing tensions. In this enabling process, managers appear flexible in the use of tactics; they negotiate and bargain, on the one hand, and use rewards and punishments, and other forms of coercion, on the other.

While Zaleznik paints a Machiavellian picture of the manager and his relationships, he is backed by much research and practical experience that supports his strong position. We are not denying this view of the effective manager; to the contrary, hopefully we have added a slightly different perspective to the enabling process that Zaleznik describes—a perspective that aims for control and the reduction of uncertainty of the organization's information systems, through the vehicle of effective human relationships.

In Chapter 6, we will apply this perspective to the total organization, as a system which imposes its own peculiarities upon the organization's information-processing requirements.

Organizational
Variables

INTRODUCTION

The three preceding chapters have examined personal and relational variables in managerial work. This chapter closes the loop with a discussion of organizational variables. With the loop closed, Drucker's analogy springs to life:

> The manager has the task of creating a true whole that is larger than the sum of its parts, a productive entity that turns out more than the sum of the resources put into it. One analogy is the conductor of a symphony orchestra, through whose effort, vision and leadership individual instrumental parts that are so much noise by themselves become the living whole of music. But the conductor has the composer's score; he is only interpreter. The manager is both composer and conductor. (Drucker, 1973)

To continue the analogy further, the organization supplies the stage upon which the manager, as conductor and composer, retains responsibility for the success of one score after another. On this stage, some musicians remain longer than others, some instruments are replaced by more sophisticated substitutes, and the stage itself may be altered from one symphony to the next. But the concert goes on, and its measure of success seldom shifts in the critic's eye.

Even the most accomplished conductor can only integrate x number of instruments to produce a coordinated musical score; similarly, we have argued that the ability to process x amounts of information is limited; and that the threat of managerial information overload has never been greater, because our organizations—our stages, if you will—have grown so large and complex.

However, in Chapter 4, we stated that Argyris's revolutionary concept of the Model II organization contains the most appropriate solution for the modern manager: an organizational system that subscribes to (*a*) *valid information*—information that is passed up-down, down-up, side-to-side, and diagonally in the organization; (*b*) *informed choice*—decisions that are the consequence of knowledge and valid information; and (*c*) *internal commitment*—commitment that is real because organization members genuinely believe that their personal goals and needs are in concert with organizational goals and needs.

Returning to Drucker's comment, anyone who has attended a symphony will recall that before the conductor comes on stage, each musician is separately and privately fine-tuning his or her instrument for the performance to follow. During this period, the concept of organization is all but absent from the collection of musicians appearing in the orchestra. But then the composer enters and takes his position. He taps lightly with his baton, raises his arms, and suddenly an organization springs to life. As if by magic, the stage produces an instant experience that is humbling to even the most informed skeptic.

In this chapter, we plan to look closely and completely at the entire organizational stage of information and communication in managerial work. Figure 6-1 supplies us with the tool to do so. For the manager, the important concept portrayed in Figure 6-1 has the value of a conductor's baton. Without it, the pieces of the complicated puzzle of human behavior and intelligence in complex organizations would never completely fit together to produce—for the manager—the success by which he or she is ultimately measured.

THE INTERNAL SYSTEM OF ORGANIZATIONAL COMMUNICATION

Figure 6-1 depicts a system that is an adaptation of the Functional Analysis System Technique (FAST). Essentially, *functional analysis* permits management to check the logical integrity of the primary and secondary systems which it employs to produce organization output. In this case, we

FIGURE 6-1. THE INTERNAL SYSTEM OF ORGANIZATIONAL COMMUNICATION

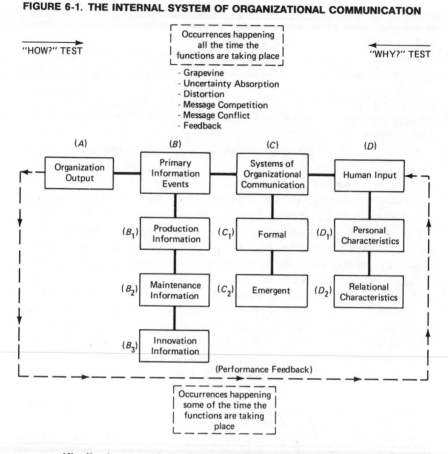

are specifically interested in the organizational communication systems that contribute to this output. There are, of course, other systems (financial, marketing/sales, manufacturing) and subsystems (costing, service, product development) to which the FAST program can be applied.

From Figure 6-1, it can be seen that FAST looks very much like a PERT (Program Evaluation Review Technique) program—except that FAST is *function-bound* and PERT is *time-bound*. Like PERT, the FAST program requires that the key program concepts be sequentially distinguished (see the heavy line in Figure 6-1). In our case, we have identified the *most basic function* of any organization as making some kind of output (in the form of a product or service to others); this we have labeled (*A*). Next to this most basic function, we identify (*B*) primary information events, (*C*) systems of organizational communication, and (*D*) human input as our *required secondary functions*—which make the accomplishment of the organization's most basic function possible.

The most basic function and the required secondary functions form the *critical path* of the FAST program. In order for this critical path to be valid, it must meet a two-way test of logic. First, from left to right, a "How?" test must be applied; and then, for the program to remain intact, from right to left, a "Why?" test must succeed. Specifically, *How* do we produce organization output? Through the use of primary information events. *How* do we make use of primary information events? Through systems of organizational communication. *How* do we make use of these systems? Through human input.

The "Why?" test works similarly. *Why* do we make use of human input? To provide systems of organizational communication. *Why* do we have systems of organizational communication? To use primary information events. *Why* do we use primary information events? To produce organization output.

Although these logic tests may appear tedious, they insure that (*a*) functions have not been assigned a critical path priority which should be realistically subordinated elsewhere in the FAST program, and that (*b*) other functions have not been inadvertently excluded from the critical path sequence. Together, then, with the logic tests appropriately applied, we can conclude that our components of the internal system of organizational communication fit a composite whole. Altogether, we believe that the critical path functions derived through this FAST procedure offer a convenient model for any manager who is embarking upon a critical analysis of his organization's system of internal communication.

Functions Not Appearing on the Critical Path

Occurrences happening all the time the functions (critical path) are taking place. Above the critical path line are listed six secondary communication-related occurrences that tend to be present any time the (*A*), (*B*), (*C*), and (*D*) functions are activated in the organization. For example, as most managers know from experience, the grapevine is always operative—in spite of management's efforts in some cases to tightly control or eliminate it.

Occurrences happening some of the time the functions (critical path) are taking place. Below the critical path line are seven secondary communication-related activities, events, and occurrences whose presence or absence is contingent upon what is happening—at a given point in time in the life of the organization—to the critical path functions. For instance, suppose a company is presented with an immediate crisis—the knowledge that its products must conform to a new governmental regulation or be removed from the marketplace (the children's pajama industry in the United States experienced such a crisis). Primary information events (*B*) in Figure 6-1 suddenly center upon "innovation information" (B_3); "What measures can we take to conform to this regulation?" Not surprisingly, communication among all levels of management concerned with the problem then short-circuits channels specified by the formal organizational hierarchy (C_1) as managers attempt to come to grips with a problem that threatens their very livelihood. That is, emergent (informal) communication systems (C_2) are spontaneously formed to supply the organizational input needed to solve the problem.

Figure 6-1 Implications

In today's complex multifarious organizations, managers are continually challenged to view the total, systemwide consequences of the uses, misuses, and, in some instances, abuses of organizational intelligence. Further, the internal features of an organization's communication and information network(s) are dynamic and constantly changing—which makes the manager's challenge still greater.

In this context, Figure 6-1 should be viewed as a conceptual tool for the manager to perform *critical analyses* relating to the performance of the organization's internal communication and information system. In Chapters 3, 4, and 5, we discussed at length the human input function (D) and the primary information events function (B). In Figure 6-1, we see that these functions constitute only two of the components necessary for a complete understanding of the total organizational intelligence process from a *communication* and *information* viewpoint. We must add the systems of organizational communication function (C)—the connecting link—which makes possible *planned* organization output. Other implications of the FAST program described in Figure 6-1 include:

1. *A problem with any one component on the FAST critical path line will undoubtedly provoke problems for one or more of the neighboring FAST components.* For example, suppose two department heads with similar authority and responsibility assignments do not get along with one another —in fact, unless absolutely necessary, they avoid each other altogether. Their personal antagonisms (reflected at D_2) produce constraints on the *formal* flow of information between their departments (reflected at C_1), but probably a very strong *informal* or emergent communication exchange has developed between subordinates of both departments (reflected at C_2) in an effort to replace the communication/information vacuum existing in the interdepartmental formal channels.

2. *The quality and quantity of organizational output increases to the extent that the critical path functions are highly integrated with one another.* This, of course, reflects the underlying premise of the Model II organization. An

enlightened management that subscribes to the creation of an information environment characterized by valid information, informed choice, and internal commitment achieves it through a highly integrated system of internal communication. It is integrated in the sense that production, innovation, and maintenance information flow spontaneously and deliberately (not randomly) through both formal and informal organizational channels, as the need arises, to meet day-to-day organizational output requirements.

3. *The system has a built-in self-correcting feature which any management can employ to reestablish itself on a desired course of organizational progression from which top management perceives it has deviated.* The final loop of any system links system outputs with system inputs. In this case, the performance of organizational output—how well products or services are accepted, in what quantity, by how many customers, in what markets, and so on—supplies important input at point (*D*) in Figure 6-1, which management uses to judge the system's overall effectiveness. Changes and corrections are then made as needed, based upon this planned feedback, to permit a reintegration of the total system.

4. *Management can exert some control over "occurrences happening all the time the critical path functions are taking place"—but not total control.* This point becomes evident from an inspection of Table 6-1. Each of the six "all the time" occurrences are listed and described, with possible management responses to these occurrences supplied. Noteworthy is the fact that in every instance, management can make a calculated, appropriate response (whether preventive or after-the-fact) to enhance the probability that its internal system of organizational communication will continue to function effectively. But it cannot exert total control over these occurrences, and this is a major point that until now most writings on the subject have simply ignored or overlooked.

5. *It is the combination of occurrences happening all the time and those occurrences happening some of the time the critical path functions are taking place that places information-overload stress on the organization.* This is perhaps the most important implication of the FAST program. Information overload tends to be a cancerous phenomenon. It attacks an organization in an unsuspected area and then spreads very rapidly. As we have pointed out, it can be attributed to difficulties occurring at the human input level, at the systems of organizational communication level, or at the primary information events level. It is not easily diagnosed as an organization problem, even with the tools we supply in Part III of this book. It is easy to see, however, that if organizational messages sent through the formal network were continually subject to a high degree of distortion, and if feedback systems were for one reason or another ineffective, so that inaccurate production information constituted the basis for production

TABLE 6-1. POSSIBLE MANAGEMENT RESPONSES TO INFORMATION-RELATED OCCURRENCES HAPPENING ALL THE TIME IN THE ORGANIZATION

Occurrence	Description	Possible management responses
Grapevine	Usually involves small clusters of people exchanging unverified information, including rumor, outside officially sanctioned organization channels.	(1) Ignore it. (2) Listen to it for information about employee attitudes and morale. (3) Attempt to suppress it by discounting, challenging, or denying the validity or significance of information carried by it. (4) Participate in it by planting select grapevine messages at different levels of the organization.
Uncertainty Absorption	Progressively increasing omission of message detail as the message moves farther away from the original message source. This phenomenon is most characteristic of upward-bound messages in the organization.	(1) Ignore it. (2) Keep messages designed for mass consumption short and simple (sentences used within the message, if written, should not be complex, and syllables should not exceed an average length of three for the entire message). (3) Recognize that information received from lower organizational levels probably contains fewer nuances and uncertainties than when the message was initially communicated (these nuances and uncertainties are typically known only by the original source of the message).
Distortion	There are three primary types of message distortion: (a) the message is recorded according to the personal rules that the message receiver applies to the information contained in the message; (b) the message is perceived in such a way that some of the information is inadvertently lost; or (c) the message is perceived in such a way that information not contained in a message is spuriously added to it.	(1) Ignore it. (2) Never act upon second-party information unless it is independently verified. (3) Build message redundancy—i.e., send the same message (or receive it) through different organizational channels or send duplicate messages through the same organizational channel. (4) Keep messages simple and short. (5) Keep the number of organizational levels through which the message must pass to an absolute minimum.

Table 6-1. Continued

Occurrence	Description	Possible management responses
Message Competition	Message-sending and message-receiving activities seem to be characterized in many organizations by a conflicting and contradictory random system of assigning message priorities. Messages sent downward in the formal system typically carry the highest and clearest priority, but this is not true for messages communicated horizontally and upward in the organization. Thus, there is continuous competition for messages of these types because of the assignment of differing priorities by message originators and recipients.	(1) Ignore it. (2) Code formal messages so that the message priority is clearly understood. (3) Set message response times realistically so that the message priority is given timely attention (e.g., "The contents of this memo must be answered in 48 hours"). (4) Distinguish between organizational messages that are designed to inform and educate and those requiring problem-solving and/or action-oriented management behaviors. (5) As a last resort, queue messages that arrive simultaneously; that is, stack them up and deal with them individually, according to their assigned or perceived priority. (6) And by all means, discourage the rerouting of messages which is ever-present in bureaucratic organization forms.
Message Conflict	When two messages support contradictory positions, claims, or directives, message conflict will occur. The most frustrating situation occurs— rather commonly—with messages emanating from the same source. Message conflict also occurs when a message is received which does not meet the expectation of the receiver (e.g., "I expected a 12% salary raise, but was informed by my supervisor that the raise will only be 7%").	(1) Ignore it. (2) Avoid suppressing bad news in the organization, because this is where many message conflicts seem to originate. (3) Insure that all preempted messages are accompanied with a concrete explanation for the preemption. (4) Confirm expectations, do not assume them. (5) When message conflicts are perceived to occur, seek a third information source to resolve the conflict. (6) Finally, remember that the informal communication system network seems to be the best communication locale for resolving conflicts of any type.
Feedback	Feedback can be planned or accidental and can be verbal (orally or in writing) or nonverbal (a gesture, tone of) voice, facial expression, and so on). Humans are, for the most part, feedback seekers, but some are more receptive and responsive to feedback than others.	(1) Ignore it. (2) Establish a Model II climate in the organization where both positive (reinforcing) and negative feedback is routinely sought, accepted, and acted upon to improve the entire system of organizational communication. (3) Provide opportunities for anonymous feedback (through questionnaire surveys, telephone speak-ups, and reward-based suggestion and safety programs).

decisions, the amount of information overload experienced at the human input level (D in Figure 6-1) would be great, if not unmanageable.

In summary, the individual parts that constitute the whole of an organization's internal communication system are intricately bound to one another. When a problem with the system occurs, the manager should be equipped to ask, at minimum, the following questions:

1. What critical path function (or functions) is most directly affected by the problem?
2. Is the problem caused by, or coincident with, any one of the six occurrences that happen all of the time the critical path functions are taking place? Why?
3. Is the problem caused by, or coincident with, any one of the seven occurrences that happen some of the time the critical path functions are taking place? Why?
4. Is the problem caused by, or coincident with, a combination of one or more of the six occurrences that happen all of the time with one or more of the seven occurrences that happen some of the time? Why?
5. Is the problem caused by, or coincident with, a combination of two of more of the six occurrences that happen all of the time the critical path functions are taking place? Why?
6. Is the problem caused by, or coincident with, a combination of two or more of the seven occurrences that happen some of the time the critical path functions are taking place? Why?

In other words, the objective here is to locate and isolate the most probable problem source so that it can be treated and remedied without disturbing the remainder of the internal system of organizational communication. We provide a point matrix in Figure 6-2, which can be used by the manager for such a purpose.

While the matrix may at first appear somewhat overwhelming, its usage is actually not at all difficult. It is designed to answer any one of the six problem-probing questions listed above. For instance, suppose that a manager suspects a problem with the "systems of organizational communication" critical path function (see Figure 6-1). Specifically, he or she has learned that the grapevine is carrying a message to the effect that the organization (a manufacturing company) is building inventories at a time when there is a decline in business activity. Speculation among those included in the grapevine network is that an impending work force layoff is at hand, and foremen are beginning to receive inquiries in that regard. In reality, the reason for the inventory accumulation is top management's

FIGURE 6-2. ISOLATING INTERNAL COMMUNICATION PROBLEM SOURCES

Cause	Effect												
	P.I.	M.I.	I.I.	Form.	Emer.	Pers.	Relat.	G.V.	U.A.	Dist.	M.C.	M.Con.	F.B.
Production Information	1.1	1.2	1.3	1.4	1.5	1.6	1.7	1.8	1.9	1.10	1.11	1.12	1.13
Maintenance Information	2.1	2.2	2.3	2.4	2.5	2.6	2.7	2.8	2.9	2.10	2.11	2.12	2.13
Innovation Information	3.1	3.2	3.3	3.4	3.5	3.6	3.7	3.8	3.9	3.10	3.11	3.12	3.13
Formal	4.1	4.2	4.3	4.4	4.5	4.6	4.7	4.8	4.9	4.10	4.11	4.12	4.13
Emergent	5.1	5.2	5.3	5.4	5.5	5.6	5.7	5.8	5.9	5.10	5.11	5.12	5.13
Personal	6.1	6.2	6.3	6.4	6.5	6.6	6.7	6.8	6.9	6.10	6.11	6.12	6.13
Relational	7.1	7.2	7.3	7.4	7.5	7.6	7.7	7.8	7.9	7.10	7.11	7.12	7.13
Grapevine	8.1	8.2	8.3	8.4	8.5	8.6	8.7	8.8	8.9	8.10	8.11	8.12	8.13
Uncertainty Absorption	9.1	9.2	9.3	9.4	9.5	9.6	9.7	9.8	9.9	9.10	9.11	9.12	9.13
Distortion	10.1	10.2	10.3	10.4	10.5	10.6	10.7	10.8	10.9	10.10	10.11	10.12	10.13
Message Competition	11.1	11.2	11.3	11.4	11.5	11.6	11.7	11.8	11.9	11.10	11.11	11.12	11.13
Message Conflict	12.1	12.2	12.3	12.4	12.5	12.6	12.7	12.8	12.9	12.10	12.11	12.12	12.13
Feedback	13.1	13.2	13.3	13.4	13.5	13.6	13.7	13.8	13.9	13.10	13.11	13.12	13.13

Key: P.I. = Production Information; M.I. = Maintenance Information; I.I. = Innovation Information; Form. = Formal; Emer. = Emergent; Pers.= Personal Characteristics; Relat. = Relational Characteristics; GV = Grapevine; U.A. = Uncertainty Absorption; Dist. = Distortion; M.C. = Message Competition; M.Con. = Message Conflict; and F.B. = Feedback.

knowledge that a competitor is very close to going out of business and their desire to maintain continuity for the competitor's customers when the shutdown occurs.

Using the matrix in Figure 6-2, the manager has several cell choices to make: (*a*) the selection of cell 8.10, if that were chosen, would indicate a belief that the *grapevine* was the main reason for the distortion that occurred; (*b*) the selection of cell 10.8, on the other hand, would indicate a belief that the *distortion* itself led to grapevine activity; (*c*) the selection of cell 5.10 would suggest the belief that the use of the *emergent* system to carry information about the inventory accumulation had led to a distortion of the facts; or (*d*) the choice of cell 10.5 would suggest the belief that *distortion* itself led to increased communication activity within the emergent communication system. In our example here, with no other information provided, choices (*a*) or (*b*) seem the most plausible.

Figure 6-2, in other words, provides for some determination of suspected cause and suspected effect in the analysis of a problem with a critical path function of an organization's internal organizational communication system. Those occurrences listed in the row designations of Figure 6-2 form the causal side of the matrix. Thus, in analyzing a particular problem, a manager need only single out from this vertically specified list those occurrences which he or she believes are responsible for those occurrences that are repeated as column (horizontal) headings. Circling the various combinations helps to pinpoint sources that are evidently influencing the detected critical path problem. We might add that getting the causal sequence in the right order (the grapevine led to distortion versus distortion led to grapevine activity) is not nearly as important as being able to specify accurately the occurrences that are associated with the problem management has identified.

A Closer Examination of the Systems of Organizational Communication Function

At this point, it is necessary to expand our discussion of the two major systems of internal communication in the organization: formal and emergent (we have also used the term *informal* to mean *emergent*). In this section, we indicate how and why individuals and groups in an organization send and receive production, maintenance, and innovation information through either the formal or emergent communication systems or both.

To this end, we introduce the concept of "structure." Figure 6-3 illustrates six structural variations or human networks found in organizations

FIGURE 6-3. ORGANIZATION STRUCTURAL VARIATIONS

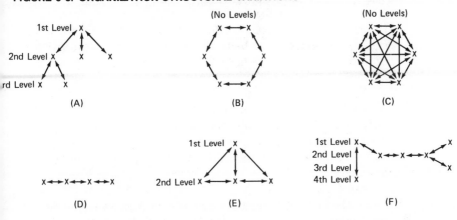

The x's in Figure 6-3 can represent either individuals or groups or even entire organizations (such as divisions or subsidiaries). The essential characteristics of the six arbitrary networks we have selected are as follows:

Net A. This net resembles a typical hierarchical relationship found in most organizations, characteristically depicted on an organization chart. In this example, three levels are represented. Noteworthy is the fact that this formal hierarchical arrangement technically limits the accessibility of some members of the network to other members. It is for this very reason that formal organizational structural systems, once established, lead to the evolution of informal structures: informal structures permit accessibility, which is not multilateral in hierarchical structures. Besides the important issue of accessibility, there are some other advantages and disadvantages to a conventional hierarchical structure:

1. *Advantages*
   -Authority and responsibility levels are easily distinguished from the top to the bottom of the hierarchy.
   -Decision-making roles are easily identified.
   -The lines of communication are clearly defined.
   -Management reporting relationships are clearly identified.
   -Accountability for actions taken can be quickly determined.
   -Technically, all individuals at a given level of the hierarchy have mutual access to information maintained at the next higher level.
2. *Disadvantages*
   -Information received at the third and subsequent management levels of the hierarchy is subject to uncertainty absorption and distortion; upward-flowing information is similarly threatened.

-The speedy transmission of information—up-down and down-up—is restricted as the number of hierarchical levels increases.
-Information bottlenecks are likely to occur at the third and subsequent levels of the hierarchy—especially if a clear system of information priorities has not been established in the organization.
-The ability of a given management level of the hierarchy to respond to a crisis on its own level is dependent upon the cooperation of the next higher level of the hierarchy.
-The perceived cohesiveness and feeling of overall unity diminishes, typically, at the third and subsequent levels of the hierarchy.
-In any formal hierarchy, at some point in the growth of the organization, a bureaucratic effect sets in (e.g., increased standardization, regimentation, intolerance of exceptions), which tends to dampen and discourage human initiative and spontaneity in organizational problem solving and decision making.

Net B. This structure, resembling a circle, could represent (*a*) an informal communication network in an organization, or (*b*) a combination of a formal and informal network. The first observation to be made about Net B is that network member accessibility is evenly distributed among the members, which is not the case in Net A; however, accessibility is still limited because the maximum number of contacts a member of Net B has with other members is two. Other advantages and disadvantages include:

1. *Advantages*
   -The perceived cohesiveness and feeling of overall unity and togetherness are typically high.
   -The ability to respond to sudden and confusing changes—crises—is typically better than in hierarchical structures.
   -Each member of the net is more or less a self-contained decision center, which tends to enhance the quality of participation and commitment to focal issues confronting members of the net.
   -Problems of hierarchical-position power are noticeably absent in this structural arrangement—technically speaking, everyone has equal status, although not equal influence.
2. *Disadvantages*
   -It is difficult for members to organize their resources efficiently.
   -While power may be distributed equally, the capacity to influence is not; unless the ground rules are accepted by all the members, political maneuverings to exert influence and possibly

achieve status can undermine the performance effectiveness of the net.

-While the ability to respond to crises is superior to hierarchical structures, the speed with which this response is made can be considerably slower.

-If a member elects to disassociate himself or herself from the net, all the advantages of this circle-type arrangement are lost until the member is reinstated or a replacement is found.

Net C. This structure represents perhaps the ideal emergent or informal type of organization structure. It offers an opportunity for maximum accessibility to information. It is most typical of small groups or management work teams. However, even with members of the net geographically dispersed from one another, use of such devices as conference calls can restore the accessibility features of groups that have immediate face-to-face contacts among members.

1. *Advantages*
    -As with Net B, morale and overall feeling of unity of this type of structure are typically very high.

    -The opportunity for immediate and multiple feedback is greater in this type of structure than with any other type of structural variation; as a result, the ability to solve complex problems is great.

    -The ability to respond to crises is high, and the speed with which this response can be made is also high.

    -The perception of individual communication freedom can be greater with this arrangement than with any other structural type.

    -The presence of distortion, blockage, and uncertainty absorption is minimized with this structure.

    -From the viewpoint of hierarchical status and the impending problems that perceptions of differing status relationships cause, this net is superior to Net A.

    -This is the only structure that reflects a Model II, consensus management orientation.

2. *Disadvantages*
    -Because communication is totally unrestricted, the potential for information overload is rather high; this is because the participation demand on individual members is great.

    -The process of organizing the net to accomplish an objective can be difficult if members do not recognize or accept the need for emergent administrative leadership.

-The net encourages influence struggles, since presumably everyone has equal status.

-Message conflict and message competition (see Table 6-1) can
be great if no self-enforced information priorities are adopted
by the structure.

Net D. Nets A, B, and C are by far the most common formal and
informal structures encountered in most organizations. Beginning with Net
D, however, we present three additional structures which to a greater or
lesser extent share characteristics in common with the three previous nets.

Net D will be recognized as a simple chain in which, again, accessibility
to information sources is unevenly distributed. In fact, if Net D were
placed vertically instead of horizontally in Figure 6-3, it would resemble
succeeding management levels of a formal organizational hierarchy. The
implications of the chain—which is found in both formal and informal
communication structures—are as follows:

1. The risk of distortion and uncertainty absorption is great (see our
brief discussion of the serial transmission phenomenon in Chapter 3).

2. A chain's message transmission and receiving characteristics will vary
depending upon whether there are an odd or even number of members
forming the chain. With an even membership, as we show in Figure 6-3, no
single individual (or unit) can balance the flow of messages that are routed
along the chain. With an odd membership, however, one person in the
center of the chain can perform this information-central function, which to
some extent can make the chain arrangement a more efficient—though not
necessarily more reliable—handler of messages.

3. A chain can pass messages reasonably fast, although as the number of
chain links increases, so does the error or distortion potential. Our research
has shown that message accuracy cannot be predicted with more than five
to seven members comprising a chain network. On this basis, we can state
that, as a general guideline, an organization with more than this number of
formal hierarchical levels is likely to experience significant distortion in its
downward and upward message flow—especially for messages originating
at the extreme vertical ends of the organization.

Net E. This net is a reproduction of a single level jump in Net A. The
only difference is that there is a horizontal or side-to-side message flow
possibility built into the net structure (if we view the net as a formal
structure). As a consequence, information accessibility is maximized for
two members of this net—that is, they can exchange information with
every other member of the net. Some other implications of Net E are:

1. The distortion potential is relatively low. With one member receiving messages from all other members, problems with message accuracy are minimized—since this individual (or unit) can verify a message by contacting all other members of the net to confirm its accuracy.

2. Messages can also be disseminated rapidly, providing that the number of members located at the second level of the net structure is not excessive. Research indicates that up to thirty five contacts can send and receive messages with one central coordinator without seriously reducing the performance effectiveness of the net. In formal structures, managers will recognize this upper limit as the frequently cited span-of-control limit.*

We mentioned the fact that Net E, if viewed as a segment of a formal organization structure, offers an opportunity for horizontal communication. As any manager knows, peer contact in an organization is perhaps the most valuable source of information concerning other functional areas of the organization which can influence what will or should occur in one's own area of management responsibility. In smaller organizations (five hundred employees or less), peer or horizontal management communication is customary—rigid formal structural rules are seldom followed. In large organizations, and in organizations that are—or resemble—bureaucracies, due to the organization's reward system, horizontal contacts are not encouraged or provided for in the organization's published formal structure (an ad hoc committee of peers is not a substitute, incidentally, for a structural system that requires horizontal communication as an essential ingredient for the maintenance of management relationships).

Net F. This net represents a mutation of the other net structures, but retains both formal and informal net characteristics. Information accessibility is largely dependent upon one-to-one contacts within the net, with the exception of the central member—who has access to three other members. Obviously, this individual (or unit) has a great degree of flow control over messages that are exchanged within the structure; because the structure is spread out—in contrast to Net E—even dominance over flow control is insufficient to insure accuracy. Other characteristics of this structure are:

1. If viewed as a formal organizational hierarchy, from left to right Net F depicts first a superior-subordinate relationship between the first (top)

---

*The state-of-the-art conclusion on the subject of span of control is: It depends. It depends upon the individual superior, members of his or her work team, and the situation, according to Van Fleet and Bedein (1977).

and fourth (bottom) levels of the organization; which, because levels 2 and 3 are not shown in the relationship, is most likely indicative of an informal contact existing between these individuals (or units). This level-1 member also has a direct relationship with a level-2 subordinate, who in turn has contact with another level-2 peer, who in turn has a direct relationship with another level-1 superior as well as with a level-3 subordinate. We supply this amplified description to illustrate the fact when an organizational network of management relationships is plotted, the network usually has elements of both the formal organization hierarchy and an emergent (informal) structure.

2. Net F has some of the characteristics of Nets A (hierarchical relationships), B (chain), and C (horizontal communication). Thus, it contains all the strengths and weaknesses of these structures that have already been discussed. It also suggests the basis for a possible management role conflict—a level-2 member enjoys higher accessibility than both of the level-1 members depicted. This observation explains a number of organizational scenarios that we have witnessed: a superior who relies upon an informer-subordinate to transmit information that is otherwise unavailable to him; a subordinate who deliberately "massages" information designed for a superior because he or she is in an advantageous message-intercept position; a superior who cannot trust or obtain needed information from an immediate subordinate and therefore elects to bypass the subordinate to acquire the information; and an informal liaison arrangement of a group of people (or units) loosely tied to the organization's hierarchy to establish a network for some predetermined purpose.

3. Finally, in odd-person groups that are structured similarly to Net F, the possibility of a majority-minority coalition is always present. In Net F, one member (the center x on level 2) is in a position to form an alliance with the three members situated on either the left or the right. Such an alliance can produce an imbalance in the net's message flow in favor of the majority coalition.

The issue of symmetrical message flow. In Figure 6-3 all message connections are depicted as two-way (↔). In real organizational communication structures, some of the contacts are one-way and others are two-way. When one-way contacts are added to a net representation, the effect is an immediate reduction in information accessibility for one or more of the members and an increased probability that messages flowing through the structure will be perceived inaccurately. As we stated earlier, in any network structure, four possible network roles can be distinguished: (*a*) *liaisons*—linking individuals who do not belong to a particular network group, but who function as a connection between two or more intact net structures; (*b*) *group members*—whose communication with one another in a defined network exceeds half of all communication directed outside the group members' network; (*c*) *bridges*—members of one network group who have communication contacts with members of other communication groups; and (*d*) *isolates*—individuals with no membership in a network group. Figure 6-4 illustrates these roles and the effect of asymmetry throughout the entire structure.

The first observation we can make is that Net 2 in Figure 6-4 is the most highly integrated network—it has the fewest number of members, and they enjoy total symmetrical relationships with one another. (In the real organization from which these net charts were constructed, Net 2 was composed of four computer-systems analysts.)

One member of Net 2 has a one-way bridge relationship with a bridge in Net 3. In fact, in the organization studied, this was primarily a reporting relationship to the EDP (electronic data-processing) systems manager. Apparently, much of the production type of information exchanged in Net 2 was needed to make decisions in Net 3 (which constituted both EDP and accounting), but the reverse was not true. From this standpoint, Net 2 is isolated, organizationally speaking, except within its own finite structure.

Net 3 has seven one-way links and five two-way links. In the real organization, this group was managed by a rather firm, autocratic individual, who was described by his people as a technical genius. His human relations skills, however, were perceived to be limited, and the general level of morale reported among his subordinates was low. The two isolates shown adjacent to Net 3 were part-time bookkeepers in the EDP and accounting department. Apparently, the department manager saw no reason to involve them in the department's communication structure. We should point out that Net 3 illustrates what we were talking about in the description of Net F in Figure 6-3: it is a mutation in the sense that the routing of messages is partially in conformity with this department's formal hierarchy (message routings between the department manager, the

FIGURE 6-4. ILLUSTRATION OF THE FOUR NET ROLES

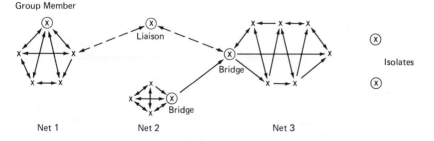

bridge, and four of his subordinates—three in Net 3 and one in Net 2), as well as informal contacts that have evolved within the net. This is true of most communication structures found in organizations.

Finally, one member of Net 3 has a relationship with a liaison between Nets 1 and 3. In the organization from which we obtained these data, the liaison was the executive vice-president in charge of finance. The bridge in Net 3 was the company's controller. Interestingly, while the organization's formal chart indicated a direct reporting relationship between the bridge in Net 3 and the liaison, none was apparent during the two-week period data were collected on communications in this organization.

Net 1 closely approximates Net C in Figure 6-3. One member of the group did not report a communication relationship with one other member; however, he was an outside consultant who had been hired by the organization for a temporary assignment. The group itself was composed of the company's president (who had contact with the liaison), the vice-president of planning, the marketing vice-president, a corporate attorney, and the consultant. During the period of study, this group was launching a new merger and acquisition program, so in this sense its formation met a specific organizational requirement.

In summary, the issue of symmetrical message flow is pertinent to both formal and informal organizational structures. We have treated the subject rather simplistically here, but we believe that an understanding of the effects of symmetry—or the lack thereof—is important to the manager who wishes to obtain a finer appreciation of the structural dynamics that affect communication relationships in his or her organization. A change in structural symmetry has one important effect worth remembering: *It alters the information accessibility opportunities available to members who comprise the structure.* Any alteration of information accessibility can produce any or all of the following consequences for a manager:

1. The ability to perform one's task effectively is reduced if a two-way symmetrical relationship is replaced with a one-way relationship.

2. The use of feedback as a self-correcting mechanism is lost in an asymmetrical relationship.

3. The accuracy of the information communicated in a one-way relationship becomes dependent upon the ability of the message sender to anticipate the communication needs of the message receiver and the ability of the receiver to decipher the message accurately.

4. The human feeling that accompanies perceived information inaccessibility (because one cannot challenge, counter, or reject messages that originate from sources who protect an incontrovertible message superiority) is counterproductive to effective information exchange in the organization.

5. Finally, when symmetry in a relationship changes, the entire structure of which that relationship is a part changes; and there is a "mushroom effect"—new channels will be formed to reestablish a human connection that will provide surrogate information to replace the loss of information that accompanied the symmetry change ("If I can't get the information I need from him, I'll find another source!").

Why information accessibility is important. Smaller companies have much less of a problem with internal information accessibility than larger ones. This is because, as was indicated earlier, smaller organizations tend to have a more fully developed and organizationally accepted informal communication system. As the organization becomes larger, information accessibility becomes a serious problem because (*a*) the original sources of information become blurred in a myriad of reports and inputs to projects of complex magnitude, thereby allowing ever-present uncertainty absorption to erode a clear statement of the facts; (*b*) the organization simply loses track of which unit or individual has the information needed; (*c*) time does not permit a thorough and exhaustive evaluation of data that are presented to make decisions; and (*d*) bureaucracy layers itself in such a way that the most profound answer to a relatively simple question is another question followed by a referral.

Why should organizations place a very high premium on encouraging maximum information accessibility—whether it is accomplished through formal or informal channels? We can cite six important reasons:

1. *To circumvent certain superiors who refuse to communicate upward good ideas from subordinate managers.* The quality of good ideas that reach the top from third- and fourth-level managers is directly proportional to the extent to which their superiors encourage and practice two-way communication relationships. If information possession in an organization is subject to a status or position determination (such as in a Model I organization), then the organization distribution of information accessibility will be quite low.

2. *To accelerate the speed of information flow in crisis situations.* In a crisis, *all* information related to the crisis immediately acquires a high priority. But if the habit of inaccessibility to information has previously characterized the organization, the introduction of a temporary crisis-accessibility policy will not eradicate old behavior patterns. Specifically, it is much more difficult to create two-way relationships than to discourage them, and it is obviously difficult to establish new information links where none previously existed.

3. *To insure that information is validated before it is transmitted through the formal structure.* It has often been said that Nixon's most serious mistakes during the Watergate controversy were to announce through

public channels that portions of his notorious tapes had been erased—and to indicate that such tapes existed in the first place. If Nixon's own information accessibility had been higher (he was protected by a small screen of advisors whose own inability to perceive reality accurately is evidenced by the fact that they all ended up with jail sentences), the opportunity for a validation process in connection with the tapes would have been greater. Or consider the admission of a number of U.S. multinational corporations in 1976 that payoffs were common to overseas suppliers and customers. Embarrassingly, the magnitude of these payoffs proved to be higher in several instances than these corporations publicly reported. Again, the information validation process apparently failed to the extent that when the information was formally disseminated, it was in error.

4. *To reduce the probability of information distortion and uncertainty absorption.* Given low accessibility to information, the likelihood that the information will be misrepresented increases. Several of our clients are continually confronted with unionization threats—a small group of employees who begin circulating union cards and/or drumming up support for a union. Typically, management receives knowledge of these activities through the grapevine, and if the first line of supervision is not strong, management's planned response to such a campaign is typically based upon questionable information. In short, low information accessibility complicates any attempt to determine just how threatening the unionization attempt really is.

5. *To allow managers to participate more fully in the organization's decision-making process.* Two major tenets of the Model II organization are valid information and informed choice; and the Model II management system is founded on the premise that consensus decision making can be no more effective than the quality of the information that is available to support the decision. In brief, qualitatively high participation in the organization's decision-making process is predicated upon high information accessibility. In small and medium-sized businesses (mostly closely held) much greater attention is now being given to the establishment of long-range business plans; however, we are also witnessing reluctance on the part of chief executive officers who spearhead this planning process to share with their operating managers balance-sheet specifics about the firm. As a consequence, the operating managers must act on the basis of certain financial assumptions (regarding profitability, debt, and capital strength in particular, and excluding the major components of working capital in general), which may or may not represent financial reality for the corporation. In short, because of this limitation of accessibility to needed planning information, the quality of the plan itself is threatened.

6. *To insure that highly complex and variable organizational tasks can be accomplished successfully.* Schneider (1971) has estimated that 30 percent of

scientific manpower is wasted or lost because important information is not accessible to the person who needs it, at the time he or she needs it. In an organization characterized by a relatively routine makeup of the way tasks are performed, most of the information needed to perform the task effectively is already possessed by those who are performing the task (an assembly line operation, for example). Unless the task abruptly changes, the need for high information accessibility is not that great. But if the task is always changing and/or highly complex (such as the designing of a new digital oscilloscope that requires the coordination of many technical personnel), high information accessibility is essential if the task is to meet a predetermined production timetable. Figure 6-5 illustrates this important relationship:

FIGURE 6-5. RELATING INFORMATION ACCESSI-BILITY TO TASK VARIABILITY AND COMPLEXITY

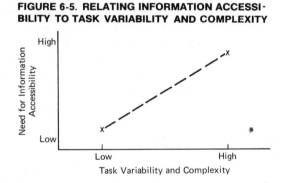

This section has presented observations within a framework that reflects both our practical experience in organizations and twenty-five years of laboratory research. Many other hypothetical network structures could have been presented, but we deliberately selected six that illustrate the concepts of formal and emergent structure, information accessibility, and relationship symmetry.

Basically, in analyzing either a series of formal and informal networks or a single network, there are four major issues to be considered:

1. *How are messages typically sequenced?* Within informal communication networks, who initiates a message is usually based upon a need that exists for a member of the network or for the entire network itself; within formal networks, however, messages are often generated—especially at the top of the organization—which have little relationship to the needs of those members who will be receiving the message at lower levels. Thus, the issue of sequencing—sequencing on the basis of need or some other criterion—is always a major issue in analyzing communication structure.

2. *In what direction do messages flow?* In a formal structure, message directions are either (*a*) *downward*—from a higher member in the formal

hierarchy to a lower member; (*b*) *upward*—the reverse of downward; (*c*) *horizontal*—side-to-side communication between members at the same level of the organizational hierarchy—providing that this side-to-side message flow is considered a part of the formal organization structure; or (*d*) *diagonal*—usually connecting a member at one level of the hierarchy with another subordinate or superordinate member at a different level of the hierarchy, neither of whom have a direct reporting relationship to one another—especially common in organizations that have adopted matrix structures. In an informal or emergent structure, message directionality gives one a clue to reciprocal relationships (if Bob seems to be a primary informant for Bill, who is a primary informant for Jane, who in turn shares information she receives from Bill with John, but the reverse is not true, then we have a one-way chain structure). It also points to the respected and creditable sources of information in the informal structure. These individuals will be "centrals" or possibly liaisons in that others seek them out for information; and when they do give it, the information disseminates rapidly in the structure. Finally, a consistent policy and practice of two-way communication will undoubtedly produce greater information-accessibility dividends than will a one-way policy. Asking the question, "In what direction do messages that affect me typically flow?" will help the manager analyze his or her own situation.

3. *How structured and rigid is the communication structure in the organization?* Both formal and informal organizational structures vary in their degrees of communication permissiveness and flexibility. In Chapter 4 we discussed the interpersonal aspects of this at length in the section "The Notion of Relationship." Essentially, the question of flexibility is a question of rules, protocol, and past experience. Beyond this, however, increasing rigidity of structure decreases the opportunity for dynamic, spontaneous, and opportunistic communication relationships (a bureaucracy, for example, discourages flexibility, while a new, entrepreneurial organization thrives on it). In a formal structure, degree of flexibility is fairly well spelled-out, and so explicitly shared by the members of the structure; in an informal structure, flexibility is a matter of abiding by implicit rules to which the members agree. A stiff structure is less capable of responding to changing organization demands than a pliable one. This is why the issue of flexibility in structure is important.

4. *To what extent are formal and informal structures subject to critical information overload points?* Message activities taking place in the formal and informal structures of organizations fall into two general categories: *budgeted* and *unbudgeted*. If an activity has been budgeted (scheduled meetings, conferences, report suspenses, letter dissemination, telephone calls), the assumption is that blocks of time have been allocated to these activities (time allocation here being analogous to the allocation of cash in

a financial budget). As with any budget, variances are bound to occur, and most commonly the variance is in the direction of insufficient time available to complete the budgeted activity. (For example, a scheduled thirty-minute meeting that lasts an hour and a half; the weekend work that is needed to prepare a report due Monday that could not be completed on Friday; or the phone call that led to several more unexpected calls to obtain the necessary information.)

The reasons for insufficient time allocations are (*a*) poor planning or no planning at all; (*b*) poor coordination of information resources; (*c*) "acts of God"—such as a plane that arrives late, a computer that breaks down, a secretary who is sick, a "missed" appointment; and (*d*) an untold number of unexpected interruptions in a typical manager's work day. Regardless of the reason, the major consequence is the subjection of the individual or the organization unit to information overload stress—stress because of the perceived variance experienced in attempting to meet an activity deadline. Both the *magnitude* of these variances and the *frequency* with which they occur can spell the difference between success and failure in coping with overload stress. Finally, the accessibility of information unmistakably plays a key role in influencing the budget constraints imposed upon these periodical organization activities. Figure 6-6 summarizes the budgeting problem:

FIGURE 6-6. EFFECTS OF BUDGETED TIME VARIANCES ON OVERLOAD

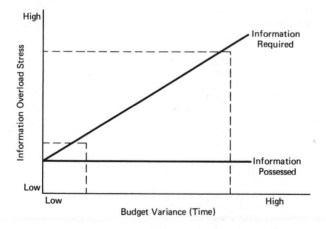

As can be seen in Figure 6-6, as the budget variance in the direction of insufficient time available to complete activities increases, so does the gap between the information possessed and the information required by the individual (or unit) endeavoring to complete the activities—and, as a

FIGURE 6-7. MANAGEMENT COMMUNICATIONS SYSTEM QUESTIONNAIRE

	YES	NO	NOT SURE
1. Have you developed your own personal approach to finding out what is going on in your organization?	___	___	___
2. Do you use informal communication networks in your organization as a source for decision-making data?	___	___	___
3. Do you know who your organization's liaisons are?	___	___	___
4. When you are experiencing conflict in your organization, do you rely upon the formal structure to help you resolve the felt conflict? (Only check "yes" if you use the formal channels as a *primary* source to resolve conflict.)	___	___	___
5. Do you keep a written record of or otherwise document information affecting your work that you receive through informal channels?	___	___	___
6. Would you consider bypassing your immediate superior if you needed an answer to an important question that he or she could not provide?	___	___	___
7. Do you regularly budget time to accomplish daily, weekly, and monthly recurring activities?	___	___	___
8. Do you routinely prioritize information you send to others?	___	___	___
9. Is the information you receive from others routinely prioritized?	___	___	___
10. Are more than 50 percent of your contacts in the formal organizational structure primarily one-way in nature (e.g., giving-receiving orders, instructions, or assignments)?	___	___	___
11. Do you find that you waste valuable time because you cannot regularly find the information you need?	___	___	___
12. Is the type of information exchanged in the informal network of which you are a part primarily social (e.g., news of what others are doing, baseball scores) or personal?	___	___	___
13. Do you believe that you are satisfactorily informed about your organization's plans and objectives?	___	___	___
14. Do your subordinates ever communicate with your superior without first clearing it with you (on job-related matters)?	___	___	___

Figure 6.7. Continued

	YES	NO	NOT SURE
15. Are there individuals in your organization who possess information which you need to perform your job effectively who do not or cannot share this information with you?	——	——	——
16. Do you regularly communicate with managers at your organizational level in other departments?	——	——	——
17. Are you interrupted more than 25 percent of a typical working day?	——	——	——
18. Do you miss deadlines more than your immediate superior believes is reasonable?	——	——	——
19. Do your subordinates miss deadlines more than you believe is reasonable?	——	——	——
20. Do meetings you regularly attend detract from meeting your own personal work schedules?	——	——	——
21. Does your physical work location restrict your opportunity to communicate with others as often as you would like?	——	——	——
22. Do you find that the information you receive from others is usually only partially accurate?	——	——	——
23. Do you routinely receive feedback from others on your performance?	——	——	——
24. Do you find that information received from the grapevine is usually accurate?	——	——	——
25. Has the formal structure of your organization undergone any changes in the past three years?	——	——	——

consequence, information overload stress heightens. The depiction of a difference between the information possessed and the information required is another way of describing the degree of information accessibility. With high accessibility to the information needed to complete an activity, using budgeted time as the major constraint, the information required is usually possessed; with low accessibility, however, the information required is not possessed, and time becomes the critical component in the information overload equation.

Budgeted message activities by definition usually occur within the formal organization structure, but when that is impossible the informal structure is utilized. In other words, message activities that cannot be accomplished within the formal structure are undertaken within the informal structure. Other unbudgeted message activities also take place in the informal structure (for example, the grapevine). Not only do most managers regard the informal structure as more flexible for these purposes, but they also realize that certain time economies can be realized with the informal structure that are impossible with the formal structure ("If I need a special computer run on a cost estimate, I can always count on Jane to get it done for me"—even though Jane works for someone else).

In summary, both the formal and informal organization structures provide a myriad of pathways through which budgeted and unbudgeted information transactions occur. When there are unexpected time variances resulting in missed deadlines or missed activity engagements, information overload stress is experienced. Many of the personal and relational factors we discussed in Chapters 3, 4, and 5 will determine if this stress is managed successfully.

A Manager's Checklist for the Effective Use of Systems of Organizational Communication

Throughout our examination of the systems-of-organizational-communication function, we have touched upon a number of areas that directly influence the manager's ability to secure meaningful intelligence in his or her organization. In this section, we supply a Management Communications System Questionnaire (MCSQ) to help the manager evaluate his or her own position in the system. At the conclusion of the section, a scale is provided to score the results obtained from completing this checklist.

Each question in the MCSQ is worth one point if answered correctly; a point is subtracted for an incorrect answer; and the "not sure" category is treated as a "0" for scoring purposes. Thus, the maximum score you could obtain is 25, the minimum 0. Listed below are the "yes" and "no" responses to each question that are required to attain a perfect score:

Questions to which you should have responded "yes"	Questions to which you should have responded "no"
1	4
2	10
3	11
5	12
6	15
7	17
8	18
9	19
13	20
14	21
16	22
23	
24	
25	

Table 6-2 supplies an explanation for the "yes" and "no" responses; and listed below is the scoring system we have devised after repeated administrations of this questionnaire to our industrial clients. While the sample is admittedly small and by no means statistically generalizable, the consistent trend of responses we have received suggests that the questionnaire is an indicator of the quality of organizational intelligence *from the manager's perspective.* The scale, incidentally, has been corrected for those managers who elected to not respond to a question at all because they felt it was not applicable to their organizational situation.

Score	Organization Trend
25	The systems of organizational communication are perceived to be *highly effective and flexible*: accurate, timely, and accessible information is available to the manager as needed, through both formal and informal channels.
20–24	The systems of organizational communication are perceived to be *highly effective in general*, with a few exceptions in particular. The exceptions by and large represent weaknesses that can be corrected before the effectiveness of the system as a whole is disturbed.
15–19	The systems of organizational communication are perceived to be *satisfactory*. At the low end of the scoring range, scores indicate a perception of system inflexibility to a degree that the effectiveness of the system as a whole is likely being disturbed. The possession of timely and accurate information is also likely to be perceived as a problem by the manager.
10–14	The systems of organizational communication are perceived to be *unsatisfactory*. The effective flow of information is being moderately disturbed by the inflexibility and rigidity that is perceived to characterize both formal and informal structures. Scores in this range are indicative of moderate communication dissatisfaction.
5–9	The systems of organizational communication are viewed as *highly unsatisfactory*. Major problems with information accessibility are likely to have been cited. Punitive conditions are perceived to exist in the organization, and it is probable that management has witnessed high turnover among personnel. Only 10 percent of our sample had scores in this range.
0–4	The systems of organizational communication are perceived to be *a dismal failure*. We can only report one instance of scores in this range—in a small consulting firm that went out of business. It is unlikely that conditions would deteriorate to this point before extraordinary management action was taken.

Internal Systems of Organizational Communication: Summary

In this chapter we have supplied an integrated description of the organizational variables which affect how well an organization's intelligence resources are utilized. We introduced the concept of the Functional Analysis Systems Technique (FAST) to integrate and show how these organizational variables relate to one another; and then we explored in detail the

TABLE 6-2. EXPLANATION OF A PERFECT RESPONSE PROFILE FOR THE MCSQ

Question	Correct Response	Explanation
1. Have you developed your own personal approach to finding out what is going on in your organization?	Yes	This indicates that the manager recognizes that entry into informal information networks in the organization requires the development of a personal approach, which will vary from one manager to the next. It may entail displaying a pleasing personality, unusual competence in some area, and an ability to maintain confidences.
2. Do you use informal communication networks in your organization as a source for decision-making data?	Yes	The informal communication networks are probably the best source for data needed to make decisions that are accepted by the organization's formal structure. The assumption is, however, that within the informal networks a manager can have better access to the original data sources than is possible through the formal structure.
3. Do you know who your organization's liaisons are?	Yes	Liaisons' information value to the organization is higher than that of most other organization members.
4. When you are experiencing conflict in your organization, do you rely upon the formal structure to help you resolve the felt conflict? (Only check "yes" if you use the formal channels as a *primary* source to resolve conflict.)	No	The most viable and speediest channels for resolving perceived conflict are not found within the formal organization structure—especially conflict between a superior and a subordinate. The informal structure contains much of the maintenance type of information that flows through an organization, and this is precisely the type of information needed most frequently to resolve perceived conflict (caused by message conflict, differing views, contradictory actions).
5. Do you keep a written record of or otherwise document information affecting your work that you receive through informal channels?	Yes	Technically speaking, the informal or emergent organization networks are not officially sanctioned entities. Thus, any information that is used which originated from within the informal structure should be documented for verification purposes. Some managers refer to this as a "JIC" (just-in-case) file.
6. Would you consider bypassing your immediate superior if you needed an answer to an important question that he or she could not provide?	Yes	This would be heresy, you say? Well, in some overly punitive organizations, it unquestionably would be; however, occasions do arise in which the logical source for information is not one's immediate superior, but someone higher in the hierarchy who has more control over the information. If they are accessible, then they should be used.

No.	Question	Answer	Explanation
7.	Do you regularly budget time to accomplish daily, weekly, and monthly recurring activities?	Yes	Information efficiencies are created when those message activities that recur on a routine basis are budgeted by the manager. (For example, allot one hour daily for dictation, review of project reports, and the previous week's business activities.) A schedule also helps others who work with you to plan their activities.
8.	Do you routinely prioritize information you send to others?	Yes	The purpose of prioritizing information is (a) to insure that message receivers will give it timely attention and (b) to help reduce overload potential by insuring that all messages are not treated as equal in importance. Many managers use standard preprinted memo slips for this purpose, but we prefer the use of multicolored tags whose only purpose is to establish the information's priority.
9.	Is the information you receive from others routinely prioritized?	Yes	The preceding explanation applies here.
10.	Are more than 50 percent of your contacts in the formal structure primarily one-way in nature (e.g., giving receiving orders, instructions, or assignments)?	No	If more than 50 percent of your communication contacts in the formal structure are of a one-way variety, your accessibility to information is limited, or the accessibility of others who have contact with you is limited. In either case, personal communication dissatisfaction will typically be high; and the communication structures within which you hold membership are probably inflexible.
11.	Do you find that you waste valuable time because you cannot regularly find the information you need?	No	Your accessibility to information is a function of freedom of movement within the organization's formal and informal structures. This movement can be limited for a number of reasons, but the net effect will always be a compromise of personal time efficiencies.
12.	Is the type of information exchanged in the informal network of which you are a part primarily social (e.g., news of what others are doing, baseball scores) or personal?	No	Both social and personal message exchanges do occur more frequently in the informal organizational structure than they do in the formal network as specified by the organization chart. Some of these exchanges constitute maintenance-type information in that they enhance the individual's personal identification with the organization. However, for the informal network to be useful, both production and innovation information should flow through these channels—for the organization's benefit—more than information that can be classified as social or personal in nature.
13.	Do you believe that you are satisfactorily informed about your organization's plans and objectives?	Yes	If you do not believe that you are satisfactorily informed, it indicates (a) that your organization has no explicitly defined plans and objectives or (b) that you do not have access to them.

Table 6-2. Continued

Question	Correct Response	Explanation
14. Do your subordinates ever communicate with your superior, without first clearing it with you (on job-related matters)?	Yes	See our explanation to question 6.
15. Are there individuals in your organization who possess information which you need to perform your job effectively who do not or cannot share this information with you?	No	Unlike question 11, which presumes that you are uncertain about the sources of information you need, this question describes a situation where the information source is known—but is not accessible to you. The reason for the inaccessibility may be deliberate (personally or by organizational design) or unintended. In either event, information deprivation is a serious threat to your successful management performance.
16. Do you regularly communicate with managers at your organization level in other departments?	Yes	Side-to-side communication (within either the formal structure or within an informal network that is also a part of the formal structure) is often one of the most valuable channels for the exchange of information that exists in the organization—because it represents an exchange among peers.
17. Are you interrupted more than 25 percent of a typical working day?	No	Some surveys indicate that a manager is typically interrupted more than 60 percent of a working day! We believe that 25 percent is sufficient to significantly disrupt the flow of planned and budgeted message activities and therefore impose unnecessary information inefficiencies.
18. Do you miss deadlines more than your immediate superior believes is reasonable?	No	The missing of deadlines is the most tangible proof a manager has that inadequate planning (and information gathering) and other unpredictable circumstances are detracting from managerial effectiveness. This is perhaps the most serious symptom of weakness in an organization's internal organizational communication system; and it looms as a major threat to the timely retrieval and dissemination of vital organizational intelligence.

19. Do your subordinates miss deadlines more than you believe is reasonable?	No	The preceding explanation applies here. We would add that if you are missing deadlines, it follows that your subordinates are missing deadlines, too.
20. Do meetings you regularly attend detract from meeting your own personal work schedules?	No	Managers typically insist that their required participation in lengthy and questionably productive meetings are a major source of the time pressures they experience.
21. Does your physical work location restrict your opportunity to communicate with others as often as you would like?	No	Information accessibility is sometimes affected by office or building geography, as well as by the distance that separates, for example, a European subsidiary from its U.S. parent. If geography is a problem, greater emphasis must be placed on the erection of alternative channels in the organization's formal structure to increase accessibility.
22. Do you find that the information you receive from others is usually only partially accurate?	No	Loss of accuracy can be due to (a) the failure to transmit complete information by the information originator, (b) distortion and uncertainty absorption, or (c) "noise" in the channel that carries the message itself. Use of feedback to verify and authenticate information should be imprinted on the first page of every manager's personal communication handbook.
23. Do you routinely receive feedback from others on your performance?	Yes	In a Model II organization, performance feedback is not just tendered once a year: it is continual, it is positive as well as constructive, and it is self-correcting. It travels in both the organization's formal and informal networks.
24. Do you find that information received from the grapevine is usually accurate?	Yes	This simply indicates that the grapevine is a viable informal communication network in your organization.
25. Has the formal structure of your organization undergone any changes in the past three years?	Yes	If your formal hierarchy is flexible and nonbureaucratized, it is adaptable to the changing functional needs of your organization. A study of most large organizations shows that they typically alter their formal structure at least once every three years (centralize or decentralize their operations).

notion of formal and informal or emergent structures, with examples and implications, to illustrate the complex, dynamic factors that influence the exchange of information and its flow in organizations. We concluded with a questionnaire for the manager to use in evaluating his or her own position within the organization's internal communication and information environment. Most of what we have tried to accomplish is aptly summarized by two of the early, distinguished contributors to our understanding of the role of formal and informal communication networks in organizations, Alex Bavelas and Dermot Barrett (1971):

> Communication is not a secondary or derived aspect of organization —a "helper" of the other and presumably more basic functions. *Rather it is the essence of organized activity and is the basic process out of which all other functions derive.* The goals an organization selects, the methods it applies, the effectiveness with which it improves its own procedures—all of these things hinge upon the quality and availability of the information in the system. (Italics added)

If the reader can accept these authors' belief that communication (we would add, "information exchange") is the "essence of organized activity" in organizations and recognize that it is a vital responsibility for all managers to accept—regardless of their organizational position—then we will have communicated well.

EMERGING TRENDS AND ISSUES

We wish to conclude this chapter with our observations about one likely design configuration that managers will encounter in the organizations of tomorrow. Some acceptance of this configuration is already well underway. Other changes are occurring and will continue to occur because management everywhere is recognizing the critical need to simplify the whole notion of organizing and to create information economies in an effort to reduce the multitude of cost overruns that are being witnessed in today's modern organization. Few managers argue with the contention that the competitive edge in the marketplace can only be retained and preserved through the creation of internal resource efficiencies affecting every operational area of the organization.

That the competitive edge is becoming more difficult to maintain is evident from a January 9, 1978, *Forbes* "Thirtieth Annual Report on American Industry," which lists performance yardsticks during 1977 for 1005 of the largest public corporations with sales over $250 million. In terms of profitability, for example, 20 percent of the companies listed did not maintain a 10 percent return on equity over a five-year average; 15 percent of the 1005 showed absolutely no earnings growth during the past five years compared to the previous five; and, for American industry as a whole, in spite of increased sales, the median profitability was only 12.9 percent, the median profit margin 4.5 percent, and the median return on total capital under 10 percent.

Financial performance, and especially the erosion thereof due to continuing unabated inflation, is just one slice of the pie. The energy crisis has placed the United States in an energy-dependent position for the first time in its two-hundred-year history. The real or imagined 1976 shortages dealt a blow to American industry that is still being felt today. Prospects for the future are not bright either. The authors have been told by Richard Anderson, a geologist and consultant on energy (formerly of the Battelle Memorial Institute, Columbus, Ohio), that the United States will face energy starvation, at present consumption rates, by the turn of the century. He maintains that a very major technological breakthrough is needed (conservation alone is not the long-term answer—it just buys short-term time) within the next decade to get us into the twenty-first century.

Aside from shortages in energy, increasing world demand has also resulted in shortages in metals, timber products, food, feed, and other essential raw materials needed to keep industry moving. These shortages have necessitated immediate management action to increase productivity per man-hour—and to find new ways to solve other old problems more economically.

Finally, increased government regulation and control—in spite of the need for it—has in many economic sectors almost totally paralyzed industry's ability to cope with the rising costs associated with compliance. According to the Environmental Protection Agency, for example, the cumulative pollution control bill from 1973 to 1982 will reach $43 billion. When industry is required to devote over 20 percent of its capital budget to meet regulation and control requirements, as has been true since 1973, it is clear that very few alternatives are left for maintaining the competitive edge we mentioned earlier. This is especially true for the American multinational; it is absolutely choking for the small business; and it is becoming more characteristic for foreign industry as well (particularly in Europe and Japan).

Turning from the issue of maintaining or preserving a competitive edge, there are two other significant developments that are and will continue to influence the emergence of the design we will discuss and the configuration the manager will see as we approach the twenty-first century.

The Direction of Technology

By the 1980s, it is estimated that technology will be able to produce a number of transformations that are not possible today—such as making steel with synthetic gas and possibly, later on, with nuclear energy; such as combining and eliminating production process stages with the advent of lighter metals, more durable and flexible plastics, and more resilient fibers; and such as providing for the instantaneous transmission and reception of information at any point on the globe, regardless of the proximity of the information users.

By far the most revolutionary technological impact, however, will be that of the microcomputer—economical, compact, and extraordinarily powerful—which is already beginning to revolutionize many industries. Its implications for controlling and effectively managing organizational information environments are staggering and awesome.

The most advanced microcomputers will have a hierarchical systems responsibility. They will combine, for example, computer control of manufacturing with computer-assisted design and the retrieval and evaluation of plant data. Each plant will have its own central microcomputer connected to the corporate data-processing system. The corporate system will issue production and control instructions to the central plant system, which will in turn instruct a number of remote microcomputers that will run individual machines or entire lines.

In office complexes, the microcomputer revolution will provide management information systems that may significantly alter present patterns of management and organizational communication. For example, office aids that are now separate functional units (typewriters, copying machines, dictating machines, word-processing equipment, videotape recorders, and even telephones) will be integrated as single systems interfacing with the organization's overall data-processing activity. One variation of this system is already installed at Sperry Rand Corporation's Univac Division plant in Roseville, Minnesota. Some managers have their own terminals, and a simplified computer language, which gives them a private information system that is linked to a central computer for file storage and retrieval. The central computer can also be used as a "memory jogger" to alert the manager to changes that he or she should know about.

The new office technology, aside from tremendously intensifying the potential volume, organization, and timeliness of data communications, promises to revolutionize the manager's workspace in still another significant way: the need for personal mobility—for going from here to there for this meeting or that conference, and so on—will almost be totally eliminated. Through these advanced data systems, it is altogether feasible that superiors and subordinates, suppliers and customers, subsidiaries and parents will be entirely linked communicatively by microcomputer systems. In short, conceivably, in the not-too-distant-future, a manager's work location—perhaps an 8- by 11 foot-room—will link him or her with every organizational responsibility directly or indirectly managed. Such contact with these operations and responsibilities will produce permanent files of management experience which, at least in theory, the microcomputers can draw upon to make decisions and conduct business as effectively and as successfully as the manager—if not more so—and in the manager's absence!

The Direction of Values

In 1917, American women still did not have the right to vote, and cigarettes were still banned in Iowa and Utah. The divorce rate at that time was about one marriage in ten, compared to one out of two, or more, now. The environment, in all its ruggedness and beauty, was not regarded seriously as an exhaustible resource. Patriotism, the Flag, mother's apple pie and sips of lemonade at grandma's—these simply and precisely reflected a congruent and unchallenged set of values which were inherited from our founding fathers.

At some point—value experts disagree, but probably in the early 1960s—as one observer remarked, "Not that many young people were seen in church anymore." Evidence of a new and different value orientation for our society culminated, for many, with the assassination of President John F. Kennedy in November 1963. Not since Lincoln's assassination had one of America's most sacred institutions been so inexplicably and mercilessly crushed. The mood of the people changed, some will argue, and a relatively passive America of the 1950s came out of a Rip Van Winkle-like slumber. The word *radical* was used to describe a sizable section of our populace for the first time. Disenchantment with the "establishment" led to an unwillingness to accept "hawkish" attitudes toward the newly developing Vietnam engagement.

As the 1960s progressed, the voice of a dissenting minority became stronger, alternating between acts of brutal violence and acts of nonviolent demonstration. The decisions of the country's political leaders became increasingly more suspect, each decision sparking more controversy and dissent than it resolved. As the country turned the corner into the 1970s, it was beset by a second major cultural shock wave: the uncovering of felonious, unethical activities by men charged with the highest responsibility this country can confer to leaders of our government.

Terrorism of unprecedented magnitude abroad as well as at home, rising crime statistics, especially among our youth, the increased reliance on and accessibility to mind-altering drugs, political scandals such as Wilbur Mills and Fanny Fox, Wayne Hays and a $15,000-a-year typist, the "Koreagate" bribery scandal, and many more—all have tested the limits of America's conscience, many say, and have eroded our ability to bounce back from crisis in values. Corporate bribery, too, a public product of the mid-1970s, substantiates a way of conducting personal and institutional affairs in a manner to which the average American and foreigner have become unfortunately accustomed.

We supply this backdrop to support our claim that American society has been subjected to a history of abrupt value contradiction. The old rules which dictated what is good and what is bad have been replaced by a new permissiveness—a permissiveness that penetrates business as well as personal affairs. With this permissiveness, some distinctive *value variations* have occurred, and these variations very definitely carry over into the work environment. The most important ones that are most frequently cited are:

1. *"You must earn my trust before I will give it to you."* Younger people, in particular, are especially skeptical about the whole issue of trust and confidence. They have grown up in a world where trust at all levels of society is routinely abused and abandoned for the sake of an individual's or an organization's self-interest.

2. *"You owe it to me."* Many claim that America's welfare mentality and its inept handling of the Social Security crisis has produced, again among younger employees, a value variation in which the individual expects more from society than he or she is willing to give in return. Translated to the workplace, this variation is expressed in demands for more benefits, wages, and so on, without a corresponding increase in personal productivity.

3. *"I prize my leisure time."* Whether it be in the form of a shorter work week, a reduction in working hours, more holidays, or longer vacations, there is this value expression for leisure among today's organization members—which is not restricted to a particular segment of the employee population either. The underlying value variation responsible for this demand for more leisure time is complex. Some believe that it is indicative of a deterioration of the work ethic; others claim that people want more time to experience vicarious satisfactions not provided at the workplace; and still others maintain that it reflects a withdrawal from the responsibilities of societal membership.

4. *"You must improve the quality of my work experience."* Numerous organizations have adopted quality of work life policies and programs in reply to governmental pressures to recognize this human need. On the surface, quality of work life implies that employees are given an opportunity to experience some form of self-actualization in their organizational environment. Job enrichment programs, flex-time working hours, continuing education opportunities, and other programs have been experimented with—with varying degrees of success and failure—to enhance the self-esteem of organization members. Here again, the underlying value dynamic is complex. It is somewhat related to the "You Owe It To Me" variation, but it also expresses a general recognition that, for the past twenty years, society has ignored the value of individualism and has substituted a collective, institutional—largely bureaucratic—norm to

govern human conduct. That norm failed, as we illustrated earlier, and perhaps a return to respect for individualism is being reflected in the quality of work life movement.

5. *"We are equals."* The value of deference to others because of rank or status has been replaced with an egalitarian spirit that strives to level incomes and lifestyles, and to shift decisions from the marketplace to a bureaucratic institutional apparatus. The demands have become especially vocal and public from minorities, from the poor, and from a raft of intellectuals who believe they know what is right for society. The underlying value of equality has had a precipitous history in American society, but the means that are now being suggested to achieve it represent a significant deviation from the past. The implications to a free market system are evident. The egalitarian movement began as a just fight for legal rights, such as the right to vote, the right to equal job opportunities, and equal pay for equal work. Somehow, this drive for rights became married to a value expression aimed at results rather than rights—such as income equality, standing in the organization, and job satisfaction equality. Some even argue that a high priority of government should be to force organizations to "equalize human competence" by reorganizing work so that this priority will obtain.

6. *"Leave me alone."* When we first heard this value variation cited along with the others mentioned, we thought there must be a mistake. The statement "Leave me alone" sounds selfish, withdrawing, nonparticipating, and antisocial at best. It was not a mistake. "Leave me alone" is an expression of *noncommitment*, a desire for independence, a need for some form of autonomy, or for an unwillingness to become involved. As one observer put it, "It's OK to send me a check, but don't ask me to come down to the office to fill out all the forms to get it." Does it reflect the accumulated effects of one disappointment after another with society at large? Is it simply a mood? We do not know, but hope that time and experience will not confirm our worst expectations.

These six value variations are among the most important ones for the manager to observe as we enter the 1980s. They are important because they describe six driving forces that, to a greater or lesser degree, will constitute the expression of tomorrow's workforce. Still, they do not paint the total picture. David Cherrington (1977) has reported a value survey in which he queried over three thousand employees in a wide variety of industrial and business organizations. His objective was to check on the status of the Protestant work ethic among both younger and older employee populations. His findings of interest include:

1. The Protestant work ethic is not dead, as some maintain. The highest-rated item on his 190-plus-item questionnaire related to pride in

one's work—although this rating tended to be higher for older than for younger workers.

2. The next grouping of value expressions included (*a*) more money, (*b*) being recognized and obtaining the respect of others, (*c*) being of service to others, and (*d*) receiving more fringe benefits.

3. Among several differences he noted between older and younger employees, one struck us as particularly revealing. He reported that younger employees do not believe that their organization makes a significant contribution to the economic strength of the surrounding community or that the community is a better place to live because of the company. Young employees (including managers who participated in the survey) do not place the same premium on their organizations that older employees do.

So overall, while Cherrington did find that the values of older and younger (and male and female) employee populations vary in strength, he did not find that his sample believed that the only way to get ahead in this world is to use the Dale Carnegie approach and "win friends and influence people." To the contrary, the values of the people he surveyed reflected an endorsement of an ethic that calls for hard work.

The competitive edge, technology, and values will indeed impose some new organization design requirements upon the manager tomorrow which he or she is probably already experiencing today. In the final section of this chapter, we review one strong structural candidate.

An Emerging Structural Configuration

Throughout this book, we have stressed that the collection of useable organizational intelligence combined with the selection of appropriate strategies and tactics to implement this intelligence will, in the long run, separate the successful from the unsuccessful organization. In the last four chapters we have concentrated upon information and communication activities that bear directly upon this intelligence function. But in Chapter 2 we established a notion that is gaining much attention among students of management—the notion of *contingency*. This important concept has been reflected in both our descriptions and prescriptions for appropriate managerial responses in Chapters 3, 4 and 5, and now in Chapter 6. It is impossible to talk about a new organizational structure without stating categorically that an appropriate organizational design must depend upon the nature of the organization's environment, internal and external, and upon the personality and/or inclinations of its membership.

Applying this contingent viewpoint to the issue of intelligence means asking the following questions—all derived from the FAST program presented in Figure 6-1:

1. *At the human input level,* how can the organization accommodate personal characteristics and improve relational characteristics in such a way that its intelligence-gathering and disseminating activities are enhanced?

2. *At the systems-of-organizational-communication level,* how can the formal and emergent communication structures be opened up to provide evenly distributed information accessibility and organizationally accepted consensus management decision making?

3. *At the primary-information-events level,* how can the need for production, maintenance, and innovation information be synchronized in such a way that when the particular need exists, it can be satisfied successfully?

4. *At the organization output level,* how can information and data about this output be circulated throughout the organization in such a way that people know the extent to which their individual and interdependent efforts combine to make this output either succeed or fail?

How can all this be accomplished if we accept the premise that the problem of the competitive edge, the problem of a changing technology, and the problem of a clarified, but new, system of human values is complicating the most basic mission or purpose of our organizations?

One prominent possibility is the establishment of a matrix type of organization structure and attitude, as well as a progressive management training opportunity and an equally progressive management reward system, combined with effective evaluation and planning schemes that are administered across the organization (including the routine use of the types of tools we report in Chapter 7).

The matrix structure. A number of organizations (especially those in the aerospace industry) and organization subsystems (such as research-and-development) already possess matrix organizational structures. Unfortunately, the mistaken impression has been formed that the matrix structure is only suitable for high-technology industries. This is not true. Even a small, three-functioned manufacturing operation (manufacturing, finance, and sales/marketing) can adopt a matrix structure. Figure 6-8 illustrates this.

FIGURE 6-8. SIMPLIFIED MATRIX STRUCTURE

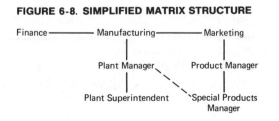

In Figure 6-8, the Special Products Manager works for two people: the Product Manager and the Plant Manager. It is his job to create a manufacturing-marketing interface with any special products that constitute exceptions to the company's regular product mix. The position was created to fill a particular need of the company: to find off-season products that were compatible with the existing manufacturing technology, and to mesh these special product introductions throughout the year on a coordinated basis that satisfied the needs of both manufacturing and marketing.

Why consider a matrix arrangement in the first place? Experience has shown that it provides an organization the best of two worlds: decentralization and centralization. In the 1950s, many larger companies adopted a decentralized organization structure, and in effect created almost fully autonomous entities. In the 1960s, however, the growing complexity of business operations forced many of these same organizations to recentralize much of their operations in an effort to obtain a more uniform system of financial controls and to realize other economies that were impossible with a decentralized arrangement. Also occurring in the 1960s was a general recognition of a systems orientation to managing many diverse businesses. The part of the systems concept entails a series of interdependent relationships among the various subsystems comprising the overall organization unit. This concept of interdependence and the concept of a flat, highly decentralized organization structure were simply found not to be practically compatible.

In a *matrix structure*, those individuals who have dual reporting assignments (their nomenclature varies from one industry to the next, but they may be called *project coordinators*, *product systems coordinators*, or *manager of special projects*, to name a few) resemble the heads of decentralized operations in that they make all the significant decisions affecting the operation. However, to accomplish these activities they make use of centralized resources to supply them with technical information, budgeting parameters, and other operational economies that are beyond their immediate areas of responsibility. In effect, the matrix manager is a coordinator and integrator for the organization. He or she typically has both line and staff responsibility and enjoys a freedom of movement across formal communication lines in the organization that traditional functional managers do not have.

Earlier, we devoted considerable time to the discussion of organizational liaisons—managers who are in a unique position from an intelligence-gathering and -dissemination viewpoint to achieve significant economies of information coordination and information interdependence. The creation of a matrix position in the organization does nothing more than legitimize this important liaison role which, as we have seen, tends to develop in the informal organization structure regardless of what the formal structure is or is not sanctioning.

Throughout this book, we have stressed that uncertainty—including the increased expectation of it in the modern organization—has led to a number of management developments during the 1970s that would have been viewed as heresy before then. The idea of reporting to two superiors, as in the matrix structure, clearly contradicts traditional principles of sound organization. And yet classic hierarchical techniques have proven inadequate in today's organizations for coping with the complex effect of uncertainty. Leonard Sayles, a distinguished professor of business administration at the Columbia Graduate School of Business and a well-known industrial consultant, supplies four reasons for the increasing attention to uncertainty—all of which make a case for matrix management. We paraphrase them here (Sayles, 1976):

1. The unpredictable problems, decisions, and technical difficulties that modern organizations experience are simply too complex and require too many nonstandardized solutions for the traditional general manager and his staff to resolve. On-the-scene experts with varying specialties are needed to cope with these frequent unpredictable occurrences.

2. Many of these unpredictable occurrences lead to divergent viewpoints concerning the most appropriate solutions. Not surprisingly, conflicting interests are brought to bear on the situation, and many of these cannot be settled unless there is a permanent mechanism to satisfy the need for ongoing deliberation.

3. These divergent viewpoints are ideally directed toward an optimal solution, one where the cost/benefit ratio is taken into practical (which may not necessarily be rational) consideration. It is unrealistic to presume that a single individual, regardless of the power he or she possesses, will possess all the knowledge needed to reach the optimal solution in the face of uncertainty.

4. For any given potential uncertainty that the organization faces, the number of operative factors involved in restoring operational stability cannot always be specified with a high degree of confidence on some master plan that provides for all contingencies. A small technical disruption anywhere in a system, because of the interdependence feature mentioned earlier, can provoke a chain reaction elsewhere in the system.

Sayles adds this important reminder:

In effect, these uncertainties require us to design a dynamic organization structure that can absorb and be quickly responsive to unanticipated changes in job definitions and allocations—a structure that will encourage rapid and continuous tradeoffs throughout the total system, not merely on a one-to-one sequential basis. This, in fact, is the strength of the matrix structure.

Once an organization has decided to put a matrix manager in place, what does such a manager do? The matrix manager is most typically not a generalist. He or she probably has a strong technical specialty as well as insight into how this specialty interacts with other specialties in the organization. The matrix manager possesses a Model II organization attitude: that is, a strong value is placed upon valid information exchange, informed choice, and dedicated commitment to organization goals. The matrix manager is also a skilled negotiator, accepts the concept of consensus decision making, and is flexible. And finally, the matrix manager has a strong capacity to perform well under stress and to accept issue-based conflict as a constructive mechanism for solving organizational uncertainty.

Typically, the matrix manager will alternate between the following roles as needed: (a) *direct specific work* and be responsible for its effective completion; (b) *stabilize*, by acting as an informed "decision broker" regarding technical difficulties that arise; (c) *evaluate* the success of organization efforts of which he or she is a part; (d) *advise* others with whom the matrix manager must coordinate workflow; (e) *provide services* for or support to the functional areas that the matrix manager represents; (f) *troubleshoot* and attempt to uncover problems before they disrupt planned organization activity; and (g) *mediate* differences of opinion reflecting the expertise of other specialists and integrate these differences into a common course of action.

In short, the matrix manager serves an identifiable organization need, is not bound to a line or staff ideology, retains results-oriented accountability, exhibits flexibility, remains highly accessible to others, and accepts the premise that pluralism of authority in modern organizations cannot flow along neatly defined hierarchical lines. One of our colleagues described a matrix manager as a "franchise player"—meaning that he or she is skillfully equipped to meet important needs of the organization at various given times.

Until now, matrix managers, especially those equipped with research-and-development expertise, have been technical specialists. In the future, the threefold challenge imposed by the issues of maintaining competitive superiority in one's industry, a rapidly changing information technology, and the increased sensitivity of organizations to the impact of employee value variations on commitment to individual and organizational performance will require the emergence of a different type of matrix manager.

This new matrix manager will continue to express technical proficiency, but will have two additional traits: first, an ability to understand the systems requirements of an advanced and complicated microcomputer technology, and second, an empathic ability to sense how human values are reflecting changing human needs. Technology is only useful if it can be applied, understood, and implemented without depressing the quality of human input needed to keep technology thriving. Which requirement will hold the higher priority? Both, in our opinion, and that leads us to a condition that must be met if the flexible matrix concept is in fact to become common practice.

Management training opportunities. The current focus of management continuing-education programs is on the development of human relations, technical, and administrative skills required of the manager on his job. These programs are simply not equipping the manager with the information needed to make the transition from the organizational methodology of today to that which is just over the horizon. This is true in our universities and colleges as well.

The development of effective matrix managers will require a concerted effort, first, to identify the need, and second, to begin providing expanded training opportunities (most importantly, on-the-job development) that will yield technically proficient and human-resource-proficient candidates for the matrix positions that will become available as organizations accept the fact that the old ways of organizing are inadequate to meet present-day organizational uncertainties. The time for such training to begin is now. Many organizations have already incorporated the matrix concept into their structures (for example, IBM and NASA), and their competitive edge in their respective industries is obvious.

What is an example of an effective management training program that meets these requirements? First, we believe that continued exposure to developments in one's specialty area is important—through professional associations or their trade equivalents; second, exposure to HRM (human resource management) seminars that stress small-group relationships is essential; and third, in-house management development programs (including job-rotation or job-enrichment activities) will meet this need. Training and development, in short, must be an ongoing commitment of organizations that recognize the competencies needed in future managers (and in those who will negotiate the transition)—not an accidental happenstance that is fulfilled once annually with attendance at, for example, a "manager-assertiveness seminar."

Management reward systems. The uncertainty levels and degrees of complexity that organizations face today show no signs of a reversal for tomorrow. The pressure on individual managers to perform will continue to increase. The motivation to perform, on the other hand, will still be linked to two primary sources, extrinsic and intrinsic. Extrinsic reward systems have a finite upper limit beyond which the organization cannot afford to compensate the manager and still remain in business. Intrinsic systems have no finite limit that we know of, and offer the greatest opportunity for exploitation in the future. These systems go beyond the cry for greater job satisfaction and job variety and in part reflect the quality-of-work-life momentum that we discussed earlier. To the extent that these systems are perceived to be unsatisfactory for the effort expended, then the commitment to the organization will be adversely affected. At present, our research indicates that a greater variety of *both* extrinsic and intrinsic rewards are possible in most organizations. They necessitate more administration, no one would argue, but the long-term result should and can make the investment in them worthwhile. We recommend to our clients that they conduct an annual audit that determines just how well the organization's reward system is functioning. Some of the tools recommended in Chapter 7 are satisfactory for this purpose.

An interesting paradox emerges when we realize that most managerial salary administration systems are administered for the aggregate, while any member of that aggregate may have different extrinsic needs at a given point in time than someone else comprising the aggregate. This means that a "total" compensation program must be hit-or-miss to some extent—satisfying the needs of some managers, but not others. Some organizations have implemented "cafeteria" total compensation plans wherein individual managers are offered a selection from which they can make choices that fit their particular needs. For example, instead of making a monthly contribution to the organization's medical insurance plan, an employee may opt to receive the equivalent of this contribution in cash. Obviously, ERISA (Employee Retirement Income Security Act) places restrictions on the amount of freedom an organization or a manager has in determining how total compensation and benefits plans will be distributed and structured.

Intrinsic rewards (satisfaction from accomplishing a difficult job, the praise received from others, increased responsibility, and so on) are much more difficult to tabulate and administrate. But it is possible. As one president confided, "We report annually that people are our most important asset, but we treat them that way each day of the year." Chapters 3, 4, and 5 contained a number of suggestions for recognizing this important reward need that is present in all of us, regardless of our organizational position. It is a discipline more than a practice, as many managers know, but it will become an absolute requirement for the survival of the future organization.

Evaluation and planning. Lastly, matrix management imposes upon the organization the need for continual evaluation and planning, continual appraisal of organizational contingencies (such as those described in Chapter 2), and continual organizational design and renewal. The testing of assumptions and the prevention of these assumptions from becoming organizational myths or unquestioned canons of faith must become fundamental to organization routine. It will be insufficient to complain that "I can't get as much out of my people as I used to"; it will be vital and necessary to ask the question, "Why?"—and then do something about it.

Planning, in particular, will enter a new dimension—one that is entirely usable by every manager in the organization. It will not dictate, "*Here* is where we are today, and *there* is where we must be five years from now." It will instead insist, "We are *here* today; and here are our alternative strategies, one of which we must commit to undertake today—hopefully, it will put us at 'such-and-such' tomorrow." This is a revolutionary perspective in terms of the way most organizations view their planning process. It implies that planning input will not originate at the apex of the organization, it will originate from below; and because of its origin, the commitment to it will be great. Chris Anderson, a representative from management consultants Arthur D. Little, Inc., tells us that this planning attitude is already accepted—and practiced—by many of their clients throughout the world.

One Step at a Time

To some managers, the contents of Part III will seem disturbing. A revolution is never comfortably accepted by the majority until it passes all the acid tests. We *are* talking about a revolution in management thinking and practice that has already begun. Those managers who are in fact now matrix managers may consider our treatment simplistic. To those managers who are witnessing many of the uncertainties that we have described in this and the preceding two chapters, and who are equally confused about the whole concept of "communication and information" in their organizations, we can only urge: review what we have said. The intelligence dynamic is not new, by any means, but its implications for the modern complex industrial organization are crucial.

In this chapter, we have attempted to present an integrated perspective for viewing, at the organizational level, the internal system of organizational communication. We have stressed organizational *structure* because of our firm belief that structure is the one critical organization resource that is, unfortunately, most misunderstood. We have described a feedback- and action-oriented system that is designed to help the manager perform an audit of opportunity, while realizing what the odds are that the audit will indeed be successful.

We began our discussion of organizational variables relating to information and communication in managerial work using the analogy of a symphony orchestra and describing how the conductor can tap ever so lightly with his baton to bring this complex organization to order. He makes it seem effortless; this ability, in fact, is the essence of an effective and organized manager who gets—and uses—organizational intelligence productively and profitably.

part three

Measurement and Development of Organizational Intelligence

7

Tools
of
Measurement

INTRODUCTION

Thus far in this book, we have described both the major variables and contingencies which form an organization's intelligence system. We have shown the importance of an optimal intelligence system to the manager who hopes to use information power in his decision making. However, information power will still be illusory unless the manager is knowledgeable about his organization's intelligence system. He will be unable to optimize its development without first knowing how it operates, without knowing its strengths and weaknesses.

Before investing large resources of time and money in the improvement of communication in an organization, a manager must gather as much valid information as possible about the present state of his communication system. In Part Three we present several measurement tools available for assessing communication in an organization and a detailed description of one measurement system with which we are intimately familiar—the Organizational Communication Development (OCD) system. Whenever particular instruments or methods are appropriate for an organization, the information provided by these methods will help the manager determine the overall communication effectiveness in his organization. Then, using the information obtained by monitoring the contingencies affecting his organization (see Chapter 2), he will be able to determine the amount of intelligence his organization possesses and needs, and thus the size of its information power gap.

Figure 7-1 (repeated from Chapter 2) illustrates the relationship between high and low communicative effectiveness and large and small information power gaps in organizations. Measurement of organizational communication variables not only helps the manager diagnose and evaluate a system, but also allows him better control of his organization by identifying problems and by developing and implementing remedial steps before the problems escalate beyond control. Some specific examples of how some organizations have used measurement of their communication systems to optimize their intelligence systems may help:

1. Pre-post measurements to determine the impact of new communication programs.
2. Assessment of the impact of ERISA programs.
3. Pre-post measurements to determine the impact of organizational innovations (addition of the computer, new Organizational Development program, restructuring).
4. Identification of current organizational structure to help in the reorganization process.

FIGURE 7-1. CONDITIONS OF ORGANIZATIONAL INTELLIGENCE

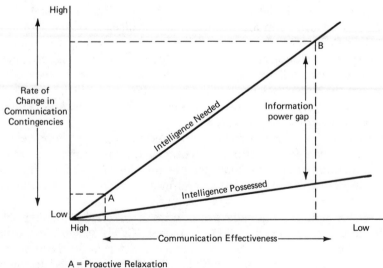

A = Proactive Relaxation
B = Reactive Stress

5. Identification of key communication groupings prior to restructuring for overseas assignments in a large multinational corporation.
6. Identification of major communication costs (telephone calls, meetings, postage, air travel involved in new expansions to other states or countries).
7. Development of new communication training programs geared to solve the problem identified in the assessment.
8. Assessment of amount of information comprehended by employees about company policies and regulations.
9. Comparison of the personality of the organization with the personality of its founder(s) and leader(s).
10. Comparison of the amount of information actually possessed by employees (about selected topics) versus the amount of information perceived to be possessed by top management.

Identification of Intelligence Needs

In Chapter 2, we outlined a procedure for determining the rate of change in communication contingencies affecting an organization. After determining whether one's organization is affected to a very great or very little extent by internal and external contingency changes, the manager must evaluate his communication effectiveness. This can be done for personal, relational, or organizational variables (as described in Chapters 3–6) or some combination, depending upon one's current needs. Later in this

TABLE 7-1. STATES OF ORGANIZATIONAL INTELLIGENCE
AND INTELLIGENCE NEEDS

When: Rate of change in communication contingencies is:	And: Effectiveness of the communication system is:	Then: The organization's current condition is:	And: The organization's current intelligence needs are:
1. Low	High	Proactive relaxation ("the honeymoon")	Low
2. High	High	Proactive coping ("the marriage")	Low
3. Low	Low	Reactive hibernation ("the time bomb")	Moderate
4. High	Low	Reactive stress ("the explosion")	High

chapter (and in Chapter 8) we will present several alternatives for conducting such an evaluation to determine whether the organizations's communication effectiveness is relatively high or low. Once the manager knows both the effect of contingencies and the effectiveness of communication, he can predict the current condition of his organization and thus its intelligence needs. Table 7-1 (repeated from Chapter 2) describes the four states of organizational intelligence. Once the manager has determined the state of organizational intelligence which most closely approximates that of his organization, he can take the steps necessary to maximize its information power.

MEASUREMENT OF PERSONAL VARIABLES

In Chapter 3, we discussed personal communication variables—those that are likely to vary considerably from one person to the next. The following suggested measurement tools and approaches can be used to monitor and describe them.

Cognitive Stretch Test

Research by McKenney and Keen (1974) has shown that managers use one of four cognitive styles in solving problems and making decisions. Although style may vary, one will tend to dominate the manager's cognitive behavior. In order to help the manager determine his dominant cognitive style, we have devised the following short test.

In the following two sets of statements, select the one in each pair which best represents your behavior.
In solving most problems or making most decisions:
    A. I prefer to begin gathering facts in a deliberate, systematic manner; or
    B. I prefer to begin going with my feelings and emotions.
and
    C. I prefer to begin focusing on one key detail or fact; or
    D. I prefer to begin studying the entire situation and then look for facts.

The following identifies the cognitive style preferred for each of the four combinations (see Table 7-2):

AC—*Systematic-Receptive*
AD—*Systematic-Preceptive*
BC—*Intuitive-Receptive*
BD—*Intuitive-Preceptive*

Consider the following situation as an example of these four styles:
A chief executive officer is contemplating whether to merge his company

TABLE 7-2. COGNITIVE STYLES IN PROBLEM SOLVING AND DECISION MAKING

In solving most problems or making most decisions:

	(A) I prefer facts first.	(B) I prefer feelings first.
(C) I prefer focusing on one detail first.	(AC) Systematic-Receptive	(BC) Intuitive-Receptive
(D) I prefer studying the entire situation first.	(AD) Systematic-Preceptive	(BD) Intuitive-Preceptive

with a larger conglomerate (Company X). Notice how the thinking process differs among the four styles:

1. *Systematic-Receptive.* "I don't know if merger is good. Although the stock of Company X hasn't reflected its earnings potential, the company does have an excellent management team. Their managers have been particularly innovative in some of the following human resources programs . . . "
2. *Systematic-Preceptive.* "Merger is bad for us and now I'll look for some facts in my Dun and Bradstreet to prove it."
3. *Intuitive-Receptive.* "Their earnings record is terrible and I just don't feel that's good for us in the long run."
4. *Intuitive-Preceptive.* "I feel merger is very bad for us now, no matter what the facts indicate."

Now the reader should try to identify the predominant style in each of the following. Imagine you are contemplating whether or not to purchase 1,000 shares of stock in a new company which is being traded over-the-counter:

1. "I'm going to buy it. It's another Kodak. I can feel it."
2. "The stock appears to have some merit, but I'd better get the facts from *Standard and Poor*'s and *Dow Theory*."
3. "I'm not interested in *Standard and Poor*'s recommendation. This company just struck oil. I'll check the growth rate of similar-sized companies who have just struck oil."
4. "My God! They've just struck oil! I'm calling my broker to buy the stock."

Here are the answers:

      1—Intuitive-preceptive
      2—Systematic-preceptive
      3—Systematic-receptive
      4—Intuitive-receptive

A caution: although most people prefer one of the above styles when confronting problems or decisions, any one of the styles may be appropriate for a particular problem or decision. It is probably best, in short, to adapt one's style to the problem rather than the problem to one's style.

Clary Organizational Script Checklist

Clary (1976) has developed a series of questions to help managers assess their self-image in relation to their organization. The following questions can help the manager check out his mental picture of what his group is or should be like as well as his adjustment processes:

1. Before joining your organization, what was your estimate of the situation? (This is a blend of fantasy and expectations based upon previous experience.)
2. How did you modify your estimate after confronting the reality of the job? (Involvement may cause adjustment of expectations.)
3. How did you further modify your behavior so it would fit with your perception of your boss's image of you? (Is your perception closely matched with your boss's expectations of you?)
4. How much have you adjusted your own individuality to the organization image since starting the job? (To what extent do you maintain your own autonomy or sacrifice it to satisfy the need for belonging? How closely do your goals now follow those of the organization?)
5. Where do you want your organization to be five years from now?
6. What are the most important changes to be made?
7. What are the desirable directions for growth?
8. What changes in you or in the organization would bring renewed enthusiasm, excitement, and creativity?
9. What changes are you going to begin making?
10. When are you going to start making these changes?
11. Where do you start with the changes?
12. Who is going to be responsible for seeing that you keep on target in making these changes?
13. How will you know when you've made these changes?

Answers to these questions will help the manager determine the extent to which his personality has adjusted to the needs of a changing organization.

Supervisory Inventory on Communication

Kirkpatrick (1968) has developed an eighty-item inventory which gives the manager personal feedback about his communication skills (listening, speaking, writing) and knowledge of basic communication principles. The inventory requires the respondent to either agree or disagree with the items. For example, to test attitudes toward listening, the respondent is asked to indicate agreement or disagreement with the following statement:

A supervisor should not take time to listen to personal problems of employees.

Concerning writing, one item is:

In written communication, a short word should be used whenever possible instead of a long one.

Concerning speaking, the respondent either agrees or disagrees with:

When talking with subordinates, a supervisor can increase understanding by using their first names.

Finally, one test of basic principles calls for agreement or disagreement with:

Semantics refers to the different meanings of a word.

According to Kirkpatrick, the inventory is useful in determining the need for communication training, as a tool for conference discussion, for evaluating the effectiveness of a communication course, for providing information for on-the-job coaching, and to assist in the selection of supervisors.

The test is self-scored (with a carbon-back answer sheet) and is accompanied with a set of norms to help the respondent compare himself with comparable workers. Most people get about 75 percent of the items "correct." The test can be purchased directly from its author.*

Personal Report of Communication Apprehension – Organization Form

Scott, McCroskey, and Sheahan (1976) have developed an instrument which measures the amount of apprehension a manager feels toward communicating in general and specifically at work. This instrument has been shown to be highly reliable. Those who are most apprehensive about communicating (as measured by this test) were found to have less desire for advancement, to be less likely to expect advancement, and to be more likely to see themselves as being in positions with low communication requirements than those least apprehensive about communicating. The test, presented in Table 7-3, is easy to administer and score. Scores can range from 20 (low apprehension) to 100 (high apprehension); in one study of 243 federal and state government employees, the authors of the test reported a mean of 50.05 with a standard deviation of 11.50. The authors of the test further advise that a score above 62 should be a cause for concern and a score as high as 72 is probably indicative of a severe problem.

*Write to: Donald Kirkpatrick, 4380 Continental Drive, Brookfield, WI 53005.

TABLE 7-3. PERSONAL REPORT OF COMMUNICATION APPREHENSION-
ORGANIZATION FORM

Directions: This instrument is composed of several statements concerning feelings about communication with other people. Please indicate the degree to which each statement applies to you by marking whether you (1) Strongly Agree, (2) Agree, (3) are Undecided, (4) Disagree, or (5) Strongly Disagree with each statement. There are no right or wrong answers. Work quickly; just record your first impression.

_____ 1.   People can usually count on me to keep a conversation going.

_____ 2.   Conversing with people who hold positions of authority is something I really enjoy.

_____ 3.* I feel self-conscious when I am called upon to answer a question or give an opinion.

_____ 4.   I am basically an outgoing person.

_____ 5.* When I have to represent my organization to another group, I feel very tense and nervous.

_____ 6.* I am afraid to express myself in a group.

_____ 7.* When I'm with other people, I often have difficulty thinking of the right thing to talk about.

_____ 8.   I enjoy fielding questions at a meeting.

_____ 9.* I'm afraid to speak up in conversations.

_____ 10. I look forward to an opportunity to speak in public.

_____ 11. In most situations, I generally know what to say to people.

_____ 12. I enjoy talking to my subordinates.

_____ 13.* I talk less because I'm shy.

_____ 14.* I am fearful and tense all the while I am speaking before a group of people.

_____ 15.* Talking to my supervisor makes me nervous.

_____ 16. I like to get involved in group discussions.

_____ 17.* Conversing with people who hold positions of authority causes me to be fearful and tense.

_____ 18. I enjoy representing my organization to other groups.

_____ 19. I look forward to interviewing people applying for a job as my subordinate.

_____ 20.* I consider myself to be the silent type.

SOURCE: Scott, McCroskey, and Sheahan, 1976. Reprinted by permission.

*Agreement with items with asterisks indicates communication apprehension. Disagreement with other items indicates communication apprehension.
To score this scale, complete this formula: Score = 60 − Total of items with *'s + Total of items without *'s.

Dogmatism Scale

Rokeach (1960) has developed a scale designed to measure individual differences in openness or closedness of belief systems. According to Rokeach, open-minded people can "receive, evaluate and act on relevant information received from the outside on its own intrinsic merits, unencumbered by irrelevant factors in the situation arising from within the person or from the outside." Although revised several times, the current version of the scale contains both a long form (sixty-six items) and a short form (forty items). Responses are scored along a $+3$ to -3 agree-disagree scale, with the 0-point excluded. These scores are converted to a 1–7 scale by adding the constant 4 to each score. Thus, the range of possible scores on the long form is 66–462, and on the short form 40–280. The higher the score, the greater the degree of dogmatism. Sample items include:

The U. S. and Russia have nothing in common.

Groups tolerating diverse opinions can't exist.

To know what's going on, rely on leaders.

I hate some people because of what they stand for.

Most printed ideas aren't worth the paper they're printed on.

So much to do, so little time to do it in.

The main thing in life is to do something important.

I don't listen.

I interrupt others to put across my own views.

The world is a lonesome place.

Similarity-Dissimilarity Test

Daly, McCroskey, and Falcione (1976) have developed a test which measures the degree to which employees are similar or dissimilar in their attitudes and values to their immediate supervisors. Their research has shown that the greater the similarity, the greater the job satisfaction. The instrument contains only eight items, scored on a 1–7 scale. Two scales make up the test (Table 7-4). Scores can range from 8 (very dissimilar) to 56 (very similar).

TABLE 7-4. SIMILARITY-DISSIMILARITY TEST

Please identify in your mind *your immediate supervisor.* Please complete the scales below describing your immediate supervisor in comparison to yourself.	
Attitude Scales	
Doesn't think like me	1 2 3 4 5 6 7 Thinks like me
Doesn't behave like me	1 2 3 4 5 6 7 Behaves like me
Different from me	1 2 3 4 5 6 7 Similar to me
Unlike me	1 2 3 4 5 6 7 Like me
Value Scales	
Morals unlike mine	1 2 3 4 5 6 7 Morals like mine
Sexual attitudes unlike mine	1 2 3 4 5 6 7 Sexual attitudes like mine
Doesn't share my values	1 2 3 4 5 6 7 Shares my values
Doesn't treat people like I do	1 2 3 4 5 6 7 Treats people like I do

SOURCE: Daley, McCroskey, and Falcione, 1976. Reprinted by permission.

MEASUREMENT OF RELATIONAL VARIABLES

In Chapters 4 and 5, we discussed relational communication variables—those factors that are likely to vary considerably as dyads and groups interact within an organization. The following measurement tools and approaches help the manager monitor and describe them.

Disparity Tests

Research by Browne and Neitzel (1952), Odiorne (1954), and Read (1962) has shown that communication problems can be inferred from the amount of disparity between a manager's estimate and his subordinates' estimates of their authority, responsibility, and problem-solving ability. The greater the disparity, the greater the probability of poor communication about the areas in question. Insufficient or low-quality information is usually the culprit. To test this variable the manager can design a short (say, ten-item) test with such questions on it as the following:

Whom do you supervise?

In what areas of this business do you have authority?

What are your major job responsibilities?

What are the major job responsibilities of your immediate supervisor?

The manager also answers these questions—as he thinks the subordinates will. Comparing the manager's answers with his subordinates' will give a quick indication of any disparity. Where great disparity is anticipated, additional or clearer information about the areas questioned may be necessary.

Accuracy Tests

The work of Funk and Becker (1952) has provided the groundwork for tests measuring the degree to which employees receive and/or understand specific information about their jobs, organizational policies and procedures, and pay and benefits. The logic behind such tests is simple. Test items are constructed which measure employee understanding of major areas of concern to the organization. The greater the number of correct answers, supposedly the greater the employee understanding. Low scores typically indicate either inadequate or poor-quality information given to employees *or* poor listening by employees. Regardless of the cause of the problem, the effect is the same—low understanding of major issues. Where areas of ignorance or misinformation are identified, corrective steps can be taken to increase employees' knowledge of organizational policies and practices.

The senior author of this book once directed a study of a telephone company in which he administered a survey to test employees' knowledge of (1) their own department's major responsibilities; (2) the major responsibilities of the other three departments (as a measure of lateral communication); and (3) companywide personnel policies.

The test (Table 7-5) contains five items for each department and five items for the entire company. Thus, for Accounting personnel, the five items of direct importance to the Accounting Department would provide an index of how well they understand their job roles and functions, the fifteen items about the other three departments of how well they understand the job roles and functions of the three other departments, and the five items about company policies of how well they understand company personnel policies. Scores on such a test allow one to compare employee understanding among various departments, as well as to pinpoint areas of misinformation and misunderstanding.

TABLE 7-5. ACCURACY QUESTIONNAIRE

Please answer each question by choosing the *best* answer listed.

1. The Accounting Department is considered:
   (1) a record-keeping service department
   (2) customer service department
   (3) employee service department
   (4) all of the above

2. The Revenue Accounting Department is responsible for:
   (1) customer billings in the city
   (2) customer billings for the entire state
   (3) customer billings for the northern portion of the state
   (4) all of the above

3. It is a responsibility of the Accounting Department to:
   (1) record the location of all telephone poles in the state
   (2) record the location of every manhole in only the city
   (3) conduct accounting procedures only
   (4) all of the above

4. The Accounting Department keeps:
   (1) records of travel expenses accrued by all departments
   (2) records of the amount of cable used in the state
   (3) records of payroll issued throughout the state
   (4) all of the above

5. The Accounting Department:
   (1) keeps track of the capital dollar for the entire system
   (2) keeps track of the money spent by all departments
   (3) does all the computer programming
   (4) all of the above

Table 7-5. Continued

6. The Engineering Department is chiefly concerned with:
   (1) the installation of telephone equipment
   (2) the provision of communication systems
   (3) providing services for Marketing to sell
   (4) all of the above

7. It is the responsibility of the Engineering Department to:
   (1) provide toll facilities based on usage and forecasts initiated by other departments
   (2) build telephone equipment
   (3) build telephone equipment and systems
   (4) none of the above

8. The Engineering Department is concerned with:
   (1) management of the capital dollar
   (2) forecasting the expense dollar
   (3) developing satisfactory facilities for the entire state
   (4) none of the above

9. It is the responsibility of the Engineering Department to:
   (1) build buildings to house equipment
   (2) purchase or lease land for buildings to house equipment or personnel
   (3) purchase all equipment
   (4) none of the above

10. The Engineering Department:
    (1) determines how much equipment is required for each fiscal year based on reports from other departments
    (2) functions as a service organization for other departments
    (3) determines equipment needs through long-range plannings for most other departments
    (4) all of the above

11. The Marketing Department:
    (1) installs telephones
    (2) installs PBXs
    (3) installs large-key systems
    (4) none of the above

12. The Marketing Department:
    (1) analyzes all types and sizes of telephone systems
    (2) contacts large business customers only
    (3) writes service orders for business customers
    (4) none of the above

13. A function of the Marketing Department is to:
    (1) promote customer relations
    (2) analyze telephone systems
    (3) recommend PBX systems
    (4) all of the above

14. A responsibility of the Marketing Department is to:
    (1) design complete communication systems for large customers only
    (2) sell and service electric equipment only
    (3) serve the larger business customers
    (4) all of the above

15. The Marketing Department is responsible for:
    (1) jointly (with Engineering) designing large PBX systems
    (2) sale of WATS lines
    (3) business customer relations
    (4) all of the above

Table 7-5. Continued

16. One of the main functions of the Plant Department is to:
    (1) maintain telephone sets
    (2) install telephone sets
    (3) maintain switching equipment and install telephone and radio sets
    (4) none of the above

17. The Plant Department is concerned with the toll and local equipment through:
    (1) maintenance
    (2) installation
    (3) both maintenance and installation
    (4) none of the above

18. A main function of the Plant Department is to:
    (1) design correct installation services for every customer
    (2) analyze maintenance and services
    (3) devise adequate safety approaches
    (4) none of the above

19. A responsibility of the Plant Department is to:
    (1) maintain all motor vehicle fleets
    (2) maintain local buildings
    (3) maintain only office areas where Plant is located
    (4) none of the above

20. The Plant Department purchases:
    (1) all supplies
    (2) all equipment
    (3) all the motor vehicle fleet
    (4) none of the above

21. A goal of the company is to strive for fewer accidents:
    (1) involving motor vehicles
    (2) in the office buildings
    (3) within private homes
    (4) all of the above

22. Company safety meetings are conducted:
    (1) every two weeks
    (2) every month
    (3) every other month
    (4) none of the above

23. It is a goal of the company to:
    (1) attain proportions of minority employees within the company equal to that represented in the state
    (2) achieve 38–50% minority group employees
    (3) attain a proportion of minority employees within the company equal to that represented within the city
    (4) none of the above

24. It is important to the company that:
    (1) a minority applicant be given serious first consideration for job opportunities
    (2) safety programs be conducted for those persons who operate company vehicles
    (3) safety programs be conducted for vacation-bound employees
    (4) all of the above

25. It is a goal of the company to:
    (1) show statistically that 47–58% of terminating employees do so for personal reasons
    (2) develop less turnover among employees
    (3) determine causes of turnover among employees
    (4) require terminating employees to file forms for their reasons of termination

SOURCE: Developed by Gene Probasco and Gerald Goldhaber.

Readability Formulas

The *readability formula* is a mathematical model of relative difficulty or comprehension of text. The formula is usually based on statistical analysis of written text coded for difficulty. The most famous of these formulas for English were developed by Rudolf Flesch during the 1940s and '50s. There are readability formulas for other languages as well. These formulas are useful for determining the relative level of difficulty of a written message. The formulas usually rank the difficulty according to the level of formal schooling by the receiver: this book, for example, represents a college graduate level of difficulty. These formulas offer a useful method of message analysis in order to optimize organizational communication situations.

As an example, we give the Flesch Reading Ease formula for English:

Systematically select 100-word samples of a written text.
Determine the number of syllables per 100 words (wl = word length).
Determine the average number of words per sentence (sl = sentence length).
Apply the following formula:

Reading Ease
$$= 206.835 - 0.846wl - 1.015sl$$

Change the score to grade levels according to the following table:

100–90	5th grade
90–80	6th grade
80–70	7th grade
70–60	8th and 9th grades
60–50	10th to 12th grades (high school)
50–30	13th to 16th grades (college)
30–0	College Graduate

SOURCE: Adaptation of Readability Formulas from THE ART OF READABLE WRITING by Rudolph Flesch. Copyright 1949 by Rudolph Flesch. By permission of Harper & Row.

As you can see, the Flesch formula measures two comprehension factors: word length and sentence length. The length of the word is directly correlated with word difficulty: long words (in most languages) tend to be difficult and seldom-used words; short words are often-used, familiar words.

Flesch was recently hired by the U.S. Federal Trade Commission to help simplify the bureaucratic language in their regulations. He concluded that most of the agency's writing was in the 30–0 range (indicating college-graduate difficulty). As an example:

No seller shall represent that it or any of its employees, agents, sales persons and/or representatives is a physician or an audiologist, unless such is fact.

He changed this to the following more readable version:

Don't say or hint, you or anyone in your firm is a doctor of medicine or an audiologist if it isn't so.

It does an organization little good to send frequent written memos, newsletters, brochures, and manuals to its employees if they can't understand the message. The 1974 ERISA regulations guarantee clarity of communication to employees about their pension and retirement benefits. The essence of this law is: *Say it in simple English!*

In organizational communication, we find an ideal background for misunderstanding messages. The members of the organization usually have widely different educational backgrounds. First of all, the educational levels usually vary significantly: there are people with high academic degrees and high school dropouts with very little other formal training. The educational background also varies horizontally: people have different specialities with corresponding education. Academic training in one area does not usually make a person expert in another field of knowledge: a Ph.D. in physics may be completely at loss with the terminology of social sciences, and vice versa.

Also, the value and norm systems of members of organizations may be quite different: facts mean different things to different people.

Because of all this, the language in organizational communication should be as simple and general as possible if the receivers of messages represent a wide variety of social groups. The communication task is easier among members of a single social group—for example, experts can use expert language when talking or writing to other experts in the same field.

Credibility Test

Falcione (1974) has developed an instrument which measures subordinates' perceptions of the credibility of their immediate supervisor. This construct is of vital importance to any organization interested in the believability of their communications. If employees don't trust or believe or find supervisors to be credible, then their messages will probably not be believed. Falcione's scale (Table 7-6) is made up of thirty items measuring four dimensions of credibility: safety/sociability, competence/expertise, extroversion/dynamism, and emotional stability/temperament. Each item has a seven point scale with the low end (1) indicating low credibility and the high end (7) indicating high credibility. The score for a supervisor is found by averaging employee ratings for a particular dimension or for the total instrument. The range in scores for the entire test is 30 (very low credibility) to 210 (very high credibility). The range for safety is 14–98, for competence 5–35, for extroversion 7–49, and for emotional stability 4–28.

TABLE 7-6. FALCIONE CREDIBILITY SCALE

Dimension	Scales								
Safety/Sociability	dishonest	1	2	3	4	5	6	7	honest
	unfriendly	1	2	3	4	5	6	7	friendly
	unpleasant	1	2	3	4	5	6	7	pleasant
	awful	1	2	3	4	5	6	7	nice
	irritable	1	2	3	4	5	6	7	good-natured
	dangerous	1	2	3	4	5	6	7	safe
	negativistic	1	2	3	4	5	6	7	cooperative
	unjust	1	2	3	4	5	6	7	just
	unselfish	1	2	3	4	5	6	7	selfish
	unfair	1	2	3	4	5	6	7	fair
	unethical	1	2	3	4	5	6	7	ethical
	headstrong	1	2	3	4	5	6	7	mild
	sinful	1	2	3	4	5	6	7	virtuous
	jealous	1	2	3	4	5	6	7	not jealous
Competence/Expertise	untrained	1	2	3	4	5	6	7	trained
	inexperienced	1	2	3	4	5	6	7	experienced
	uninformed	1	2	3	4	5	6	7	informed
	inexpert	1	2	3	4	5	6	7	expert
	unskilled	1	2	3	4	5	6	7	skilled
Extroversion/Dynamism	slow	1	2	3	4	5	6	7	fast
	timid	1	2	3	4	5	6	7	bold
	aggressive	1	2	3	4	5	6	7	meek
	hesitant	1	2	3	4	5	6	7	emphatic
	cautious	1	2	3	4	5	6	7	adventurous
	forceless	1	2	3	4	5	6	7	forceful
	passive	1	2	3	4	5	6	7	active
Emotional Stability/ Temperament	nervous	1	2	3	4	5	6	7	poised
	anxious	1	2	3	4	5	6	7	calm
	excitable	1	2	3	4	5	6	7	composed
	tense	1	2	3	4	5	6	7	poised

SOURCE: Falcione (1974). Reprinted by permission.

Communication Climate Measures

In recent years, several researchers have developed instruments which measure the communication climate of an organization, that is, the degree of supportiveness, trust, confidence, openness, and candor present in an organization. Dennis (1974) has developed one instrument, in particular, which measures most of the dimensions of communication climate described in Chapters 4 and 5. The instrument (Table 7-7) contains forty five items representing five factors of communication climate. These factors are:

Factor 1 (twenty-one items): Superior/subordinate communication, particularly the supportiveness from a superior perceived by the subordinate.

234

TABLE 7-7. DENNIS COMMUNICATION CLIMATE INVENTORY

FACTOR I: Superior/subordinate communication
____ Your superior makes you feel free to talk with him/her.
____ Your superior really understands your job problems.
____ Your superior encourages you to let him/her know when things are going wrong on the job.
____ Your superior makes it easy for you to do your best work.
____ Your superior expresses his/her confidence with your ability to perform the job.
____ Your superior encourages you to bring new information to his/her attention, even when that new information may be bad news.
____ Your superior makes you feel that things you tell him/her are really important.
____ Your superior is willing to tolerate arguments and to give a fair hearing to all points of view.
____ Your superior has your best interests in mind when he/she talks to his/her bosses.
____ Your superior is a really competent, expert manager.
____ Your superior listens to you when you tell him/her about things that are bothering you.
____ It is safe to say what you are really thinking to your superior.
____ Your superior is frank and candid with you.
____ You can "sound off" about job frustrations to your superior.
____ You can tell your superior about the way you feel he/she manages your work group.
____ You are free to tell your superior that you disagree with him/her.
____ You think you are safe in communicating bad news to your superior without fear of any retaliation on his/her part.
____ You think that your superior believes that he/she really understands you.
____ You believe that your superior thinks that you understand him/her.
____ Your superior really understands you.
____ You really understand your superior.

FACTOR II: Quality of information
____ You think that people in this organization say what they mean and mean what they say.
____ People in Top Management say what they mean and mean what they say.
____ People in this organization are encouraged to be really open and candid with each other.
____ People in this organization freely exchange information and opinions.
____ You are kept informed about how well organizational goals or objectives are being met.
____ Your organization succeeds in rewarding and praising good performance.
____ Top Management is providing you with the kinds of information you really want and need.
____ You are receiving information from those sources (for example, from superiors, department meetings, coworkers, newsletters) that you prefer.
____ You are pleased with management's efforts to keep employees up to date on recent developments that relate to the organization's welfare—such as success in competition, profitability, and future growth plans.
____ You are notified in advance of changes that affect your job.
____ You are satisfied with explanations you get from Top Management about why things are done as they are.
____ Your job requirements are specified in clear language.

FACTOR III: Superior openness/candor
____ You believe your subordinates are really frank and candid with you.
____ You believe your colleagues (coworkers) are really frank and candid with you.

Table 7-7. Continued

_____ You think your subordinates feel free to "sound off" to you about things that bother them.
_____ You believe that you really understand your subordinates' problems.
_____ You believe that your subordinates think that you really understand their problems.

FACTOR IV: Upward communication opportunity
_____ Your opinions make a difference in the day-to-day decisions that affect your job.
_____ Your superior lets you participate in the planning of your own work.
_____ Members of your work group are able to establish their own goals and objectives.
_____ You believe your views have real influence in your organization.
_____ You can expect that recommendations you make will be heard and seriously considered.

FACTOR V: Reliability of information
_____ You think that information received from your subordinates is really reliable.
_____ You think that information received from your colleagues (coworkers) is reliable.

SOURCE: Dennis (1974).

Factor II (twelve items): Perceived quality and accuracy of downward communication relationships with subordinates, especially the affective aspects of these relationships, such as perceived openness and empathy.

Factor III (five items): Superiors' perceptions of communication relationships with subordinates, especially the affective aspects of these relationships, such as openness and empathy.

Factor IV (five items): Perception of upward communication opportunities and degree of influence.

Factor V (two items): Perception of reliability of information received from subordinates and colleagues.

The instrument is designed to be administered to all employees, who would be asked, for each item, to indicate the extent to which they agree with the statement. The five-point scale used with each item is:

1—to a very little extent
2—to a little extent
3—to some extent
4—to a great extent
5—to a very great extent

The range of scores, therefore, is from 45 (indicating a very poor communication climate) to 225 (indicating a very good communication climate). Each factor can also be scored independently. The ranges are:

Factor I (Superior/subordinate communication)—21 to 105
Factor II (Quality of information)—12 to 60
Factor III (Superior openness/empathy)—5 to 25
Factor IV (Upward communication opportunity)—5 to 25
Factor V (Reliability of information)—2 to 10

MEASUREMENT OF ORGANIZATIONAL VARIABLES

In Chapter 6, we discussed the organizational communication variables—those factors that are likely to vary considerably as a function of the entire system. The following measurement tools and approaches help the manager monitor and describe these systemwide variables.

Observation Techniques

Observation techniques involve perceiving and recording the behavior of either oneself or other people. When we observe and record our own behavior, we are involved in a "duty study"; when we observe the behavior of others, we are acting as "trained observers." These techniques can give the manager information about the amount of communication, or *communication load*, carried by key personnel, as well as *which network* is utilized and the *direction* of the flow. Such techniques reveal such information as the average length of time spent interacting with certain people, differences in topics of discussion between various people and their significance, and the major media or channels used to exchange messages among certain people. Hinrichs (1964) used observation techniques in his duty study in which employees kept a diary or log of their daily communication activities over a period of eleven days. The major dimensions covered were:

1. Where the individual was at the observation time.
2. Whether he/she was communicating or not.
3. If communicating, the method being used:
   oral communications
   writing
   reading
4. Who the other participants in the communication were:
   their organizational level and affiliation
   the number of people involved
5. Why the communication started:
   who initiated it
   its major function

6. What the subject was:
   technical matters
   nontechnical matters
7. How much time had been spent on the communication.
8. How important the respondent felt the communication to be, and what further action was required.

   An employee would fill out a form for every logged communication. The amount logged would depend upon the degree of desired detail. One could log only a sample of communication or all communications transacted over a period of time. Results would be summaries, in frequency or percentage format, which described the communication behavior of the sample of people maintaining diaries.

   Some of the major problems associated with such diaries, however, are the amount of time required to keep them, the amount of training necessary to familiarize personnel with the instrument, the amount of monitoring required to check on respondents' filling out the forms, the degree to which it depends upon the willingness of respondents to complete the diary for confidential communications, and the large amount of data generated by the instrument, much of which may not be useful for a particular manager.

ECCO Analysis

Keith Davis (1952) developed ECCO (Episodic Communication Channels in Organization) analysis as a means of tracking a particular message or set of messages through an organization. The instrument focuses on a message and follows it through time and space from the time it is initially sent until it is completely diffused. With its output one can map communication networks and measure rates of flow, distortion of messages, and redundancy.

   Administration of the instrument (Table 7-8) is relatively simple. Respondents are asked to fill in the ECCO form in the presence of an interviewer. This generally takes three to four minutes and can be done at the place of work. If a respondent has a question, he or she may freely converse with the interviewer. Questionnaires are then coded, tabulated, and analyzed. Among its chief advantages are that it is a convenient, fast, reliable instrument. It allows for respondent-interviewer interaction and is inexpensive, simple, and clear. Finally it deals with a concrete message that the manager may be interested in testing for effectiveness in both diffusion and understanding. Its major disadvantage is that it sometimes can take several weeks for a message to be totally diffused within an organization.

TABLE 7-8. EXAMPLE OF AN ECCO ANALYSIS INSTRUMENT

Prior to receiving this questionnaire did you know the information in the box below or any part of it?

```
┌─────────────────────────────────────────────┐
│                                               │
│                  (Message)                    │
│                                               │
└─────────────────────────────────────────────┘
```

Please check one:
____ Yes, I knew all of it.
____ Yes, I knew part of it. (If so, please list the numbers of the parts you knew:____ ____ ____ ____ ____ .)
____ No, I did not know any of it.

If your answer above was "Yes, I knew all of it," or "Yes, I knew part of it," please complete the questionnaire by providing the information requested below.

If your answer above was "No, I did not know any of it," you have completed the questionnaire. Please return the questionnaire to me or drop it in the information box. Thank you very much for your cooperation.

If you had the information in the box but the facts you heard were different, please write the facts you heard below:

1. _____
2. _____
3. _____
4. _____
5. _____

Question 1.
From whom did you first receive the information in the box? Please place the source's code number (from your code sheet) on this line._____

Remember that by using the code number *you never identify* the specific person who gave you the information because *each* code number is assigned to *several* persons (in the operator group).

Question 2.
Where were you when you first received the information in the box above? Please check one:
11. ____ At my desk, board, or other location where I carry out my job duties.
12. ____ Elsewhere in the room where I work.
13. ____ Outside this room but still working.
14. ____ Away from my unit department but still working.
15. ____ Away from my unit department but not while working (coffee break etc.)
16. ____ Away from the building and not working for this company.

Question 3.
How long ago did you first receive the information in the box? Please circle the approximate time:

Today	Yesterday	3 4 5 6 7	days ago
		2 3 4 5 6	weeks ago

Question 4.
By what method did you first receive the information in the box above? Please *check only one of* the following methods:
Written or visual methods
20. ____ Personal letter from the Chief Executive Officer
21. ____ Letter, memo, or service program

Table 7-8. Continued

22. _____ Annual report
23. _____ Company newsletter
24. _____ Company magazine
25. _____ Videotape message
26. _____ Company film
27. _____ Public newspaper or magazine
28. _____ Company records
Talking or sound methods
29. _____ Talking with one other person in his presence
30. _____ Talking over the telephone
31. _____ Talking (and listening) in a small group of two or more
32. _____ Attending an organized meeting or conference
33. _____ Overhearing what someone else said
34. _____ Radio or television
Miscellaneous
35. _____ I am the subject/source of the message
36. _____ Other, (Please explain.)

Thank you very much for your cooperation. Please return the questionnaire to me or drop it in the information box.

SOURCE: Adapted from a similar form used by Rudolph (1972).

Questionnaire-Interview Technique

Questionnaire-interview techniques generally seek data about respondents' perceptions, attitudes, and knowledge about information within the organization. Earlier we presented examples of how Scott, Falcione, Dennis, and others have used written questionnaires and surveys to gather their information about communication. Such approaches have the advantage of collecting a lot of information in a very little time. Typical problems associated with surveys are getting a return rate representative of the population, biased responses, and problems coding open-ended questions into appropriate and quantifiable categories. Many of these problems are alleviated by interviewing, especially using the in-depth interview lasting several hours. Foltz (1973) has published an interview guide which has been used successfully by Towers, Perrin, Forster and Crosby, a management consulting firm headquartered in New York City. He uses a different interview guide for each of the four groups interviewed: chief executive; personnel and communication manager; managers for other functions; rank-and-file employees. Table 7-9 presents a sample of some of these questions.

As with any interview guide, interaction between interviewer and respondent is possible, thus improving the chances of getting valid and reliable responses. The major disadvantage of interviewing is the cost, represented by employee or manager time, required to get valid data.

TABLE 7-9. SAMPLE FOLTZ INTERVIEW GUIDE

For the Chief Executive Officer:
1. What are your views on the value of developing and maintaining effective internal and external communications programs?
2. To what extent are you, as a chief executive, directly involved in your organization's communications programs? Would you rather be involved to greater or lesser extent? Why?

For the Personnel and Communications Manager:
1. Construct an organization chart depicting titles, organization levels, reporting relations, and functional responsibilities throughout the organization for major communications activities.
2. Do you have formal, written communications objectives and policies? If not, what do you believe the key ones are?
3. What means have you used to check the effectiveness of your various communications programs?
4. During the past year, which of the following subjects have you developed a communications program for?

   Personnel policies and practices
   Overall organization goals
   Compensation policies and practices (benefit plans, salary administration plans, executive compensation plans)
   Recruiting and orientation program
   Management development program
   Educational refund program
   Labor relations program
   Safety, cost-saving, recreational programs
   Community relations program
   Others (list)

For Managers of Other Functions:
1. Do you think the organization does a good job in keeping its employees informed about its plans and developments?
2. How do you communicate your plans, activities, and suggestions to departments and units outside your functional area?
3. How do you feel about the way employee suggestions or complaints are handled?
4. Do you have any ideas on how your organization could improve its employee and community relations communications programs?

For Rank-and-File Employees:
1. How do you feel about the fairness and honesty of management?
2. How do you feel about the way employee complaints are handled?
3. Do you know, in general, what is going on in other departments?
4. How do you feel about the information you get about your pay and benefit plans?

SOURCE: Foltz (1973). Reprinted by permission.

The ICA Communication Audit

In 1971, the International Communication Association (ICA), a non-profit professional communication society, started its Communication Audit Project in response to the lack of a standard procedure for assessing organizational communication systems (see Goldhaber, 1976; and Goldhaber and Krivonos, 1977). The ICA Communication Audit is unique as a measurement approach. A standardized system of five instruments, it uses both computerized analysis and feedback procedures and a normed data bank to enable comparisons among organizations' communication systems.*

Products of an ICA Communication Audit include:

1. An organizational profile of perceptions of communication events, practices, and relationships. This profile can be further analyzed according to such demographics as age, sex, education, supervisory status, and division/department.
2. A map of the operational communication network for rumors and social and job-related messages, listing all group members, liaisons, and isolates, identifying potential bottlenecks and gatekeepers.
3. Verbal summaries of successful and unsuccessful communication experiences used to explain some of the reasons for communication problems or strengths identified in the above profile and networks.
4. An organizational and individual profile of actual communication behaviors summarizing major message sources, receivers, topics, channels, lengths, and qualities, thus allowing comparisons between actual and perceived communication behaviors.
5. A set of general recommendations, derived from the results of the audit, indicating which attitudes, behaviors, practices, and skills should be continued, added, changed or eliminated.
6. Several personnel from the organization familiar with the ICA Audit instruments and procedures, helping the organization to take the major initiative in conducting future audits themselves.
7. Permanent future access (on a confidential basis) to the ICA audit data bank, allowing the organization to compare the results of present and future audits with those of similar organizations.

---

*For additional information about the ICA or the ICA Communication Audit, contact Gerald Goldhaber, Department of Communication, State University of New York at Buffalo, Amherst, NY 14260.

The ICA Communication Audit's five measurement tools, each of which can be administered independently or in any combination, are as follows:

1. Questionnaire Survey. This consists of 122 items and 12 demographic questions plus up to 34 questions of any type determined by the organization. The reliability of the scales on the 134-item set ranges from a low of .73 to a high of .92. The validity of these scales is based upon their self-evident relationship to organizational communication, their ability to predict organizational outcomes, and their consistency with previously validated measures of organizational communication. Respondents answer the survey anonymously in group sessions lasting about forty five minutes. The survey allows respondents to indicate their perception of the current status of their communication system as well as their needed or ideal status. This greatly helps in the identification of communication uncertainty in the organization. Table 7-10 summarizes the topics and item distribution on the survey. Table 7-11 illustrates the survey format.

2. Interviews. Randomly and/or purposively selected members of the organization are asked to participate in one-on-one interviews, the principal purpose of which is to corroborate and/or expand upon concerns reported in other audit tools. Two interview schedules are used: one that is structured to provide exploratory information, using open-ended questions; and a follow-up guide which is specifically tailored to each organization to explain findings revealed through the use of other audit tools. Most interviews last sixty to ninety minutes, and all are conducted confidentially (sometimes using tape recorders to facilitate data analysis). Table 7-12 presents the exploratory interview guide used in the ICA Audit.

TABLE 7-10. ICA COMMUNICATION AUDIT, SURVEY TOPICS

Topic	Number of Items
1. Amount of information received/needed from others on selected topics	26
2. Amount of information sent/needed to be sent to others on selected topics	14
3. Amount of follow-up or action taken/needed on information sent to others	10
4. Amount of information received/needed from selected sources	18
5. Timeliness of information received from key sources	6
6. Amount of information received/needed from selected channels	16
7. Quality of communication relationships	19
8. Satisfaction with major organizational outcomes	13
9. Demographic information	12
Total	134

TABLE 7-11. SAMPLE FORMAT OF ICA COMMUNICATION AUDIT SURVEY

RECEIVING INFORMATION FROM OTHERS											
	This is the amount of information I receive now.						This is the amount of information I need to receive.				
Topic Area		Very little	Little	Some	Great	Very great		Very little	Little	Some	Great	Very great
How well I am doing in my job	1.	1	2	3	4	5	2.	1	2	3	4	5
My job duties	3.	1	2	3	4	5	4.	1	2	3	4	5
Organizational policies	5.	1	2	3	4	5	6.	1	2	3	4	5
Pay and benefits	7.	1	2	3	4	5	8.	1	2	3	4	5
How technological changes affect my job	9.	1	2	3	4	5	10.	1	2	3	4	5
Mistakes and failures of my organization	11.	1	2	3	4	5	12.	1	2	3	4	5
How I am being judged	13.	1	2	3	4	5	14.	1	2	3	4	5
How my job-related problems are being handled	15.	1	2	3	4	5	16.	1	2	3	4	5
How organization decisions are made that affect my job	17.	1	2	3	4	5	18.	1	2	3	4	5
Promotion and advancement opportunities in my organization	19.	1	2	3	4	5	20.	1	2	3	4	5

3. Network Analysis. Respondents indicate the extent to which they typically communicate with each individual in their unit or department (or with key individuals outside their unit). A computer examination of all communication links identifies the operational communication network (for rumors and social and job-related messages) and places individuals into communication roles of isolate, liaison, or group member. The instrument is completed in group sessions lasting about thirty minutes. Table 7-13 presents the ICA Audit network analysis form.

4. Communication Experiences. Respondents describe critical communication episodes which they consider representative of typically successful or unsuccessful incidents. From these descriptions and the type of incident each represents, a set of examples are developed to help illustrate why a given unit or department is experiencing good or bad communication. These qualitative data complement and help explain information from other audit tools. Respondents complete this instrument in group or individual sessions lasting about one hour. All data are

TABLE 7-12. ICA COMMUNICATION AUDIT EXPLORATORY INTERVIEW GUIDE

1. Describe your job (duties, function). What decisions do you usually make in your job? What information do you *need* to make those decisions and from where should you get it? What information do you *actually get* to make those decisions and from whom? Are there formal (written) or informal policies in your organization which determine how you get this information? Should any policies be added, changed, or abandoned?
2. What are the major communication *strengths* of this organization? Be specific. (Begin with the larger system and work down to your work unit.)
3. What are the major communication *weaknesses* of this organization? Be specific. (Again, begin with the larger system and work down.)
4. Describe the *formal* channels through which you typically receive information about this organization. What kinds of information do you tend to receive? How often?
5. Describe the *informal* channels through which you typically receive information about this organization. What kinds of information do you tend to receive? How often?
6. How often, if ever, do you receive information about this organization which is of low value or use to you? If and when you do, what kinds of information do you receive? Be specific. From whom do you receive this?
7. What would you like to see done to improve information flow in this organization? Why hasn't it been done yet?
8. Describe the way decisions are typically made in this organization.
9. When conflict occurs in this organization, what is its major cause? How is conflict typically resolved?
10. Describe the communication relationship you have with your immediate supervisor; with your coworkers; with middle management; with top management; with your subordinates (if appropriate). (Ask for specific examples of *behavioral* evidence of trust, openness—"How do you know that he/she trusts you?" "What has he/she done to indicate that he/she is being open and frank with you?" etc.)
11. How do you know when this organization has done a good or bad job toward accomplishing its goals? What measures of effectiveness are used in this organization?

computer-analyzed confidentially. Table 7-14 presents the ICA Audit communication experiences form.

5. Communication Diary. Each participant is asked to maintain a diary of specified communication activities (conversations, phone calls, meetings, written materials received and sent) over a one-week period. Forms are provided to simplify the recording of these communication events. Cumulative time required per person for the entire week is approximately ninety minutes, including a short training period. These data are confidentially analyzed by computer and provide indications of actual communication behavior among individuals, groups, and the entire organization. Table 7-15 presents the ICA Audit diary form.

TABLE 7-13. ICA AUDIT NETWORK ANALYSIS INSTRUMENT

	ID	Formal organizational structure	Informal (grapevine) organizational structure
During the typical work day, I usually communicate about work-related matters with the following people through the:			
Executive			
Steno. Secy.	0001	____ A B C D E	____ A B C D E
Sr. Steno.	0002	____ A B C D E	____ A B C D E
Exec. Secy.	0003	____ A B C D E	____ A B C D E
Asst. Ex. Dir.	0004	____ A B C D E	____ A B C D E
Asst. Hsg. Mgr.	0005	____ A B C D E	____ A B C D E
Telephone Op.	0006	____ A B C D E	____ A B C D E
Ex. Director	0007	____ A B C D E	____ A B C D E
Administration and Finance			
Asst. Dir. for Admin.	0008	____ A B C D E	____ A B C D E
Typist	0009	____ A B C D E	____ A B C D E
Acct. Clerk	0010	____ A B C D E	____ A B C D E
Acct. Clk. Typ.	0011	____ A B C D E	____ A B C D E
Asst. Acct.	0012	____ A B C D E	____ A B C D E
Sr. Acct.	0013	____ A B C D E	____ A B C D E
Typist	0014	____ A B C D E	____ A B C D E
Steno.	0015	____ A B C D E	____ A B C D E

A = not at all important
B = somewhat important
C = fairly important
D = very important
E = extremely important

Key Audit Logistics and Timetable

In order to complete the ICA Communication Audit within a reasonable time (usually about three months), the following timetable is suggested:

Activity	Duration
Finalize contract; prepare tools	1 week
Conduct exploratory interviews	1 week
Transcribe interviews and prepare for analysis	1 week
Analyze exploratory interviews	1 week
Administer survey, communication experiences, and network analysis questionnaires	1 week
Analyze survey, communication experiences, and network analysis data	2 weeks
Preliminary interpretation of data; formulation of follow-up interview guide, communication diary log	1 week
Conduct follow-up interviews; administer communication diary	1 week
Transcribe interviews and prepare for analysis; prepare diary data	1 week
Analyze follow-up interviews, communication diary	1 week
Interpret data; draw conclusions; prepare recommendations; write final report	2 weeks
Present final report (orally and in writing); discuss future steps	2 days
Total elapsed time:	13.3 weeks

TABLE 7-14. ICA COMMUNICATION AUDIT COMMUNICATION EXPERIENCE FORM

While you were filling out the previous section,* the questions may have brought to mind a recent work-related experience of yours in which communication was particularly effective or ineffective. Please answer the questions below and give us a clearly printed summary of that experience.

A. To whom does this experience primarily relate? (Circle *one.*)
   1. Subordinate
   2. Coworker
   3. Immediate supervisor
   4. Middle management
   5. Top management

B. Please rate the quality of communication described in the experience below. (Circle *one.*)
   1. Effective
   2. Ineffective

C. To what item in the previous section does this experience primarily relate? (Write down item number.)

Describe the communication experience, the circumstances leading up to it, what the person did that made him/her an effective or ineffective communicator, and the results (outcome) of what the person did. (*Please print. Thank you.*)

_____

_____

_____

_____

_____

This refers to previous section of the questionnaire survey.

During the conduct of the audit, the ICA recommends that the organization establish an audit liaison committee composed of a diagonal slant of seven to nine persons whose functions would be:

1. to help implement audit logistics (set up interviews, etc.);
2. to receive interim audit reports;
3. to communicate information to the organization before, during, and after the audit; (via newsletters, memos, meetings);
4. to receive the final audit report; and
5. to begin to prioritize conclusions and recommendations.

Feedback of Results and Follow-up

The results of the audit are reported orally and in writing to appropriate personnel. A brief report, containing conclusions and recommendations, is prepared for general dissemination throughout the organization. A detailed report, prepared in accordance with customary conventions for the reporting of survey-participant data (i.e., percentages, tabular presentations, and

TABLE 7-15. ICA AUDIT COMMUNICATION DIARY INSTRUMENT

Your name: _____ Date: _____ Other party: _____								
			Communication					
	1	2	3	4	5	6	7	[etc.]
Initiator Self Other party								
Channel Face-to-face Telephone Written								
Kind Job-related Incidental Rumor								
Length Less than 3 minutes 3–15 minutes 15 minutes to 1 hour Over 1 hour								
Qualities Useful Important Satisfactory Timely Accurate Excessive Effective								

content summaries) is also prepared, primarily for the audit liaison committee and other appropriate personnel. Unless specifically requested, descriptive statistics are the only calculations applied to the data.

After top management has reviewed the results, the data are commonly shared next with other subordinate supervisory personnel in the organization. Then the findings of the audit (both favorable and unfavorable) are condensed and distributed, with recommendations, to all members of the organization. Next a committee (usually the audit liaison committee) is typically formed to study the audit results and make recommendations to management. Finally, an action program is undertaken to implement approved recommendations.

Network Analysis

Although the ICA Communication Audit uses network analysis as one of its five measurement tools, the study of communication networks is neither unique to organizational communication research nor a recent development by communication scholars. Grounded in the laboratory studies of communication networks conducted primarily by sociologists and psychologists, network analysis is now possible in large, complex organizations primarily due to advances in computer technology by Richards (1975, 1976) and Lesniak, Yates, and Goldhaber (1977).

The *goals* of network analysis are:

1. to identify the particular pathways through which information flows in a particular organization;
2. to compare these operational pathways (communication networks) with planned or formal networks identified on organization charts or in job descriptions;
3. to determine potential bottlenecks and gatekeepers of information by comparing actual communication roles of key personnel (isolates, liaisons, group members) with expected roles provided by job descriptions or organizational chart placements; and
4. to use the above information to help organizations operate more effectively as they attempt to accomplish their goals.

The major *products* of a computerized network analysis are:

1. computer-generated maps of all operational communication networks relevant to the particular audit;
2. computer-generated comparison of actual and expected networks;
3. computer identification of all organizational personnel as work group members, liaisons between groups, or isolates within the organization; and
4. computer-generated comparisons of actual and expected communication network roles.

As with the ICA network analysis, data collection involves respondents, using a self-reporting form, indicating the extent to which they typically communicate with each individual in their unit or department (or with individuals outside their unit). They do so either by checking off names on an alphabetical roster or, in larger organizations, writing in the names of persons with whom they frequently communicate. Additional data are often collected concerning the frequency, importance, and effectiveness of the interactions. The instrument is typically completed in group sessions lasting about thirty minutes, including instructions. Data are then keypunched and analyzed by computer.

Implications of Network Analysis. When interpreting the data from a network analysis, one may combine these findings with those of a survey instrument to ask such questions as: Does network role influence or determine communication satisfaction? communication need? worker performance? Specifically, do isolates have greater communication needs than centrals? liaisons? group members? bridges? Do they have better relationships? higher morale? more job satisfaction? In a broader sense, data from network analysis may be used to answer questions about the entire organization, certain groups, or specific individuals.

REVIEWING MEASUREMENT

In this chapter we have presented several different tools and methods for evaluating and describing the various components and variables in an organization's communication and intelligence systems. We encourage the managers to be careful in selecting only the tool or approach which is specific to the current needs of his organization. It is only important that he take *some* steps toward measurement on a regular basis in order to determine the size of his organization's information power gap (see Figure 7-1) and calculate its intelligence needs (see Table 7-1). Just as an accountant audits the books of a large organization to determine its financial health by computing the ratio of cash resources and reserves to cash flow, just as a doctor regularly examines a patient to assess his health, so should the manager regularly audit his communication and intelligence systems. Only in this way can the manager and his organization receive the advance information needed to prevent major breakdowns that can limit his overall effectiveness.

In the next chapter, we present another audit system in detail which can help the manager collect this information.

The OCD Audit System

INTRODUCTION

As we pointed out in the last chapter, there are several tools and approaches which can be helpful to an organization when it assesses its communication system. In this chapter we describe in detail the Organizational Communication Development (OCD) Audit System, a procedure based upon the results of several studies conducted in European organizations by Osmo Wiio and his colleagues.* It is a practical approach intended quickly and cheaply to evaluate organizational communication and provide the basis for improving organizational intelligence. Although the OCD Audit was developed in Europe, we believe it is valid for use in North American organizations since the concepts it is measuring are universal to most organizational communication systems.

THE OCD AUDIT QUESTIONNAIRE

Description of the Instrument

The OCD Questionnaire consists of sixty-three items plus ten demographic questions. The questionnaire collects attitudinal and perceptual data about an organization's communication system and allows for later analysis by

---

*The OCD Audit is based on an earlier procedure called the LTT Audit developed by Osmo A. Wiio and Martti Helsilä at the Helsinki Research Institute for Business Economics in 1972–73. By 1977, 230 organizations had been audited with this method with a sample of 5500 persons.

relevant demographics. Its major advantages include its simple structure, brevity, and ease of use. The standard format allows both computer and noncomputer analysis and easy comparison with other organizations. Another advantage is that all of the coding, after it is administered, fits onto a single IBM card with eighty columns. The card is coded as follows:

FIGURE 8-1. CODING THE QUESTIONNAIRE

Column number	Questionnaire number	Other functions
1–6		Organization and person code
7–52	Communication items (minimum 1 and maximum 5 in each column)	
53–63	Communication items (minimum 0 and maximum 1 in each column)	
64–69	Job satisfaction items (minimum 1 and maximum 5 in each column)	
70–79	Background information items (minimum 1 and maximum 2 in each column)	
80		Card code

All scales are unidirectional—negative end to the left (indicating bad communication) and positive end to the right (indicating good communication). As indicated above, the first six columns on the card are reserved for an organization and/or personal code or ID number. We begin our description of the actual questionnaire with number 7 (representing column 7 on the IBM card). Columns 7–63 are reserved for data from items assessing the communication environment of the organization. Columns 64–69 are for data assessing job satisfaction. Columns 70–79 are for demographic data, and column 80 indicates which card is being coded.

Communication Items (7–63). The questionnaire starts with a general question about satisfaction with communication and availability of information in the organization. Then follow items about the amount of information that employees receive and want to receive.

Items 11–20 are the same as items 21–30. In the first case, we ask: "How much information about your work and organization do you get now from . . . ?" (items 11–20). In the second case, we ask: "How much information about your work and organization would you like to get from . . . ?" (items 21–30).

Items 31–46 measure the amount of information received and desired on selected topics. The first item is: "This is the amount of information I receive now about the following job items: . . . " (items 31–38). Next we assess the "ideal amount" of information by asking for a response to:

"This is the amount of information I should like to receive about the following job items: . . . " (items 39–46).

Items 47–52 identify those sources and receivers most in need of communication improvements: "I should like to see improved communication in the following areas: . . . " This set is followed by an open-ended question about other areas of improvement.

Items 53–63 give the respondent the opportunity to identify leading causes of poor communication: "These are the worst defects in communication of my organization: . . . " The set is followed by an open-ended question.

These items and the open-ended questions form a very primitive *critical incident analysis* about specific communication contingencies in the organization. The cumulative number of choices for each item can be used for ranking defects in organizational communication. That is, subjects can select one, two, or three items on the list. For 100 persons, the minimum number of choices would be 100 and the maximum 300. The more dissatisfaction there is, the closer to 300 the total will be. Rank correlations can be computed to compare different groups of personnel.

Job Satisfaction Items (64–69). Items 64–69 measure job satisfaction: "Are you satisfied or dissatisfied with the following aspects of your job? . . . " This set of items allows the organization to test the relationship between communication satisfaction and job satisfaction.

Background Information (70–79). Demographic information has been placed at the end of the questionnaire in order to avoid intimidating personnel before they have completed the questionnaire. All items here contain only two choices. Analysis of the audit data has shown that this is sufficient information to reveal the relationships between demographic variables and research variables in different contingencies. This technique offers a computational advantage.

The OCD Audit procedure does not contain network analysis. However, item 76 offers a simple way to measure the "communication activity" of a person. We ask the person to give a rough estimate of the number of his daily contacts. Three contact persons may seem a small number for dichotomous classification, but it is enough to separate a "communicative work environment" from a "noncommunicative work environment."

Columns 78–79 are used to indicate the position of the individual in the organization. As organizations vary, no general advice can be given on how to number departments and so on. There are ninty-nine positions for this information.

If nine positions are enough for this purpose, then one of the columns can be used for organization-specific purposes.

Column 80 is used for card indication.

FIGURE 8-2. THE OCD QUESTIONAIRE*

Instructions: The purpose of this questionnaire is to ascertain opinions of personnel concerning internal communication in your company. We ask your *personal* opinion about some problems connected with internal communication and inter-personal relations.

How to answer:
1. Please put an X in the appropriate box.
2. We'd like your opinion according to the scales below. Please write only *one* X for each scale in the box which you feel is closest to your opinion about the matter in hand. *Example:*

Question ↓	Scale → Opinion ↓	very or entirely	quite	I cannot tell	quite	very or entirely	Scale ← Opinion ↓
Do you read bulletins?	OFTEN						SELDOM

Your answer→ could be	If you read bulletins very often mark:					
	X					
	If you read bulletins quite seldom, mark:					
				X		

3. Please use the whole scale, including the extremes. Avoid the middle or "I cannot say" if possible; only in cases where you feel that it is impossible to give any other choice should you give such an answer.
4. Answer all the questions. Correct any errors by erasing out the whole box.
5. Other scales will be explained as they appear. Please put an X into the appropriate box.
6. The numbers before the questions are used for statistical purposes; pay no attention to them.
   Your answers are *completely confidential.* The questionnaire is anonymous; you need not sign it. In the research reports, it is impossible to recognize individual answers.
   Please take careful note of the direction of the scale.

1. Are you satisfied or dissatisfied with communication and the availability of information in your organization?
   7

	1	2	3	4	5	
Very dis- satisfied						Very Satisfied

2. Do you read:
   8 Bulletin boards?
   9 Circular letters and other written material?
   10 Newsletters and house organ?

Very seldom						Very often

*The OCD Audit questionnaire copyrighted for commercial use is owned by the Institute for Human Communication, Mechelininkatu 15 A 10, 00100 Helsinki 10, Finland, which owns the OCD data bank. The instrument may be used without permission for research purposes by scientific institutions.

Figure 8-2. Continued

3. How much information about your work and organization do you get now from:
   11 Superiors and management?
   12 Shop stewards and liaison persons?
   13 Fellow employees?
   14 Bulletin boards?
   15 Newsletters and house organ?
   16 Joint committees?
   17 Meetings and negotiations?
   18 Rumors?
   19 Circular letters and other written material?
   20 Newspapers and other mass media?

Very little	1	2	3	4	5	Very much

4. How much information about your work and organization would you like to get from:
   21 Superiors and management?
   22 Shop stewards and liaison persons?
   23 Fellow employees?
   24 Bulletin boards?
   25 Newsletters and house organ?
   26 Joint committees?
   27 Meetings and negotiations?
   28 Rumors?
   29 Circular letters and other written material?
   30 Newspapers and other mass media?

Very little	1	2	3	4	5	Very much

5. This is the amount of information I receive now about the following job items:
   31 Economic situation of the organization
   32 Employment situation of the organization
   33 My own work
   34 Changes in production
   35 Training and courses
   36 Social welfare in the organization
   37 Sales of our products
   38 Expansions and other large investments of our organization

Very little	1	2	3	4	5	Very much

Figure 8-2. Continued

6. This is the amount of information I should like to receive about the following job items:

	Very little	1	2	3	4	5	Very much
39 Economic situation of the organization							
40 Employment situation of the organization							
41 My own work							
42 Changes in production							
43 Training and courses							
44 Social welfare in the organization							
45 Sales of our products							
46 Expansion and other large investments of our organization							

7. I should like to see improved communication:

	Very little	1	2	3	4	5	Very much
47 From personnel to superiors and management							
48 From superiors and management to personnel							
49 With my own superior							
50 Among fellow employees							
51 Between shop stewards or liaison person and personnel							
52 Between joint committees and personnel							

8. Somewhere else (where?): _____

9. We should like you to select from the following list at least one but not more than three (one, two, or three) items about the worst defects in communication of your organization.
   These are the worst defects in communication in my organization (one, two, or three items):
   53 ____ Information is not readily available.
   54 ____ Information reaches me too late.
   55 ____ Information is not reliable and accurate.
   56 ____ Information is often useless and not important.
   57 ____ The language in information material is often difficult.
   58 ____ I get too much information.
   59 ____ Information does not reach me.
   60 ____ Management conceals important information.
   61 ____ Management does not know what the employees think and feel.
   62 ____ I cannot express my opinions freely in my organization.
   63 ____ My opinions do not count and nobody listens to what I say.
   Are there other defects in communication? What?

10. Are you dissatisfied or satisfied with the following aspects of your job:

	Very dis-satisfied	1	2	3	4	5	Very satisfied
64 Supervision of work?							
65 Chances for promotion and advancement?							
66 Wages and salary?							
67 Social benefits?							
68 My work in this organization?							
69 Participation, my possibilities to influence matters concerning my work?							

Figure 8-2. Continued

Background Information: Finally, we should like to have some background information for statistical purposes. The questions are very general and the answers will not identify you. We do not want your name.

11. 70 What is your sex?
    1 _____ Male
    2 _____ Female
12. 71 How old are you?
    1 _____ under 35 years
    2 _____ over 35 years
13. 72 How long have you worked with this organization?
    1 _____ under one year
    2 _____ over one year
14. 73 What is your classification?
    1 _____ hourly
    2 _____ other
15. 74 What is the last level you have completed in school?
    1 _____ high school or less
    2 _____ more than high school
16. 75 Do you supervise the activities of at least one full-time employee in your organization?
    1 _____ yes
    2 _____ no
17. 76 Think about a regular working day. How many people do you regularly communicate with on your job (about any subject at all)?
    1 _____ 0–3 persons
    2 _____ 4 persons or more
18. 77 Are you a union member?
    1 _____ yes
    2 _____ no
19. 78-79 What is your department (or equivalent)?
Thank you for your valuable help.

How to Administer the OCD Audit Questionnaire

Differences in organizations and social systems make it very difficult to give anything but general recommendations about how to administer the OCD Audit questionnaire:

1. Cooperation between management and personnel is vital for a successful audit. In most cases, the audit should be planned and supervised by a joint committee representing management and personnel.

2. The sample should basically be a random sample: all members of the organization should have the same chance to be selected. We recommend systematic sampling based on personnel files: every nth person is selected if the names are in alphabetical order. In small organizations, however, all persons should be included in the sample. It may be a negative factor if a person has the feeling that "almost everybody else is included, why not me?" We recommend the following sample sizes according to the size of

the organization:

Size (number of employees)	Sample size
Under 500	All
501–1000	Every 3rd person
1001–1500	Every 4th person
1501–2500	Every 6th person
2501–10,000	10% of total
10,001 and over	5% of total

These are only recommendations; different circumstances may require different approaches. The more detailed breakdowns of data required, the larger the sample should be. Further, the more precise one wants to be in generalizing the findings to the total organization, the larger the sample should be.

3. We recommend two procedures: group survey and explained survey. The subjects are gathered in both cases in groups where the audit procedure is explained and possible questions answered. In the *group survey*, the subjects then answer the questionnaires in writing and the questionnaires are sealed in an envelope and dropped in a sealed box provided by the research staff or the joint committee.

In the *explained survey*, the subjects take the questionnaires with them (or they are mailed to them), and they are given a few days to answer. They are provided an envelope in which they can mail the questionnaire to the research staff of the joint committee. They are asked not to discuss the questionnaire with anyone.

In most cases, one hour should be enough time to complete the questionnaire; most people manage it in fifteen to thirty minutes.

DATA ANALYSIS OF THE OCD AUDIT PROCEDURE

Data analysis of the OCD Audit is relatively easy: most standard survey computer programs can process the coded information.* Programs will typically compute distributions for all scales as well as a number of contingency tables with a chi-square analysis. Additionally, we give a few recommendations about OCD Audit data analysis.

---

*Readers who will rely upon others to conduct the OCD Audit's data analysis may skip to Chapter 9.

Distribution, Means, and Deviations

We recommend that a histogram be made of all scale distributions. The histograms are a very useful and simple way to see differences in distributions as well as to find out nonnormality.

Means and standard deviations should be computed for each scale. Although we caution about the overzealous use of means for statistical analysis, means and standard deviations have their valid uses. A profile of means and deviations on the questionnaire is often useful to show changes in the scales.

Contingency Tables and Coefficients

There are 549 possible contingency tables if all background variables are used with all research variables. (Actually more if item 77 is used.) By hand or hand calculator such a computation is excessive; for a computer it is an easy task.

If computer services are available, we recommend that all these contingency tables be computed; they are often vital for the treatment of organizational communication problems. The program should compute:

1. Contingency tables 2 × 5 for each of the background variables 68–77 and each of the research variables 7–49 and 59–67 as well as 2 × 2 tables for background variables 68–77 and research variables 49–58.

2. Chi-square analyses for each table. We suggest the 5% level of statistical significance. This means an F-value of 9.49 for 2 × 5 tables and of 3.84 for 2 × 2 tables. The 1% level requires an F-value of 13.28 for 2 × 5 tables and of 6.64 for 2 × 2 tables.

3. Cramer's phi coefficient (ϕ) to show relationships between distributions. It is computed from the following formula:

$$\text{Cramer's } \phi = \sqrt{\frac{\chi^2}{N(k-1)}}$$

where k is smaller than rows and columns, N is the number of observations, and χ^2 is the computed chi-square value.

This coefficient always has values between 0 and 1: 0 shows no relationship. In the case of 2 × k tables, the coefficient is the same as the traditional phi coefficient for 2 × 2 tables and the formula is:

$$\Phi = \sqrt{\frac{\chi^2}{N}}$$

In our case, we actually compute the phi coefficient for 2 × 5 and 2 × 2 tables, but if the five-step scales are to be compared, then Cramer's ϕ should be used; Φ and ϕ can be directly compared in such a case.

The phi coefficient (or ϕ) is statistically significant if the *F*-value from the chi-square test is significant. Values 0–.10 show very weak relationships; values over .10 are recommended for further analysis, even though smaller values might be statistically significant.

This form of analysis is also used in case one wants to compare any five-step scales between different groups of personnel within an organization. Chi-square tests of the relevant 2 × 5 contingency tables are computed and used for phi computation. If the phi value is, for example, .07, there is very little difference in the opinions of two departments; if the phi value is .32, there is quite a significant difference in the opinions.

4. Ranking can be used effectively as a method of analysis in our procedure. The most obvious use is the ranking of items 49–58 (defects in communication). The ten items are ranked according to the number of "votes" they get. This ranking shows the relative importance of communication problems for different groups of personnel. The computer program can perform this ranking for the desired groups: departments, hourly and salaried, women and men, and so on.

Ranking can also be used to compare the means of the five-step scales. This analysis, however, can be performed easily without a computer.

Analysis without Computers

If a computer service is not available, or there are no resources for it, distributions and means are often quite enough for a relatively good analysis. A simple tally can be used for the frequency distribution:

Scale	Tally	Frequency
1	⊩⊩⊩ 111	8
2	⊩⊩⊩ ⊩⊩⊩ ⊩⊩⊩ 11	17
3	⊩⊩⊩ ⊩⊩⊩ 1	11
4	⊩⊩⊩ ⊩⊩⊩ ⊩⊩⊩ ⊩⊩⊩ ⊩⊩⊩	25
5	⊩⊩⊩ ⊩⊩⊩ 111	13
		Total: 74

The arithmetic mean is computed so that the frequency is multiplied by the corresponding scale value, and the products are summed and divided by the total number of scores:

$$\overline{X} = \frac{\Sigma fX}{N}$$

where $\overline{X}$ is the sample mean, fX is the X score multiplied by the frequency of that score, $\sum fX$ is the sum of fX values, and N is the total number of scores. In our case, this could be:

Scale		Frequency		fX
1	×	8	=	8
2	×	17	=	34
3	×	11	=	33
4	×	25	=	100
5	×	13	=	65
Totals:		74		240

$$\overline{X} = \frac{\sum fX}{N} = \frac{240}{74} = 3.24$$

The arithmetic mean for our distribution is 3.24.

Computation of the standard deviation is not very difficult. There are many techniques for doing it. Some of the modern scientific and programmable pocket calculators have programs for calculation of means and standard deviations. However, they are not always convenient to use when the data are in frequency tables. They use raw-score data, which means that in our example, score 4 (scale value 4) has to be repeated 25 times. A program for calculation of the standard deviation from frequency tables can be written for the advanced programmable calculator.

The standard deviation in our sample distribution can be computed from the formula:

$$s = \sqrt{\frac{1}{N-1}\left[\sum fX^2 - \frac{(\sum fX)^2}{N}\right]}$$

Scale X	X²	Frequency f	fX	fX²
1	1	8	8	8
2	4	17	34	68
3	9	11	33	99
4	16	25	100	400
5	25	13	65	325
		74	240	900

$$s = \sqrt{\frac{1}{74-1}\left[900 - \frac{240^2}{74}\right]} = \sqrt{.014(900 - 778.38)} = 1.30$$

The standard deviation of our sample distribution is 1.30 on both sides of the mean 3.24 which was computed before. We repeat the steps in calculation of the means and standard deviations of the five-step scales in the OCD Audit.

Steps in Calculation

1. Write a table where the first column (X) will be the scale 1, 2, 3, 4, 5.
2. The second column contains the squares of the scale scores (X^2): 1, 4, 9, 16, 25.
3. The third column contains the frequencies for each score (f).
4. The fourth column is the products of the frequency and the score (fX).
5. The fifth column is the products of the frequencies and the squares of the scores $(fX^2 = f \times X^2)$.
6. Write the sum of columns 3, 4, and 5 under the columns. Column-3 sum will be (N), column-4 sum will be (ΣfX), and column-5 sum will be (ΣfX^2).
7. Divide column-4 sum by column-3 sum to get the mean $(\overline{X})$.
8. Square column-4 sum and divide by column-3 sum. Subtract the result from column 5. Multiply the result by 1 divided by column-3 sum minus 1.
9. Take a square root of the result of step 8 and you have the standard deviation(s).

Analysis Without Computers: Chi-square Test and Phi Coefficient

Our standard contingency table is a 2×5 table. It is used for the analysis of the influence of background variables as well as to compare two scales from different organizations or different groups of persons in an organization.

Let us take an example. We have a sample of 432 persons from an organization. We want to investigate whether sex has any influence on the general satisfaction about communication as expressed by item 7: "Are you satisfied or dissatisfied with communication and the availability of information in your organization?" There are 117 women and 315 men in the sample.

There are several computational formulas for chi-square analysis. We use McNemar's formula for $2 \times k$ tables:

$$\chi^2 = \frac{N^2}{A_t B_t} \left[\Sigma \frac{B_i^2}{A_i + B_i} - \frac{B_t^2}{N} \right]$$

The formula can be expressed also in the form:

$$\chi^2 = \frac{\Sigma C_3^2}{\Sigma C_1 \Sigma C_2} \left[\Sigma C_5 - \frac{\Sigma C_2^2}{\Sigma C_3} \right]$$

where C refers to columns in the following table (see below: "Steps in Calculation"):

(Fictional data)

q	c_1	c_2	c_3	c_4	c_5
1	25	65	90	.72	46.94
2	20	76	96	.79	60.17
3	7	19	26	.73	13.88
4	33	44	77	.57	25.14
5	32	111	143	.78	86.16
	117	315	432		232.29 = ΣC_5
	ΣC_1	ΣC_2	ΣC_3	.73	229.69
					2.6

Example: Column 1 = women; column 2 = men; scale = communication satisfaction.

$$\frac{432^2}{(117)(164)} = 5.06 \qquad \Sigma C_1 + \Sigma C_2 = \Sigma C_3 = N$$

$$\chi^2 = (5.06)(2.6) = 13.17 \qquad (df = 4)$$

$$\phi = \sqrt{\frac{13.17}{432}} = .17$$

The chi-square test gives an F-value of 13.17, which is statistically significant at the 2% level of confidence with 4 degrees of freedom. The phi coefficient (ϕ) is .17.

The interpretation of the result is that the null hypothesis (there is no difference in the opinions of men and women) can be rejected. Sex seems to have an influence on general communication satisfaction in this contingency. We can see from the contingency table that men seem to have more dissatisfaction than women.

This conclusion can be seen also from the histogram. We change the distribution into a percentage distribution and draw a histogram:

1	Women	ooooooooooooooooooooooo
	Men	xxxxxxxxxxxxxxxxxxxxx
2		ooooooooooooooooooo
		xxxxxxxxxxxxxxxxxxxxxxxx
3		oooooo
		xxxxx
4		ooooooooooooooooooooooooooooooo
		xxxxxxxxxxxxx
5		ooooooooooooooooooooooooooooo
		xxxxxxxxxxxxxxxxxxxxxxxxxxxxxxxxxxxxx

We can also see that there are more men than women in the "very satisfied" category, although, in general, men are more dissatisfied. However, the phi coefficient is rather low (.17), which means that the relationship between communication satisfaction and sex is not very strong.

We repeat the steps in the chi-square analysis and calculation of the phi coefficient:

Steps in Calculation

1. Write a table of the two five-step scales: scale 1 will be column C_1 and scale 2 column C_2.
2. Add the frequencies on each step of the scale. The sums will be column C_3:($C_{1_1} + C_{2_1} = C_{3_1}$).
3. Sum each of the columns C_1, C_2, and C_3 and write the sums on the bottom of the columns (ΣC_1, ΣC_2, ΣC_3).
4. Divide each frequency in column C_2 with the respective value in C_3. The results will form column C_4; do not sum column 4: $C_{2_1}/C_{3_1} = C_{4_1}$.
5. Multiply each frequency in C_2 by the respective value in C_4. The products will form column C_5: $C_{2_1} \times C_{4_1} = C_{5_1}$.
6. Sum column C_5.
7. Divide ΣC_2 by ΣC_3. Write this quotient (q) below column C_4: $\Sigma C_2/\Sigma C_3 = q$.
8. Multiply ΣC_2 by q and write the product under ΣC_5: $\Sigma C_2 \times q$.
9. Subtract the product above from ΣC_5.
10. Square ΣC_3 and divide the result by the product of ΣC_1 and ΣC_2:

$$\frac{\Sigma C_3^2}{\Sigma C_1} \times \Sigma C_2$$

11. Multiply the result of step 10 by the result of step 9. This value is the *chi-square value* (χ^2).
12. Test the statistical significance of the chi square. There are 4 degrees of freedom. If we accept the 5% level of significance, the chi square is 9.49; the 1% level of significance means a chi square of 13.28.
13. Divide the chi square by N (total number of observations of ΣC_3) and take a square root of the result. This is the *phi coefficient*.
14. The phi coefficient is statistically significant if the chi square is significant.

About the Use of Contingency Tables and the Chi-square Test

General rules about the use of the chi-square test apply, of course. The observations must be independent, and any subject must fall in only one category. The computation must be based on all the subjects in the sample (total N of the contingency table). In our 2×5 contingency tables, all but one frequency must be 5 or more; the one must be 1 or more. If this is not the case, then two adjacent categories may be combined. Our formula applies as well to 2×3 and 2×4 tables as to 2×5 tables.

In cases where we use a 2×2 contingency table, all frequencies should be at least 5.

Analysis Without Computers: Ranking

Ranking of the items is a useful and simple method of analysis. It indicates the relative importance of items for different groups of personnel in the organization.

Ranking can be based on arithmetic means of the scales. Another method is to compute the number of people in the first or last category of a scale and to use this frequency as the basis for ranking. For example:

Item	Means			
	Organization A		**Organization B**	
11	(7)	2.69	(4)	3.00
12	(1)	3.57	(1)	3.57
13	(5)	2.83	(3)	3.07
14	(3)	3.46	(2)	3.36
15	(8)	2.33	(6)	2.61
16	(4)	2.97	(7)	2.57
17	(6)	2.72	(8)	2.40
18	(2)	3.50	(5)	2.65

Note: Ranking in each case is indicated in parentheses.

The data are from two audit studies, and the items measure how much information the personnel receive from different sources of information. Score 1 is very little; score 5 is very much.

The rankings show that in both cases item 12 was perceived as the best source of information about one's own work. The item means: "shop stewards." In organization A (a publisher) the second-best source of information was "rumors" (item 18). In organization B (a manufacturing industry) the second-best source was "bulletin boards" (14). In organization A, the worst source was the "newsletter" (15), and in organization B the worst source was "meetings" (17).

The rank correlation between the two distributions is .62, which shows that information sources are perceived differently in the two organizations.

The use of frequencies in category 1 would have given almost the same results as the use of arithmetic means.

COMPARISON WITH NORMS

Data analysis cannot be primarily based on norm comparisons because of different organizational contingencies. This does not mean, however, that comparisons using norms are useless. When combined with other methods, norms are a valuable tool of interorganizational comparative analysis.

We have computed norm values for 29 OCD items. The norms are based on data from twenty-four organizations in Finland with a total sample of 5800 persons. The sample is drawn from a population of 35,000 persons. The organizations represent manufacturing industry, service industries (restaurants, car dealers, consulting), banking and insurance, printing and publishing, public administration, and hospitals.

Table 8-1 shows the frequencies of answers for each item as well as the sum total of the net sample, the mean values of each scale, and the standard deviation. Table 8-2 shows the percentage distribution for each item.

The norms can be used in several ways. The means can be used to plot the profiles of the norm and of the organization under examination. The statistical significance of the difference should be tested with a chi-square test between the norm and the results of the audit.

Let us take an example. We have a net sample of 323 persons for item 7 ("general communication satisfaction") in organization A and we want to compare the results with the norm. The mean value of organization A data is 2.45; the standard deviation is 1.20. The mean value of the norm is 3.03, and the standard deviation is 1.29.

The difference is highly significant; the chi-square value of 102.75 is well above the critical value for df (degrees of freedom) 4 of 18.46 for .1%

FREQUENCY DISTRIBUTIONS

Item-7 Scale	Norm	Org. A Data
1	865	71
2	1372	142
3	940	19
4	1854	76
5	708	15
Totals:	5739	323

Chi Square = 102.57
Phi coefficient = .13

TABLE 8-1. NORM VALUES FOR OCD ITEMS 7–16, 31–37, 47–52, AND 64–69 FREQUENCIES, MEANS, AND STANDARD DEVIATIONS

OCD Item	1	2	3	4	5	Sum	$\bar{X}$	s
7	865	1372	940	1854	708	5739	3.03	1.29
8	607	597	339	1501	2567	5611	3.86	1.36
9	593	328	292	1145	3137	5495	4.07	1.35
10	261	236	285	1250	3492	5524	4.35	1.07
11	2026	1375	672	1000	535	5608	2.40	1.38
12	1445	1302	879	1197	753	5576	2.73	1.40
13	595	983	794	1900	1390	5662	3.44	1.31
14	995	1300	868	1601	835	5599	3.00	1.35
15	848	1279	765	1660	954	5506	3.11	1.35
16	1827	1354	1037	798	460	5476	2.40	1.30
31	2096	1240	675	923	722	5656	2.46	1.44
32	1555	1520	681	1210	733	5699	2.66	1.40
33	1075	1266	513	1666	1241	5761	3.13	1.45
34	1899	1423	587	944	502	5355	2.39	1.36
35	1614	1348	591	1272	851	5676	2.72	1.45
36	1389	1605	756	1302	629	5681	2.68	1.35
37	2176	1213	658	910	698	5655	2.42	1.44
47	441	750	934	1648	1720	5493	3.63	1.27
48	326	492	663	1558	2488	5527	3.98	1.21
49	458	602	539	1506	2484	5589	3.89	1.30
50	814	1065	935	1340	1399	5553	3.26	1.40
51	451	717	817	1510	2008	5503	3.71	1.30
52	347	645	1060	1586	1804	5442	3.71	1.22
64	816	1266	852	1758	1031	5723	3.16	1.34
65	1870	1442	961	875	415	5563	2.37	1.29
66	2152	1646	657	1019	307	5781	2.25	1.27
67	571	1047	805	2078	1269	5770	3.42	1.28
68	289	527	683	2316	1967	5782	3.89	1.12
69	2134	1236	526	1228	585	5709	2.46	1.43

Note: These are norms for twenty-nine OCD items based on data from twenty-four organizations (n = 5800) in Finland. The first column indicates the OCD item of the OCD questionnaire; columns 1–5 refer to frequencies of answers on the corresponding scales, followed by the sample sum, item mean value, and standard deviation.

TABLE 8-2. NORM PERCENTAGE VALUES FOR OCD ITEMS 7–16, 31–37, 47–52, AND 64–69

Percentage Distributions OCD Item	Scale				
	1	2	3	4	5
7	15.07	23.91	16.38	32.31	12.33
8	10.82	10.64	6.04	26.75	45.75
9	10.79	5.97	5.31	20.84	57.09
10	4.72	4.27	5.16	22.63	63.22
11	36.13	24.52	11.98	17.83	9.54
12	25.91	23.35	15.76	21.47	13.51
13	10.51	17.36	14.02	33.56	24.55
14	17.77	23.22	15.50	28.59	14.92
15	15.40	23.23	13.89	30.15	17.33
16	33.36	24.73	18.94	14.57	8.40
31	37.06	21.92	11.93	16.32	12.77
32	27.29	26.67	11.95	21.23	12.86
33	18.66	21.98	8.90	28.92	21.54
34	35.46	26.57	10.96	17.63	9.38
35	28.44	23.75	10.41	22.41	14.99
36	24.45	28.25	13.31	22.92	11.07
37	38.48	21.45	11.64	16.09	12.34
47	8.03	13.65	17.00	30.00	31.32
48	5.90	8.90	12.00	28.19	45.01
49	8.19	10.77	9.64	26.95	44.45
50	14.66	19.18	16.84	24.13	25.19
51	8.20	13.03	14.85	27.44	36.48
52	6.38	11.85	19.48	29.14	33.15
64	14.26	22.12	14.89	30.72	18.01
65	33.61	25.92	17.27	15.73	7.47
66	37.23	28.47	11.36	17.63	5.31
67	9.89	18.15	13.95	36.01	22.00
68	5.00	9.11	11.80	40.06	34.02
69	37.38	21.65	9.21	21.51	10.25

level of significance. Thus, the organization A data show a clear negative difference between the norm and the organization A research result: the general communication satisfaction in organization A is worse than the norm.

Another method of comparison is the visual comparison of the percentage distribution histograms. In any case, it is a useful technique to see exactly where the differences are.

When all the distribution differences have been tested with the chi-square test, then the items can be ranked (for each item group) according to the magnitude of the difference between the norm and the research result. The direction of the difference is shown with + if the result is larger than the norm, and − if the result is smaller than the norm.

REPORTING THE RESULTS

It is essential that the OCD Audit report be useful for the persons in the organization responsible for organizational communication development. Rather than being a sophisticated scientific report, it should be a down-to-earth description of the findings. All heavy statistical material should be relegated to an appendix.

Here is a sample table of contents of an OCD Audit report:

1. Introduction
   1.1 Why this study was made.
   1.2 How it was made.
   1.3 How to read the report.
2. Conclusions and Recommendations
3. Communication Satisfaction
   3.1 General communication satisfaction (7)
   3.2 Amount of information (11–30)
   3.3 Information about what? (31–46)
   3.4 What should be improved? (47–52)
   3.5 What is good and bad in our communication? (53–63)
4. Job Satisfaction
   4.1 Subsistence items (64, 66, 67, 68)
   4.2 Incentive items (65, 69)
5. Appendix
   5.1 Background information
   5.2 Statistical information
   5.3 Questionnaire

A very important aspect of the report is its readability. Very few people are familiar with methods of statistical analysis or the terminology of the behavioral sciences. After the report is finished, the important and delicate process of feedback of the results must begin. Decisions about who should get what information and what should be done with the information are now in order. This entire process is discussed in great detail in our final chapter.

SUMMARY

In this chapter we presented the OCD Audit questionnaire an instrument used successfully to assess communication systems in Finnish organizations. In addition to reprinting the survey and instructions for administering it, we provided details for analyzing the data both with and without a computer. Whatever instrument, survey, or measurement tool management uses to assess their communication system, taking such action constitutes a major step toward preventive maintenance of the organization's intelligence system.

9

Developing Organizational Intelligence

INTRODUCTION

Our final chapter will deal with developing organizational intelligence. Essentially, the development and implementation of organizational intelligence involves making "kinetic" what the manager has learned about communication systems in complex organizations—formulating both policy and actions necessary to enhance currently effective systems and/or to modify ineffective ones. Since such implementation requires the bringing of previously discussed theory and principles into clearer focus, let us briefly highlight earlier chapters.

Review of Earlier Chapters

We began by positing the notion that formal organizations are living through a revolution characterized by the shift of power from line to staff, from traditional decision makers to traditional knowledge workers; by the shift from coercion-based or tradition-based power to that of information-based power; by the establishment of a free information economy whose leaders gain power through the legitimate process of accurately diagnosing internal and external contingencies or options and fusing those contingencies into policies, plans, and actions which enhance the organization's ability to survive. We held that this newly emerging power base, which we termed *reality-bound power*, while difficult to formulate, is not beyond the capabilities of most managers and administrators. Such a power base is dependent in the final analysis upon expansion—upon the willingness of individual managers, both line and staff, to stretch themselves beyond the day-to-day bureaucratic machinations of their roles. The new manager must first assimilate and then integrate knowledge about human communication behavior, organizational theory, and organizational environments into a new comprehensive model of his organization.

In succeeding chapters, we presented the concepts, theories, principles, and tools necessary for establishing this information-based, reality-bound source of power. We turned initially to the need for managers to clearly identify communication contingencies confronting their organizations, both internally and externally. We offered a series of self-reflective probes to induce the reader to consider such internal organizational communication contingencies as *structure* (the degree of formality characterizing individual, group-to-group, and interorganizational relationships), *outputs* (the extent of diversity or differentiation among the organization's products or services), *demographics* (the sociological mix of the work force or membership), *spatiotemporal factors* (variations in the structuring of space and time within and between organizational subunits), and *traditions* (cultural norms based upon precedent or historical values and assumptions about human and material resources).

External communication contingencies considered were *economic* (both organization-specific or industry-specific as well as macro), *technology* (science-based interventions in the forms of equipment, work methods, and processes impinging upon the organization, as well as its ability to assimilate such inputs), *legal* (the impact of regulatory agencies and subsequent legislative constraints upon the organization), *socio/political/cultural* (societal change and its commensurate demand for change within the organization); and *environmental factors* (the unique effects of climate, geography, and, of recent import, energy sources/availabilities upon the organization's ability to perform its major functions).

Goals—their establishment and articulation throughout the organization—were given a pivotal role within our communication contingencies model. In essence, goals were viewed as the formally stated mechanism for integrating or fusing internal and external contingencies into the "art of the possible"—a game plan for insuring the organization's continued survival and enhancing its growth. We stressed that while goals can be differentiated among subunits of the organization, they nonetheless must be complementary, avoiding "zero-sum" conflicts, and ultimately contributing to the organization's ability to remain in equilibrium with its environment.

Having devised this conceptual view of organizations as composites of internal and external communication contingencies, constantly seeking homeostasis with their environments, we turned to a more focused set of contingencies—the individual communication variables and behaviors of which managers must be cognizant if they are to successfully develop systems of organizational intelligence.

Chief among these personal communication variables are:

1. *The individual's cognitive complexity.* Here we identified cognitive complexity operationally, discussing its relationship to coping with information overload. Essentially, the more cognitively complex a manager or worker, the greater his or her ability to process larger quantities of information (ofttimes conflicting information) without impairing productivity or effective decision making.

2. *The individual's personality.* Here we described communication behaviors of authoritarian, information-compulsive, "Machiavellian," submissive, and neurotically "anxious" personalities, identifying the ways in which these personality types cope with information overload, and describing the communication styles they employ within the organization.

3. *The individual's past experience with the information stimulus.* Here we focused on specific ways in which administrators and managers can use their own past experiences with the information's content or source in coping with increased information flow, thereby better coping with overload. Essentially, we suggested that much new (and therefore more demanding) information can be set accurately within already existing frameworks of knowledge or past experience.

4. *The individual's motivation, need, and goal configuration.* Finally, we explored the relationship between individual motive and ability to withstand information overload, indicating the importance of complementary individual and organizational goals. Essentially, we observed that the more closely individual and organizational motives and goals approximated one another, the greater the individual's ability to cope with information overload.

Just as we determined that at the systems level effective organizational intelligence requires knowledge not only of internal communication contingencies but of external contingencies as well, so we determined that at the human level an understanding of personal communication variables alone is inadequate. Thus, the managerial architect of organizational intelligence must also understand *relational* communication variables.

Our views on important relational variables of human communication in organizations are much influenced by Argyris's hypothesis that within the healthy organization, interpersonal relationships are mutually rewarding and organizationally effective because three key conditions exist: (1) *valid* (not necessarily popular) *information* is generated and processed; (2) organizational members are permitted a *free choice in decision making*; and (3) there is *internal commitment* toward acting on this valid information and implementing the decisions made. Such a view demands that managers move toward greater agreement between what they may espouse as their management philosophy (participative, consensus-seeking, delegative)—what Argyris calls Model II—and what they may practice as their management philosophy (a win-at-all-costs mentality, suppression of dissent, suppression of emotion)—what Argyris calls Model I.

From the standpoint of communication relationships, we contended that Model I management styles (and accompanying communication behaviors) tend to beget Model I subordinate responses—the self-fulfilling prophecies at work in too many organizations within which strategy displaces spontaneity, gamesmanship displaces trust, and defensiveness displaces supportiveness.

We advanced the belief that managers desiring to develop truly effective intelligence systems must expand their understanding of why communication relationships are so critical to organizational functioning. Here we referred to Homans's pioneering views that interpersonal relationships in organizations can be viewed as exchanges of *activity* (due to the interdependence of tasks in order to accomplish organizational goals); *interaction* (the predictable response of one individual to another's actions/activities); and *sentiments* (the human tendency for affect—feelings, attitudes, emotions—to accompany activity and interaction).

As important as Homans's three reasons for the formation of relationships, however, is his view of their interdependence. That is, a change in one dimension of a relationship (sentiment) has a synergistic effect on the other two dimensions. Is it small wonder, then, that subordinates whose sentiments are negative toward supervisors will predictably avoid activities (assignments) which might bring them into closer contact with such supervisors—despite the fact that they may have skills for carrying out the assignment? And despite the fact that such behavior may not be in the best interests of the organization?

Another issue of significance in communication relationships discussed is that of *control*. In the overwhelming majority of human relationships in organizations, one of the parties is likely to gain greater control of the relationship at a given point in time. In the Model II organization, however, the controller/controllee roles are frequently interchanged as individual talents, competencies, and expertise are recognized as legitimate sources of power at a particular moment. The Model II manager is able to subordinate himself to those he manages when such role taking is appropriate. Control was described as *complementary* (that is, appropriate movement down in the relationship to complement another's movement up in the relationship); *symmetrical* (mutually escalating relationships, in which one's attempt to move up is counteracted by another's movement up as well); and *holding* (a truly peer-level, egalitarian relationship in which neither party moves up or down).

Control in communication relationships was also seen to include the "what" that is communicated (initiating the topic, outlawing other topics) as well as "how" information is communicated (face-to-face versus memoranda, private office versus corridor or open space, termination of the exchange).

Finally, the concept of *coorientation* in communication relationships was explored. Key components within coorientation were identified as *agreement* and *accuracy*. Here we posited the notion that four basic agreement/accuracy conditions are possible in any communication relationship:

1. high agreement/low accuracy (*pluralistic ignorance*)—the notion that, even though we express agreement, we are inaccurately perceiving one another's views
2. high agreement/high accuracy (*monolithic consensus*)—despite the "ideal" quality of this condition, here again both parties may fall prey to self-fulfilling prophecies
3. low agreement/low accuracy (*false consensus*)—this condition often surfaces in labor relations, resulting in escalation of adversary roles with both sides further misunderstanding, thereby further disagreeing with one another's views
4. low agreement/high accuracy (*dis-sensus*)—a condition which may be evidence of healthy conflict within the organization, often characterizing such intraorganizational relationships as manufacturing and production control, sales and credit

Not everyone in an organization can be constantly in touch with multiple internal and external contingencies, seeing their relationships and sensing their implications. Rather, a unique breed of communicator must perform this function in formal organizations—the *liaison*. Moreover, as we have seen, the more complex the organization's environment becomes, the greater the differentiation becomes among its internal cultures—and the more critical to organizational intelligence becomes this liaison, "linking" role.

In describing the unique contribution of liaisons, we provided an orientation toward the likely hierarchical, role, and psychological characteristics of these key communicators. Perhaps more important to managers attempting to develop organizational intelligence, however, we described specific liaison behaviors, as well as the research methodology of network analysis for accurately identifying liaisons in their organizations.

Liaisons, it was seen, tend to specialize in types of information—tend better to sense unique sets of internal and external communication contingencies. We identified a brief taxonomy of liaison specialization, focusing on the three basic information functions of *production* (information concerned with tasks or activities, such as work processes, shop rules, policies, procedures), *maintenance* (information concerned with the ways in which human resources are linked to the organization, such as reward systems, career planning, working conditions, compensation systems), and *innovation* (information concerned with new ideas—new products, new markets, new technologies).

These three basic information systems—necessary for the survival and growth of the organization—were explored both at the human level (discussing relevant individual, interpersonal, and small-group variables) and the system level (organizational and interorganizational variables)— again through self-reflective probes, enabling the reader to identify those gaps or uncertainties in information flow within these systems which may exist in an organization.

Lastly, we explored the three basic information systems of production, maintenance, and innovation at each organizational level of analysis: at the individual (personal) level, at the dyadic (two-person) level, at the group level (stressing the importance of group cohesiveness), and at the organizational (systemwide) level. "Acid test" questions were posed, encouraging the manager to identify in which of the three basic information systems the greatest degree of uncertainty, the greatest lack of shared knowledge and expectations, exist in his organizations.

In addition to the basic information systems themselves, we investigated the importance of credibility—what we termed *information authentication* —between and among members of the communication network. Information authentication deals with the extent to which information sources and information itself are judged accurate and reliable by members of the organization. In the effort to enable the manager to assess his organization's information authentication, we established criteria for credibility of source, message, context, and receiver factors composing the communication system.

An important general dimension of information authentication proved to be proximity or distance, both physical and psychological, between communicators. Here we hypothesized that the greater the distance, the greater the likelihood of *information uncertainty*, the greater the difficulty in establishing information authentication.

Critical source characteristics for authenticity were found to be his or her expertise, good intent, interest in others, similarity to receiver in values/beliefs, dynamism, sociability, trustworthiness, and a means-end rationale approximating that of the receiver's.

We stressed the obvious absence of status or hierarchical position in this list of source authenticity. Rather, those qualities of source credibility were found to be charismatic, as opposed to tradition-bound in the contemporary organization. Again, given the free economy of information of which we have so often spoken, one's position in the organization is not necessarily indicative of one's personal authentication as a communication source.

Message variables in authenticity were categorized as either content or presentation-related. *Content* factors include linking familiar information with new information, distinguishing assumptions from facts, documenting inferences, stating key elements early in the message, presenting two-sided arguments where appropriate, introducing internal summaries periodically, soliciting feedback from receivers, and couching the message in language with which the receivers are conversant.

Presentation factors discussed were the attention to message length, careful selection of most effective organizational structure (spatial, topical, chronological), and consideration of medium (face-to-face versus memorandum, letters versus telephone, computer printout versus narrative).

Regarding context factors, we also discussed unique environmental or situational variables, such as organizational crises—mergers, reductions in force, major reorganizations, and the like—indicating how the context of a communication system can affect the authenticity of its components. Intergroup conflict, line-staff relationships, and the organization's reward and reprisal systems were also shown to significantly affect information authentication.

At the systems (organization-wide) level, we explored the relationship between organizational climate and communication climate, two pervasive influences on organizational functioning which tend to complement one another closely. *Organizational climate* was described as a composite of (1) human resources primacy (the extent to which human resources are treated as assets), (2) communication flow (the ease with which information moves up, down, and across the organization), (3) motivation climate (the extent to which policies and practices encourage personnel to perform), (4) decision-making practices (the degree to which decisions are made as close to primary information sources as possible), (5) technological readiness (the use of state-of-the-art equipment and work processes), and (6) lower-level influence (the extent to which those at lower hierarchical levels can influence the course of the organization).

Communication climate was viewed as a composite of (1) supportive communication (the tendency for higher levels to be responsive to information from lower levels), (2) quality and accuracy of downward information (focusing on the timeliness, authenticity, and utility of messages received from higher levels), (3) superior-subordinate communication relationships (the openness of communication between hierarchical levels), (4) upward communication/information flow (the opportunities provided for initiating upward-directed messages and the extent to which they are acknowledged and acted upon), and (5) information reliability (focusing here on information received from subordinates and peers/colleagues).

These two climates, working together, were seen as determining the general atmosphere of the workplace, both at the system (organization-wide) and subsystem (individual department) levels. Moreover, we hypothesized that when system-level and subsystem-level climates are seen as different from one another, the latter more likely determined individual communication behavior.

Finally, we focused our attention on the receiver as a determinant of information authentication. Here, we explored the notion of status in depth. Essentially, we posited that the receiver's perception of source, message, and channel status heavily influenced his/her acceptance of and response to information. We provided guidelines for assessing status perceptions and predicting receiver responses, citing the tendency for higher-status persons to more readily initiate contact with lower-status persons, conceal information from lower-status persons, receive less accurate information from upward-mobile or upward-aspiring subordinates, have difficulty in establishing openness with lower-status persons, perceive exchanges with lower-status persons as more successful than do lower-level counterparts, and become defensive when their status is threatened by those lower in the hierarchy.

A second receiver variable of significance was the extent to which he/she is capable of processing and interpreting information received—understanding. Two methods were provided managers for determining the degree to which understanding by the receiver has, in fact, been achieved. First we discussed *feedback receptivity*—displaying verbal and nonverbal cues to subordinates and others which indicate one is open to feedback. Second, managers were encouraged to practice *feedback responsiveness*—providing evidence that feedback received is appreciated and acted upon, thus encouraging further feedback from receivers.

The third receiver variable in information authentication we reviewed was the degree to which the content of the message received appears to be in concert with the organization's stated values, goals, mission, and motives. Here we stressed the necessity for linking information from management to the value systems of employees—indicating clearly how compliance with messages will result in "win-win" organizational outcomes.

A fourth variable discussed was that of the individual receiver's personal value, belief, and motive systems. Here, managers were encouraged to link their objectives to those of their receivers, evidencing the mutual benefits to be gained by acting on the information received.

Since an important trend in organizations is that of growth and accelerated change (half the *Fortune* 500 of 1967 were no longer on the list in 1977), we treated the significance of growth in size for communication behavior in considerable depth. We reviewed research indicating that as organizations become larger in terms of human resources, the following communication variables become operative:

1. Power and its uses (and abuses) more likely become issues of concern, particularly as coalitions form and in-group/out-group stereotypes develop.
2. Intragroup conflict increases, since arithmetic changes in the group present geometrically proportionate opportunities for splinter groups to form.
3. Production, maintenance, and innovation information systems become more difficult both to identify and manage, since liaisons and those persons whom they link into networks increase.
4. Communication relationships and information flow become more formalized, as the organization's leadership relies more and more on bureaucracy to control organizational processes.
5. The grapevine takes on greater significance to satisfy maintenance communication needs of organization members, given its highly informal (and thus more flexible) information flow.
6. Feedback systems (those both of receptiveness and responsiveness) become increasingly difficult to maintain, again due to the geometrically increasing communication relationships which accompany arithmetic increases in the workforce.
7. Group cohesion and mutually satisfying interpersonal relationships become more and more difficult to sustain, given the increased tendency toward alienation and mobility or turnover of human resources.

The role of relationships in organizational intelligence, then, received considerable attention at individual, dyadic, small-group, and (where possible) organization-wide levels. We attempted to demonstrate how ignorance of the relational variables at work in organizational communication systems severely limits the manager's ability to establish effective organizational intelligence.

Earlier in Part Three we provided a variety of tools and methodologies for measuring or assessing the state of organizational intelligence in an organization. Having described the organization's environment, the free economy of information surrounding the organization, the salient internal and external communication contingencies to be optimized, and the personal, relational, and organizational communication variables at work in the organization, we described science-based instruments aimed at sensing these factors as they currently operate in a given organization. Essentially, all of these tools and methodologies are aimed at determining the discrepancies between organizational intelligence systems as they exist and as they are needed, given the organization's contingencies.

At the individual/personal level, we described the following:

1. *Cognitive Stretch Test*—focusing on problem-solving and decision-making styles used by individual managers.
2. *Clary Organizational Script Checklist*—enabling managers to assess their individual relationship(s) to their organization.
3. *Kirkpatrick's Supervisory Inventory on Communication*—providing feedback on individual communication skills of listening, speaking, and writing.
4. *Tests of Communication Apprehension*—evidencing individual tendencies to avoid positions of high communication demand.
5. *Rokeach's Dogmatism Scale*—reflecting individual tendencies toward open- versus closed-mindedness in processing information.
6. *Daly's Similarity-Dissimilarity Test*—providing information on the extent to which superior-subordinate pairs are akin to one another on work-related values and attitudes.

Relational level measurement approaches discussed were the following:

1. *Disparity Tests*—aimed at identifying discrepancies between hierarchical levels in terms of assumed authority, responsibility, and competencies.
2. *Accuracy Tests*—measuring the extent to which information assumed to be understood on an organization-wide basis is, in fact, understood at all levels.
3. *Readability Formulas*—developed originally by Rudolph Flesch, mathematically assessing the level of education required to accurately interpret or decipher a specific message.
4. *Falcione's Credibility Test*—determining the perceived credibility of managers, along the dimensions of sociability, competence, dynamism, and temperament.

5. *Communication Climate Measures*—various instruments/questionnaires providing information about employees' perceptions of the communication atmosphere characteristic of total organizations or subunits.

Measurement at the organizational level included the following:

1. *Direct Observation Techniques*—the careful observation and accurate recording of individual communication behavior, focusing on amount and direction of information flow, as well as specific networks used.
2. *Davis's ECCO Analysis*—a system for tracking specific messages as they ascend or descend the hierarchy; this technique also provides insights into specific grapevine networks and the manner in which they function.
3. *Questionnaire-Interview Techniques*—used primarily for obtaining qualitative data (perceptions, attitudes, feelings) and offering the researcher/questionner the advantage of in-depth probing for information.
4. *The ICA Communication Audit*—a multimeasurement process, incorporating interviews, questionnaires, network analysis, and critical incidents, resulting in communication maps, profiles, summaries, and recommendations based upon comparisons with normative data from similar organizations.
5. *OCD (Organizational Communication Development) Audit System* —a process developed and used extensively in Europe, characterized by mutual management-labor support and implementation of measurement tools assessing organizational communication, human relations, and organizational climate variables.

The OCD Audit procedure was described in depth in Chapter 8, providing a "hands-on" orientation toward the nature of communication research aimed at assessing organizational intelligence.

Regardless of the measurement tools selected for analyzing an organization's communication systems, the state of the organization's intelligence, we emphasized, can be described as falling into one of four broad categories. First is the condition we termed *proactive relaxation*: here, in "honeymoon" fashion, we find an organization content with processing relatively superficial information, enjoying an external environment of unusual stability, and thus satisfying present demands for intelligence.

Second, we described the condition of *proactive coping*: at the "marriage" stage of relationship to its environment, organizations in this intelligence posture are in optimal equilibrium with internal and external demands. These organizations are among our more efficient and effective. They have in place adequate communication systems for sensing significant shifts in activities, interactions, and sentiments of workers, as well as external systems for anticipating significant changes in markets, technologies, and environments. Here, again, organizational intelligence is adequate and, since the "honeymoon" phase is over, the organization processes more than superficial data.

The third organizational intelligence condition was termed *reactive hibernation*. Despite the "time bomb" nature of internal and external contingencies, organizations in this category operate on the basis of traditional or institutional power, relying upon bureaucratic mechanisms and historical precepts and precedents to manage the enterprise. Few or no attempts are made to monitor important shifts in environmental demand or internal need for greater intelligence. Senior management and boards of directors in such organizations likely suffer from the "groupthink" phenomenon described in Chapter 1—suppressing negative information rather than using it for the manufacture of organizational intelligence.

Finally, and perhaps terminally, we identified a category of organizational intelligence we termed *reactive stress*, that possessing "explosive" qualities. Here, since likely this is an organization formerly in the reactive-hibernation category, we find an entity whose internal communication systems have atrophied, whose external intelligence networks are so outmoded that sudden environmental demands cannot be adequately accommodated. Interestingly, the crisis state of such an organization has often been signaled earlier by lower organizational levels—those closer to the action of customers, clients, products—but inattention to the communication imperatives described earlier in this book insulated top management from upward-flowing negative information. And, as we saw in Chapter 1, the newer those at the top of the organization are to this unfamiliar organizational culture, the greater the likelihood that such insulation--by design or through insensitivity—can and will develop.

Having provided concepts, principles, and specific methodologies for assessing an organization's intelligence posture, let us now turn to the necessity for accurate feedback of one's findings in improving that posture where necessary.

FEEDBACK AND ORGANIZATIONAL INTELLIGENCE

We have talked much about the importance of feedback in any communication or intelligence system. In essence, feedback is the sine qua non of learning. Without feedback, there is no communication. Without feedback, there is no intelligence. Without feedback, change is only random.

Unfortunately, given the nature of complex organizations and individual motives, unbiased, constructive, objective feedback is a rarity in most organizations—public and private sectors alike. Invariably, for example, one of the most highly resisted and poorly handled management responsibilities in contemporary organizations is that of performance appraisal.

Most managers/supervisors are particularly reluctant to discuss poor performance eyeball-to-eyeball. In part this reflects, perhaps, a training deficiency. Effective courses in performance appraisal and commensurate follow-up are relatively few in number. Also in part, however, our natural human desires for acceptance, warmth, and affection mitigate against communicating information which we know will hurt feelings or disconfirm self-images, even when such feedback would be a catalyst for interpersonal growth.

The giving and receiving of unbiased feedback simply demands courage —a unique brand of courage that many an aggressive, high-risk, take-charge executive—bold in nearly every arena—cannot muster up until some type of crisis dictates that he or she do so. Recognizing the difficulty, yet simultaneously the necessity, for feedback, some firms have embarked upon management development/organization development systems aimed at increasing executives' awareness of how they, as individuals, and their performance are perceived by relevant others in the organization. Two such programs with which we are familiar (each in multibillion-dollar companies) use third-party consultants (1) to conduct in-depth interviews of key executives regarding their views on the company and its direction, their functional role in the organization, their performance within that function, their interpersonal style, and their motives, wants, and needs; then (2) to conduct in-depth interviews of members of a key contributor group, consisting of immediate superior, peers, immediate subordinates, and others deemed to have valuable input, covering essentially the same five dimensions. Ultimately, an executive profile is developed, pointing up areas of agreement and discrepancy between how the executive thinks he is perceived and how, in fact, he is perceived by others. Those executives having been through this experience consider such an exercise a valuable vehicle for self-development in an objective, highly confidential form.

Companies such as the two cited above likely function in the proactive-coping intelligence condition. Recognizing the need for organizational intelligence, they initiate communication systems to provide information to key decision makers in innovative fashion—keeping risks involved within tolerable levels yet confronting decision makers with important discrepancies between self-image and public image.

The Dennis Feedback Model

Having briefly described the critical role of feedback in improving communication and organizational intelligence, let us turn to a graphic model designed to describe research findings and prescribe actions for developing an organization's intelligence systems.

Harry Dennis (1975) has designed the model in Figure 9-1 to enable managers and/or staff specialists to quickly identify actions on one axis

FIGURE 9-1. DENNIS FEEDBACK AND PRESCRIBED ACTION MODEL

	Attitudes/Feelings	Behaviors	Policies/Practices	Skill Levels
Create	1	2	3	4
Sustain	5	6	7	8
Change	9	10	11	12
Restore	13	14	15	16
Eliminate	17	18	19	20

SOURCE: Dennis (1975).
Note: Numbers in cells (1 through 20) are for identification purposes; they are not numerical values.

commensurate with research findings on the other. Through the use of one or more of the research tools described in Part Three, we now have a "snapshot" of the organization's communication system(s) and subsequent intelligence shortfalls. We have identified important communication-related attitudes, behaviors, policies or practices, and skill levels operating in the organization. This knowledge, coupled with information about the nature of the organization's environment, enables us to categorize the organization in one of the four intelligence postures described earlier (proactive relaxation, proactive coping, reactive hibernation, or reactive stress).

Within each of the four organizational intelligence postures that are possible, there are likely certain attitudes, behaviors, skills, and policies which are enhancing the organization's ability to survive and grow, others which are threatening its survival or impeding its growth. On the other hand, our research may indicate that there is an absence of certain attitudinal or behavioral characteristics which account, in part, for the organization's inability to function at near or maximum effectiveness. Thus, as the Dennis model illustrates, feedback of research findings operates on an action continuum from creating certain attitudinal/behavioral/policy-level activities to eliminating certain others found to exist in the organization.

Applying the Dennis Model to Organizational Intelligence

A key strength of the Dennis model is its economy—a single matrix can be employed both for feedback and for prescribed actions warranted by those data which are fed back to the organization's decision makers. To best illustrate the use of this device, let us provide examples appropriate for each of the twenty cells in the matrix, drawing upon actual consulting experiences from government, business, and educational organizations, while couching our discussion within the appropriate organizational intelligence conditions found to operate in these organizations.

Cell 1. Likely the most difficult cell in which to operate, the creation of attitudes commensurate with an organization's intelligence posture demands inordinate amounts of time, money, and human energy. Essentially, such creation must begin at the very top of the organization, usually in the form of a group meeting in which key decision makers are confronted with new information or intelligence which heretofore had not been considered. For example, senior management of a northeastern bank with which we have worked were confronted with data suggesting that lower-level officers in the organization were alienated by their superiors' perceived unwillingness to share disclosure-type information. While senior management's attitudes (individual and collective) on the issue of disclosure had been formed in terms of the bank's external publics, they had not formed feelings toward the sharing of disclosure information internally. Given the organization's proactive relaxation intelligence posture, senior management explored the feelings of its members toward internal disclosure in a full-day off-site meeting with the aid of a third-party consultant. The consultant, using a variety of oral as well as anonymous paper-and-pencil interventions, aided the group in the formation of and, more importantly, articulation of attitudes toward disclosure. Individual and collective attitudes were thus formed where none existed earlier. These attitudes, of course, were later forged into policy statements and then management practices aimed at lessening the feelings of alienation at lower management levels.

Cell 2. Interestingly, the creation of behaviors can and frequently does lead to the creation of attitudes and feelings, rather than the more commonly assumed "attitudes-lead-to-behaviors" formula. Leon Festinger (1964) has, in fact, conducted a series of experiments which tend to support his theory of cognitive dissonance—that is, the notion that behavior may form attitude, rather than the reverse. One of the more famous of his experiments involved college students who were asked to perform a highly routinized, tedious task—specifically, the placing of little wooden pegs in a pegboard, dumping them out, and repeating the exercise for long periods of time. After several trials, each student was taken into confidence by the experimenter, who explained that the actual purpose of the study was to see the effects of expectations (attitude) on performance (behavior). Students were told that another party waiting outside was about to experience the same exercise. To study the impact of attitude on performance, would the present student be willing to tell the incoming subject how "interesting" or "challenging" or "enjoyable" the task was? If so, in fact, the experimenter was prepared to offer the present student a reward

—in some cases a couple of dollars (preinflation vintage), in other cases ten dollars.

What none of the students realized, of course, was that the study had nothing to do with expectations and performance. Rather, the study focused on this notion of the effects of behavior on attitude. Some thirty days later, each of the students was interviewed and asked to rate the task itself (putting round little pegs in round little holes over and over again) in terms of its being interesting, fun, and challenging. The $64,000 question: Which student-subjects now felt better about this obviously tedious and boring exercise? Which student-subjects were more likely to feel it was a positive experience—those who received one or two dollars for misleading one of their peers, or those who received ten dollars for their cooperation as requested? "Why, the ten-dollar student, of course—his was the greater reward," you say? Wrong! Festinger and his colleagues determined that invariably the greatest attitudinal change came about among the poorer-rewarded group of students. Why? Because here was a group of young people who had behaved in a fashion ostensibly against their well-conditioned values about right and wrong. They had lied to another person— wrong in itself by societal standards, but to make matters worse, they had done so for a measly dollar or two. How low can you get? The ten-dollar liars at least could justify lying by the size of the economic reward. Their "easier-made" counterparts couldn't justify lying on this basis. Their only recourse was thus to alter their attitudes toward the task itself, thereby feeling that they had not lied after all—it really was an interesting and challenging task.

Team-building interventions used in some of our consultations are prime examples of the impact of new behavior patterns on the formation of new or different attitudes. The simple but personally risky behavior of turning face-to-face to other members of the management team and openly expressing praise or criticism of them—openly and jointly exploring the affective realm of the relationship—often leads to an attitude that feelings, and their expression within agreed-upon parameters, are a legitimate part of the management process. Managers sometimes also learn that such expression is "easier," "less painful" than they had anticipated, thereby forming new attitudes about their ability to confront one another and to deal effectively with confrontation from others.

Cell 3. The creation of new policies or practices in organizational communication systems can take a variety of forms. At the systems level, some of our clients have articulated broad, comprehensive statements of communication policy—identifying channels, subjects, sources, and disclosure practices to all members of the organization. At the relational level, systematic yet informal mechanisms have been installed to increase the flow of upward and lateral information. For example, the chief operating officer of a manufacturing concern has begun to host luncheons on a revolving, periodic basis with middle managers three and four levels below himself in the hierarchy. This organizational-sensing mechanism enables him to impart important operating and managerial information or philosophies directly to those who would otherwise not receive his attention, while at the same time providing him ample data with which to begin to assess the depth of management talent in the bowels of the organization. Moreover, since this has become practice, the "in-between" senior and middle-management levels have overcome their initial understandable concerns about being bypassed. Here again, behavior has forged attitude.

Cell 4. One of the more successful skill-development interventions we have observed was among the senior management of a large metropolitan hospital. Clearly in the reactive hibernation condition, formal goal-setting activities existed in few functional areas and, where in place, were difficult to coordinate among the vested interests of the three primary power-broker groups: physicians, nurses, and administrators. Working first with senior administration and then at departmental levels, goal-setting and subsequent authority-determination activities were initiated with the help of a third party interventionist. More beneficial than the articulation and consensual validation of goals and lines of authority, however, was the learning how to reach group consensus—a group dynamics skill which could readily be employed in other areas of participative decision making.

At the individual level, skill development may take the form of "shadowing" a senior executive—actually living with him or her through the course of days or weeks, observing communication behavior and providing timely feedback on effective and ineffective actions and strategies. Working with a vice-president of a large automobile manufacturer, for example, one of the authors provided insights into an executive's tendency to shut off communication, register nonverbal cues likely to affect the ensuing discussion from his subordinates, and the like, helping him to gain skills for active listening and drawing out quiet members of his staff. In yet another example, the top management of a chemicals manufacturing company were trained in public address skills, emphasizing the more effective use of television in keeping with the firm's growing visibility.

Cell 5. The sustaining of attitudes or feelings usually requires only the confirmation from survey or interviewing data that such attitudes are perceived favorably at lower levels of the organization. Attitudes or feelings perceived to exist at the top of the organization have significant impact on forming the organizational climate of lower hierarchical levels. Human resource primacy, for example, has been found by other researchers to be an important ingredient of perceived organizational climate. If research data from an organization suggests that those at lower levels of the hierarchy believe that top management view human resources as assets, and willingly invest time, money, and energy toward maximum utilization of those assets, such confirmation will unquestionably reinforce this basic attitude.

Even when other portions of the data suggest problems or concerns among the workforce, the belief that those at the top do care and are concerned about the growth and welfare of those at lower levels can aid in the feedback of negative information. For example, in a large midwestern university with which we have consulted, a variety of communication shortfalls and problem areas were identified. Simultaneously, however, our data also confirmed confidence from those at middle and lower hierarchical levels that, once informed of problems, senior administrators were caring, well-intentioned people who would act to rectify issues which surfaced. Such information communicated to top administrators not only made negative data a bit more palatable to receive, but likely acted as a catalyst for tackling some of the problems our research revealed.

Cell 6. Akin to the sustaining of attitudes, the simple overt recognition of effective communication behaviors is a powerful form of reinforcement. In several organizations studied, the management style employed by the chief operating officer or head administrator included periodic, seemingly random walks through departments or shop floors or cafeterias—pausing to chat informally with those present. In complex organizations in which pressures of time and command performances virtually control the actions of top executives, it is quite easy to become the "name at the bottom of memos," the "invisible hand" that guides the enterprise from remote offices and is seen in the flesh only at groundbreaking ceremonies or the company picnic. When those executives who do maintain a degree of personal contact receive objective data which attest to the importance and impact of such contact, they are likely to sustain the activity.

Cell 7. Particularly, survey research is likely to reveal data on communication practices and policies which should be sustained. A comprehensive survey instrument such as the OCD or ICA Communication Audit (see Chapters 7 and 8) can provide information valuable to determining those communication systems (house organs, bulletin boards, departmental meetings, top management briefings) which are yielding the greatest return on management's investment.

Specific unconventional communication or intelligence systems deserve special note in some organizations. For example, at NASA's Marshall Space Flight Center, then Center Director Wernher Von Braun initiated a mechanism known simply as the "Monday Notes." As a rapid, distortion-free method for sensing problems at levels far below his own, Von Braun encouraged front-line supervisors and higher-level managers to report, in cryptic, handwritten form, "exceptional" information they felt he should be aware of each Friday, covering the week's activities. Such notes would be passed up, in raw form, from level to level, simply stapled together and forwarded to Von Braun from each laboratory director. Von Braun would read through them over the weekend, react with comments in margins, and reverse the process on Monday (hence the "Monday Notes"), thus establishing a nearly real-time communication system from chief operating officer to all other managers directly. Here is a somewhat unique source of organizational intelligence, employed in a proactive coping organization, which was rightfully sustained throughout Von Braun's tenure at the Marshall Center.

Cell 8. As in Cells 5, 6, and 7, the greatest guarantee that effective communication skills—individual, group, and organizational—will be sustained is the formal recognition of their effectiveness and contribution to the organization. Within this cell, however, the opportunity may emerge to align communication research findings with internal or external training and development interests. That is, not only should the manager feed back to his organization research findings that suggest that certain members or groups are perceived as having advanced communication skills, but he or she might also advance two lines of thought in terms of development: (1) Would those possessing the notable skills be willing and able to provide assistance or counsel to those not so perceived—thus developing others' competencies? and/or (2) What should management do to help these individuals or groups in sustaining their skills? Such feedback can be used for the development of others, as well as the further development of already notable communication skills.

Cell 9. The changing of attitudes or feelings remains, despite massive amounts of research, one of the least understood and most tenuous of ventures. While we know a good deal about the formation of attitudes, we cannot predict with high probability when attitudes are likely to change, or why in fact they do change, except in general and theoretical terms. But we do know this—only when individuals become aware of the discrepancy between what they assume is so and what the consensus of other relevant and/or admired observers agree is so are they motivated to change attitudinally or behaviorally.

The role of communication research in identifying shortfalls in organizational intelligence, through the use of tools presented in this book, is to confront decision makers with discrepant views of what is so—to make evident the "arc of distortion" between how they perceive organizational realities and how others within the system perceive those realities.

One other truism about attitude change is that people are far more likely to embrace new ideas, new policies, or new practices which they have had a hand in forming. *Involvement* is a somewhat overworked term in management and behavioral terminology, yet those successful sociotechnical experiments on quality of working life or codetermination (see the Appendix) are marked by the obvious contributions of all parts of the change system—management, labor, line, and staff—working in concert to design the intervention. Thus, information gleaned from a study of an organization's communication systems should be shared with as many members and groups of the organization as possible—ascertaining their reactions to findings and soliciting their ideas for enhancing strengths and/or addressing problem areas. As a guide toward feeding back information to the organizational client, remember simply that "those who generated the data have a right to see the results."

Cell 10. As in cell 2 (creating behaviors), the changing of behaviors frequently pays dividends in the commensurate changing of attitudes. A case in point: While consulting in a large manufacturing operation, one of the authors and his colleagues were confronted with a situation in which the client organization was losing ground to its competition in the manufacturing and marketing of a fuel pump. When asked for our opinions, we suggested that the hourly employees involved in manufacturing the part be involved in the solution of the problem—be permitted to generate their own cost-savings ideas.

Initially, management considered this an abdication of their "right to manage." What is more, they said, this would mean providing specific information on the costs involved and the exact margins between their costs and those of the competition. Our response was, "How else are they to know the severity of the problem?" The outcome was a rewarding one —for our own credibility, and, more importantly, for the profits of the organization and job security of employees building the fuel pump.

Briefly, the hourly employees formed a problem-solving team, headed, in fact, by a heretofore radical worker (elected by his peers) through whom their ideas for cutting costs would be channeled to management. Though management was particularly reluctant toward behaving in a shared-power mode, after some ten months their costs were within a few cents of the competition, simply because those individuals in the best position to know the operations were permitted to share that knowledge with management. We should even add (at the risk of adding a soap opera quality to this case history) that the radical informal leader elected by his peers to the critical liaison role became a highly productive employee in the process. The same energy level which had been used to harass management was channeled into accomplishing work-group, and ultimately, organizational goals. And again, behavior both by management and labor undoubtedly altered attitudes toward one another.

Cell 11. Required changes in policies and practices identified by research in the organization's communication systems will usually revolve around the dissemination of information which has heretofore been unavailable to large portions of the workforce. Government intervention into the workplace has, of course, been a source of impetus in disclosure of information. Employees may now have access to personnel records and request salary information on minimums, midranges, and ceilings for their respective job grades. In fact, recent newspaper articles have chronicled a trend toward managers bringing suit against their firms in the area of upward mobility or lack thereof. Specifically, some managers have sought legal counsel to obtain lists of high-potential candidates supposedly having been identified by management for grooming or specific career-pathing toward higher-level positions in the company. Managers not on the "high potentials" list or its equivalent are demanding to know why their names are absent. They are demanding to know the selection criteria by which those listed made it among the chosen few. While litigations in this arena are pending and this upward-mobility issue lacks clarity at present, it nonetheless is evidence of a new era of information disclosure. In a related vein, some companies have given up on performance appraisals because of the tremendous costs in time, energy, and potential court action in defending their validity and utility.

The sharing-of-information issue is not fraught only with "downsides," however. Our fifty-some man-years of consulting experience has convinced us that, for the most part, the desire for information by employees is due primarily to a motivation to contribute—to better understand the issues facing the enterprise and thereby determine areas in which they, too, might participate in helping to resolve those issues. Our use of the ICA Communication Audit survey indicates, with great consistency across organizations, that among the primary subject areas of interest to employees is problems management faces. Thus, wherever possible, and particularly in those organizations existing in the reactive-hibernation or reactive-stress intelligence postures, more and more information should be appropriately packaged and shared with more and more segments of the enterprise.

Cell 12. Changing communication skill levels, individually and in group settings, is essentially creating new skills, discussed earlier in Cell 4. However, we would add what we sense to be a trend taking shape in skill development in many progressive organizations—supplementing those formally responsible for training and development with highly competent line and staff managers who are effective role models in the skill area being addressed. More and more we are finding even high-level management (vice-presidential or director levels) conducting training sessions in their areas of expertise. The vice-president for finance, for example, may personally conduct a seminar in "Finance for the Nonfinancial Manager." We are not suggesting that training's traditional role be usurped, of course. What we are suggesting, however, is that a degree of credibility is enjoyed by those who "do," as opposed to those who "teach," which should be exploited when possible and appropriate. What is more, the involvement of high-level management occasionally in the development process communicates the importance with which development is held in the organization.

Cells 13–16. A not-uncommon finding in organizational communication research is the need for restoration—of policies and practices, behaviors, and subsequent skills and attitudes. The old notion of "not realizing what you have until it's gone" is as true of organizational life as it is of personal life. What is more, sometimes economic realities require cutting back in what some would term "nice-to-haves" like house organs, development programs, only to bring back in "better" flovonic conditions. Others would hold that it is precisely during difficult times that such activities should be maintained. Nonetheless, organizational needs change, and so also do their communication imperatives.

A good communication-sensing device can often identify the degree to which defunct systems are currently missed by members of the organization. For example, the workforce of a small retail shoe company in the Midwest indicated the desire to restore a communication channel which earlier they had elected to discontinue—a weekly "speak-up" session which exposed them face-to-face with top management. Apparently, employees did not fully appreciate the efficacy of this communication channel until it was no longer available to them.

Similarly, house organs in a couple of organizations with which we have consulted have been resurrected—albeit in a meatier form. Instead of pictures of company bowling champions and personal notes, the new versions address economic, marketing, and political issues affecting the company, often including alternative views of such issues. Or in another example, a management association whose invited speakers had formerly been primarily of the motivational, after-dinner variety now provided its membership with talks by economists, government analysts, and the like, since survey data indicated that employees desired their meetings to satisfy developmental as opposed to social needs.

Such self-analysis and introspection by organizations helps them maintain a proactive-relaxation or proactive-coping intelligence posture—even if such an inner view requires reinvestment in systems which were discontinued for whatever reason earlier in the organization's growth.

Cells 17–18. We know of no method (save a lobotomy) for eliminating attitudes or feelings unless the object of the attitude or feeling is itself eliminated. Thus we see again the counterintuitive notion of behavior leading to attitude, rather than attitude leading to behavior.

Cell 19. Almost by definition, ushering in new policies, practices, or activities means the exodus of other policies, practices, and activities— some of which are probably near and dear to a significant segment of the workforce. The elimination of behaviors (cell 18) should thus not be taken lightly by those in the change-agent role. Whether the change involves a new computer system, a new department, a new product line, or whatever, some displacement of existing systems is inevitable. Moreover, there is usually much greater management attention focused on the new than thinking through the ramifications of displacing or terminating the old. Here, the emphasis should be on providing a sound rationale for the elimination of whatever system or practice is being eliminated. Otherwise management's actions will likely appear precipitous, leading to the "sure isn't like the good old days around here" mentality that can form a strong wall of resistance to the change effort. An illustration may help to illuminate the role of "rationale" behind eliminating traditional policies or practices.

The president of a public utility decided that in place of giving away turkeys each Thanksgiving to all members of the workforce, the same costs would instead be devoted to a company-sponsored fair or carnival each spring. An announcement that the turkey-giving policy or practice would be discontinued in favor of a newly initiated spring outing was made, without giving the reasoning behind this change. The inevitable happened —negative employee opinion suggested that, once again, they'd been had by management, that no one wanted a spring outing, that the turkey-giving was another tradition being eroded away.

In ascertaining at least an ad hoc rationale for the change, however, a curious personnel manager conducted a survey among employees which discovered that (1) 33 percent of employees typically gave the turkey away to someone in greater need; (2) 24 percent judged the turkeys received as either too large or too small for their family's Thanksgiving dinner; (3) 40 percent registered negative opinions about the quality of the turkey received—too lean, too fat, not buttered; and (4) 5 percent of employees reported that they typically returned the turkey to a local supermarket in exchange for another purchase.

Obviously, had such research preceded the announcement, the spring outing would likely have been more favorably embraced. If we eliminate a behavior or practice to which organizational members have grown accustomed, such action must be accompanied with reasons behind the decision.

Cell 20. While this cell maintains the symmetry and purity of the Dennis model, rarely in our consulting experience are levels of communication skill—individual or relational—actually eliminated. By definition, *skill* suggests expertise or competence and is thus far more likely to be added to, rather than eliminated. An exception, of course, is when work skills are outmoded, leading perhaps to a reduction in force or reassignment and thus loss of whatever accompanying communication skills may have been possessed by those affected by the cutback or restructuring.

In viewing the Dennis matrix within the four conditions of organizational intelligence, it is important to note that each condition requires a different combination of cells for feedback and action. Proactive relaxation, for example, would likely involve predominantly cells 5–8, sustaining those well-functioning components of the intelligence system, with perhaps some activity in cells 1–4 (creation of appropriate attitudes, behaviors, policies/practices and communication skills) or the restoration cells (13–16).

Proactive coping, the healthiest organizational intelligence condition, would suggest the nearly exclusive focus on cells 5–8, that is, fine-tuning those sustaining components of the intelligence system which enable the organization to maintain its maximum equilibrium with its environment.

Organizations in the reactive-hibernation intelligence posture need initially to operate in cells 17–20—investigating and eliminating ineffective components of the communication system which are impeding the flow of information to key decision makers, on an internal basis. Externally, such organizations should focus on cells 1–4, creating new intelligence network components which will better place them in touch with the realities of their environments.

Finally, those organizations laboring in the reactive-stress intelligence mode are literally on the edge of a precipice. To attempt to operate on too many levels (for example, attacking issues in ten or more of the cells in the Dennis model) may serve only to exacerbate their overload problems and result in a near-catatonic state of doing nothing. Rather, here the focus should be on the "creating" continuum, specifically in cells 1 and 2. Research data must be accepted as an accurate portrayal of what is, despite preexisting attitudes of top management toward what ought to be. The predictable explaining-away, denying, and blame-projecting behaviors which often exist at senior levels of organizations in this condition must be broken through. New communication behaviors and their subsequent new attitudes must precede any attempts to work elsewhere in the system. Only through courage to change behavior by top decision makers can subsequent changes in policies and practices throughout the system be initiated.

Change activity at this highest of organizational levels need not be put on hold while we straighten out those "lower-level folks who got us into this mess." In fact, the change effort can begin simultaneously with the feedback of data using the Dennis model or a similar model. For example, those "groupthink" phenomena from Janis's work described in Chapter 1 may be put up on newsprint or a blackboard in the conference room for all to see as the discussion of research findings unfolds—as a reminder of old behaviors or attitudes that have likely brought the organization to the edge —and as motivation for adopting new behaviors and attitudes which can perhaps keep the organization from falling into the abyss.

POSTSCRIPT

We have stressed throughout this book that the organizational revolution of which we are all a part has spawned new and increasingly complex internal and external contingencies.

While there is undoubtedly some degree of commonality or universality among these contingencies, there will continue to be unique challenges to different industries and sectors of the economy. In each instance, such contingencies will require unique strategies and uses of organizational intelligence. In fact, the quality of an organization's intelligence system will in large measure determine the extent to which it recognizes its contingencies as unique—thus calling for individual effort, or for efforts similar to those of other organizations and consequently a sharing of interorganizational intelligence with which to confront industrywide or sectorwide challenges.

One of the authors has had the opportunity to study first-hand one industry's (Sweden's automobile manufacturing) and one company's (Volvo's) development and utilization of organizational intelligence in coping with a unique combination of internal and external contingencies. We provide a case discussion of Volvo's effects in the Appendix of this book, not as a solution model for all organizations—for the unique relationships between Sweden's management, labor, and government are unlike those in other societies—but rather as a process model for developing and using organizational intelligence.

Nevertheless, we believe the future will demand and see more experiences like Volvo's—more creativity and risk taking among managers and workers faced with new contingencies; more attention to the accelerated rate of economic, technical, and sociocultural change in organizational environments; more emphasis upon the role of communication and information flow in developing organizational intelligence. For our organizations are but composite mirror reflections of ourselves. And like ourselves, they will survive and grow and prosper only so far as their systems of intelligence allow.

appendix

From Theory to Practice

The Scandinavian Experience

DIFFERENT CONTINGENCIES—DIFFERENT SOLUTIONS

Since 1974 there has been much publicity about the new industrial production methods used in Swedish industry, especially in the Volvo and Saab car-manufacturing plants. There have been both positive and negative evaluations of these experiments, and managers in other countries have expressed doubts about using similar methods elsewhere. Further doubts have been voiced about whether lasting positive results have been achieved even in Sweden.

We shall briefly describe what has happened in Scandinavia with new industrial production methods: why have they been applied, what were their origins, and what has happened after they have been applied. An entirely different question is whether these new work methods should be tried elsewhere.

In one respect the Swedish experiment is revolutionary: it has, perhaps for the first time since Henry Ford, shown that new and obviously profitable production methods can be found to replace established work procedures.

When new contingencies, new circumstances, reveal negative consequences through the continuation of old work methods, then the production system has to be modified. In the Swedish case, the production system was adapted to the Swedish social system. Different contingencies may require entirely different solutions. We want to emphasize that the Scandinavian solution was created to meet specific problems: rapid turnover, absenteeism, and avoidance of industrial work.

The Swedish system seems, however, to work well in other Scandinavian countries with quite similar social systems and equally high educational levels. The Volvo experiment has inspired similar solutions in many other Scandinavian companies. From our perspective in this book, the Volvo and Saab experiments illustrate how an organization uses *proactive coping* to maximize its organizational intelligence.

BACKGROUND FOR THE SCANDINAVIAN EXPERIMENTS

Participation Systems in Business Organizations

Since about 1960, there has been increasing discussion of the possibilities of employee participation in decision-making processes of business firms. The Yugoslavian system of self-determination and the West German system of codetermination have been living examples of the trend, and demands for similar increased participation have appeared in most European countries. In the United States as well, many theorists have advocated a shift toward participatory management systems (McGregor (1960); Likert (1967)).

Existing systems of participation—"industrial democracy"—represent a four-stage continuum:

1. *Authoritative system.* A common system at the beginning of capitalism in its purest form, this system is impossible to apply in many modern industrialized societies where decision-making power is determined by legislative actions.
2. *Coinfluence system.* Employees can influence decision making through bargaining, shop stewards, work councils, politics, and public opinion. Employees have the right to get information and to be heard, but decision making is reserved for management. *Example:* Scandinavia.
3. *Codetermination system.* In addition to the methods of participation of the coinfluence system, the employees take part in the decision-making process through representation, and they may also elect some managers. *Example:* Federal Republic of Germany.

4. *Self-determination system.* The employees have the highest decision-making power. They also elect and dismiss the management. *Example:* Yugoslavia.

Some theorists, such as McGregor and Likert, have argued that there should be a positive correlation between the amount of employee participation in decision making and job satisfaction. Were this the case, it would seem that people are happiest and work best in a self-determination system. The reality is not as simple as that, however—in fact, there is very little scientific evidence to support such a claim. On the contrary, it appears that organizational behavior is dependent upon a large number of factors or contingencies, both within the organization and within its environment.

There exists a work culture within which the most important organizational decisions are made by the employees: Yugoslavia. Begun in 1968, the Yugoslav system of self-determination is an effort to implement total "democracy" in work. "Workers' self-management" enables employees to make all work-related decisions within the framework of general law. The system also provides the opportunity for employees to own the means of production. Thus, the Yugoslav environment should foster ideal conditions for job satisfaction and maximum efficiency with a minimum amount of alienation. However, this is not the case. The Yugoslav National Report for the International Labor Organization seminar in Belgrade in 1969 stated:

> In the last few years, there have been more than 2000 strikes in various Yugoslav undertakings. This form of protest included approximately 2 percent of the total number employed in the socially-owned sector of the economy. The most frequent reason for striking was unsolved or wrongly solved problems, primarily of income distribution. (Unpublished report)

The Yugoslav example suggests that the self-management system does not necessarily mean maximization of job satisfaction and efficiency. Many other conditions must be met.

Mass Production and Henry Ford

It has been said quite often that the "second Industrial Revolution" started when Henry Ford began to use mass production with his Model-T car. Before that industrial work had been more or less "multiplied craftsmanship"—many workers in a factory organized as a collection of small workshops with one worker producing a complete product.

In the beginning of this century a motorcar was an expensive and rare toy for rich people. Ford had a vision of the car as an everyman's vehicle: he wanted to produce a light, cheap, and reliable means of transportation. This would be possible only if cars were produced in large numbers in a short time. What was needed was mass production and mass consumption. He wrote:

> The necessary, precedent condition of mass production is a capacity, latent or developed, of mass consumption, the ability to absorb large production. The two go together, and in the latter may be traced the reasons for the former.
> As to shop detail, the key word to mass production is simplicity. Three plain principles underlie it: (a) the planned orderly and continuous progression of the commodity through the shop; (b) the delivery of work instead of leaving it to the workman's initiative to find it; (c) an analysis of operations into their constituent parts. (Private correspondence)

According to Ford, mass production required analysis of the work process and breaking the process into small parts which could be taught to unskilled workers.

Ford's key to mass production was an assembly line, a moving transportation belt which carried the work piece from one worker to another. Every worker added his part to the product. Every phase of the process required only a very simple performance: setting a part on a certain place, tightening a nut. The work was easy but sometimes deadly monotonous and forced: the assembly line determined the speed of the work process.

Ford's principles revolutionized industrial production, transportation, and American society. He sold 15 million Model-T cars in twenty years: in 1909 a Model-T cost over $900, in 1922 it cost under $300.

Man or Machine?

Mass production led to new theories of organization. The organization theories of the beginning of our century were so-called machine theories: the notion that the human organization performs at its best when it functions as a machine. The individual human being was viewed as more or less a part of a machine, and thus dehumanized in the process, as depicted dramatically by Charlie Chaplin in his film *Modern Times*.

Mass production has been, in effect, a necessary phase in the history of industrial development. No other method has been invented for the use of large number of nonskilled workers for highly developed technological production. Mass production and assembly lines have been essential to the economic growth which has increased the living standard for millions of people in only a couple of generations. Economic growth has been such an important goal of industrial societies that people have willingly endured the hardships of monotonous and machine-paced work processes. Money has compensated for boring work: when people work for their survival, they are willing to sacrifice job satisfaction and higher needs. Man has not, however, accepted this dehumanization without protests.

For the situation is different when the basic needs have been satisfied, when the standard of living is moderately high and there is a basic social security system for coping with unemployment and illness. Then the unpleasant sides of the work situation become important. The monotonous assembly line work is avoided, if possible, and more interesting work is preferred. This has happened in the top countries of industrial development: the United States, Sweden, and Western Germany. Their mass production has been partly possible only by the use of foreign workers or workers coming from underdeveloped parts of the country. These countries have also seen the first strikes against assembly line work methods.

The dehumanization of assembly line work has been recognized for a long time, and social scientists have warned about its dangers. However, no viable alternative methods have emerged: mass production and assembly line processes have been accepted as necessary for economic growth. A partial remedy has been found in automation: some of the most boring mechanical work has been transferred from humans to automated machines. Ironically, however, automation has often meant replacing monotonous assembly line work with equally monotonous monitoring work.

The new production systems developed in Scandinavia during 1970 are promising new alternatives for the integration of machines and humans in industrial work. While the traditional assembly line was based on the principle of adapting human to machine, the Scandinavian model reverses that process—machine is better adapted to human needs.

Humanizing Mass Production

Since World War II, Sweden has been one of the world's industrial leaders. In the middle of the 1970s, its average living standard was probably highest in the world. Sweden's well-developed social security system has, for all practical purposes, abolished poverty. Before the beginning of the 1970s, however, there were severe labor problems, one of which was a constant shortage of manpower. During the 1960s, Sweden had imported a large number of foreign workers from less-developed European countries to work in its industry.

This development meant, however, that the large mass production factories in Sweden employed many foreign workers: Swedes avoided heavy and monotonous industrial work and preferred light industry and services. A contributing factor to this trend was the rapidly increasing Swedish educational level. As early as the 1950s, about 80 percent of the Swedes already had between ten and twelve years of school. "You don't go to school for twelve years and come out to turn a bolt for a living," was the comment of a Swedish industrial leader.

During the early 1970s, the worldwide recession was felt also in Sweden, although not as severely as in most industrial countries. However, importing still more foreign workers for unskilled jobs was made difficult. Moreover, many foreign workers already in Sweden soon obtained a higher standard of living and left the assembly lines as soon as there were more interesting jobs available. The result was seen especially in the Swedish car industry, evidenced by an unusually high rate of absenteeism and turnover.

There was additional pressure for new production methods from other directions as well: the demands for "industrial democracy" and "worker's participation" have been traditionally strong throughout Scandinavian industry. The labor unions have always demanded better and more humane working conditions.

Something had to be done. The answer was the application of job rotation and job enrichment in the design of the work process and partial self-determination in the social system on the shop floor. These principles had been known for a long time, but now they were applied together for the first time on a large industrial scale.

Job enrichment, job enlargement, and job rotation are based on the ideas of Frederick Herzberg (1959), who claimed that meaningful work as a motivation factor has long-lasting positive effects for job satisfaction. Herzberg's idea was that monotonous work processes can be made more motivating by enlarging work assignments to include more than simple assembly line operations, as well as rotating jobs among workers.

The Swedish pioneers of new production methods have merged present knowledge about work motivation and self-determination into a production system aimed at "humanizing" industrial work processes. They recognize that present results in Scandinavia are by no means final and that their new interventions may not suit other production technologies and social systems. However, there appears to be general validity in the basic principles employed, and these principles are being increasingly applied in other Scandinavian countries.

The search for new production methods is by no means over: these applications are experimental. Some industrial leaders (Henry Ford and Fiat's Agnelli) contend that the Volvo experiments are expensive and cannot be practically applied in mass production on a really large scale. Also, these applications are inextricably woven into the particular culture in which they are used. However, these criticisms do not negate the importance of searching for more humanistic industrial processes. There is no doubt that such a search will be further necessitated by the increasing complexity of contingencies with which we have dealt in this book.

APPLICATION OF THE NEW METHODS

The Cultural Context:
Labor and Management Organizations in Scandinavia

The role of the labor and management organizations is highly significant in Scandinavia. In fact, companies usually regard unionizing as a positive factor which stabilizes labor relations.

In all Scandinavian countries, labor negotiations are centralized: agreements are reached in negotiations between the central labor unions and employers' confederations. Usually, the National Confederation of Trade Unions (LO in Sweden) and Employers' Confederation (SAF in Sweden) reach a general agreement on wage increases and social benefits; specific details are worked out by branch organizations representing the metal and woodworking industries. The agreements reached centrally are binding on all member organizations.

The member organization principle for labor in Scandinavia is the so-called industrial union principle. All workers in a plant belong to one union regardless of their job. For example, if the plant is in the metal industry, all blue-collar workers belong to the metal workers union, even if their job is to drive trucks or install electric wiring. Thus, there is usually only one labor contract for all the blue-collar workers in a plant, and another for all white-collar employees.

The Industrial Context:
The New Production Methods

The following description of the new production methods is based on the Volvo experiments in Sweden. Similar developments are to be found in other Scandinavian companies as well. Our specific case is the Volvo assembly plant in Kalmar, on the east coast of Sweden. Formed in 1974, the plant employs about five hundred workers.

The design of the Kalmar plant incorporated the following requirements:

1. Workers should be able to work in teams.
2. It should be possible to rotate jobs on a voluntary basis.
3. There should be a possibility to change the rate of the work process.

4. Workers should be able to better identify with the product.
5. Workers should feel responsible for the quality of the production.
6. Workers should be able to influence their own work environment.
7. Workers should be able to communicate freely with other members of the team.

To achieve these goals, the following forms of job enrichment and participation were used:

1. Job rotation.
2. Job enrichment (through increasing the number of work steps performed by each worker).
3. Small work groups, team work, and partial self-regulation.
4. Human-oriented technological facilities.
5. The formation of management-employee councils.

These principles were applied immediately; even in the design of the plant, employees were consulted. They were systematically asked what was wrong with previous work methods and what their wishes were for new facilities. Table A-1 summarizes the Volvo experiments.

TABLE A-1. THE VOLVO EXPERIMENTS

Starting Points
Difficulties in recruitment of personnel for industrial assembly line production
High absenteeism and turnover of assembly line personnel
High costs of reserve work force and training of new personnel
Demands for participation and "industrial democracy"
New ideas of behavioral studies of work organizations during the 1960s: McGregor, Maslow, Herzberg, Likert
Hypothesis that development of work methods can increase the productivity of industrial organizations

Development of Work Methods and Work Organization
New Work Methods:
    Job rotation—systematic rotation of work among members of the work team
    Job enlargement—work steps made longer by combining several steps
    Job enrichment—introduction of more difficult work phases: planning, material handling, maintenance duties, and control
Participation:
    Teamwork in partly self-regulating work groups
    Management-employee council
    Special seminars for training and information
Improved job environment:
    Attractive work facilities
    Flexible organization
    Possibilities for advancement

The Volvo Experiments

Teamwork. The production is based on independent teams of fifteen to twenty persons. Each team has a certain amount of self-determination:

team members elect their own spokesman and decide among themselves how the work will be distributed. They also elect the members of the team. The team takes care of the work process in its work area and handles all necessary material. It also has the responsibility for the quality of the car.

Supervision. The work group negotiates its own issues and the foreman negotiates with a group spokesman about problems between the group and the company.

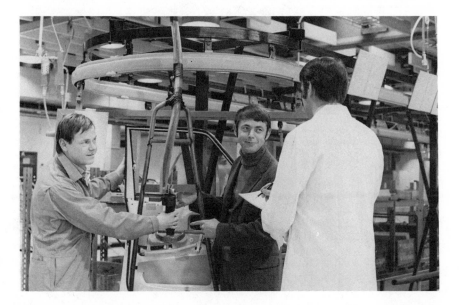

The Process Flow. Figure A-1 illustrates the physical layout of the Volvo assembly plant at Kalmar. There is no assembly line in a traditional sense. Assembly of cars takes place in the group areas where the teams work. Each area has about fifteen workers (fitters). The chassis travels on low assembly carriers or platforms which are computer-controlled. Each carrier travels independently and is self-propelled and controlled by cables embedded in the floor. The cars can be turned sidewise to make it easier for fitters to work on the underside of the cars.

Each team has a buffer zone of carriers both in the input side and the output side of the group area. These buffers allow workers to regulate the work rate to a certain extent. If there are extra cars in the output buffer, workers can take a break or drink coffee. The work rate has been agreed upon by management and the unions and is announced by a computer terminal in the work area: if a red light is on, this indicates the team is behind its schedule; if the light is green, they are ahead of schedule. When the team has performed its role on the chassis, the relevant information is fed to the computer terminal by one of the group members and the computer directs the carrier to the next operation.

Each team thus controls its own work. However, there is final inspection as well, and the result of this inspection is fed to the computer. If there are many mistakes in the work of a team, the computer terminal will alert the team and identify the problem.

FIGURE A-1. VOLVO ASSEMBLY PLANT LAYOUT (KALMAR)

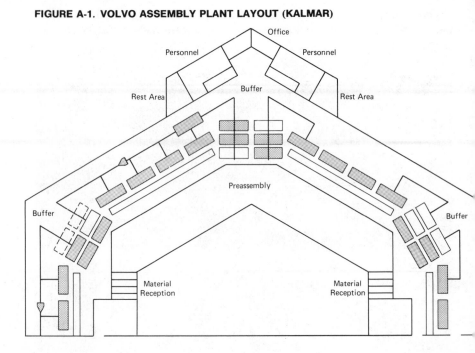

The conventional assembly line has essentially disappeared. In a traditional assembly line process, one step in the process may take a few seconds or even less than a second. The shortest step in the Kalmar process is three minutes, but some steps can be much longer. A team takes care of a whole work phase. For example, one team may assemble all electrical systems of a car. In addition, the teams may rotate jobs among themselves so that the workers eventually learn all phases of the car assembly. Nonskilled assembly line workers become semiskilled car fitters.

There are two basic types of assembly operations: straight assembly and dock assembly. In *straight assembly*, the team area is divided into working stations and assembly is carried out with the platforms stationary. The work moves from station to station through the team area at the rate set by the team on its computer terminal.

In a *dock assembly* system, the team is subdivided into smaller groups of three to five people. These groups carry out all the work for which normally an entire team is responsible. The platform is "docked" beside the track through the team area. The advantage of this system is that it provides each individual with a working period of 20–30 minutes at a time.

New Production Technology. There are several technological innovations involved in the new production methods. The basic principle has been to adapt the technology to people and not the other way around.

The cars travel on independently controlled platforms; the control may be manual or by computer. The platform is unique in industry; it has eliminated heavy lifting work and created improved physical positions for work. The car can be turned sidewise for easy access to the underside of the body. A high platform is used for assembly of the car chassis.

Flexibility in the Work Process. Greater flexibility is achieved in the work process instead of the fixed and forced work rate in a traditional assembly line process. The platforms can be controlled by team members and the order of production can be changed to fit their schedule. Because of the buffer zones in the input and output of the team area, the group can take breaks whenever they wish. The computer follows the progress of the work process and reports to the team.

Because of the structural flexibility, the organization can meet unexpected challenges. If personnel are absent or there is a shortage of material, the production rate can be slowed down or workers can be moved to other teams. The number of members in a group can be easily increased to allow for an increase in production.

Restructuring of Jobs. Job enlargement, job enrichment, and job rotation are all used to combat monotony of the industrial work. All team members learn all phases of the work. The shortest work phases are several minutes. The teams are free to rotate jobs in any way they like: some groups change every day, some groups every week.

Self-determination and Participation. The team work is based on partial self-determination within the team. The team elects its own spokesman. It decides freely about job rotation. It elects the members of the team. It has responsibility for the work process and the quality of the project. The team is free to act as a social system without outside interference. A very important factor in job satisfaction is the informal communication system among team members.

At the companywide level, a variety of policies and systems encourage employee participation in the decision-making process. First of all, there is a company council, a joint committee which deals with a wide range of subjects from company finances to industrial safety. In 1976, a law was also accepted which provides seats for the blue-collar workers on the board of directors.

In addition, the company provides for development groups which discuss problems, changes, improvements, and new products on a company wide basis.

Finally, the company has articulated policy for increasing self-determination of its employees:

1. One must know what is to be done and how it is to be done.
2. One must have the necessary means and resources to influence the result.

3. There must be feedback of the results:
   Success or no success
   Amount of deviation
   Feedback with sufficient frequency
   Feedback in an easily understood form

   Work Environment. An important part of the whole innovation is also
the new work environment. In Kalmar, the new plant made it possible to
design the plant itself to meet the requirements of the new production
methods and the humanizing of the work process. The teams work in small
workshops where they see only their immediate team area. Each team has
its own entrance and its own facilities: shower room, sauna, lockers, and
coffee room. Everything has been done to cut down the noise level; in fact,
it is quite easy to talk and listen in the work area.

   Information System. The new production system relies heavily on a
computer-based information system. There are, in fact, two information
systems: production control and quality control. Figure A-2 illustrates
these.

   Production control performs the following tasks:

1. Direction of control of the platforms through the plant
2. Starting and stopping of processes

FIGURE A-2. VOLVO INFORMATION SYSTEMS

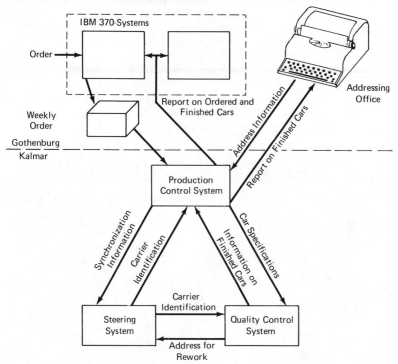

3. General control and registration of points of trouble
4. Recharging of batteries
5. Supplying of information about production and assembly

The quality-control information system (KVIK) has turned out to be one of the main bonuses of the new production system. Complete functional systems are tested at special quality-control stations. All this information is processed by a computer system KVIK (Quality Information, Kalmar) making it easier to take rapid, corrective actions. KVIK provides:

1. Rapid reference of defects to responsible assembly teams
2. Priority inspection points adapted to quality situation applying to each type of car
3. Good statistical data for quality appraisal
4. Basic material for decisions concerning special inspection efforts.

KVIK provides information to the quality manager:

Each day:
Summary of all alarm reports
A list of valid alarm reports older than two days
The ten costliest faults with age identification

At weekend:
The ten oldest valid alarm reports
The ten costliest faults with age identification
The ten most common faults
The five costliest modules
The total cost of repairs with trend analysis
Quality report
The ten most common safety faults
Answers to questions

Information to the general manager:
The ten costliest faults with age identification
The ten most common faults
The five costliest modules
The total cost of repairs
Trend analysis of total costs
Quality report
Answers to questions

Effective Communication

An essential element in the Scandinavian experiments of new production methods is effective communication. It is critical to all phases of the process. The new methods were devised together with the employees, and their application required extensive training. Internal communication in the work teams must be as free as possible; otherwise, the team does not function as a team. Also, communication between the teams and the company has to function without friction in order to link these parts to the whole.

The following remarks about the Kalmar experience by Pehr G. Gyllenhammar, General Manager of Volvo, Sweden, were obtained in an interview with Osmo Wiio:

In the beginning of the Kalmar project I perceived the following objectives: It must be possible to create an environment which better meets the need of modern man for finding meaning and satisfaction in his work life. This goal must be reached without impairing efficiency.

A manager seldom has time to stop and consider really deeply the different aspects of management. I had this opportunity when I came to Volvo. It so happened that the plans for a new plant in Kalmar were in preparation. The plans did not meet my requirements for the development of the work organization.

In the Spring of 1971, I devised a so-called social balance, which showed in clear numbers what the turnover, absenteeism, and retraining really meant to Volvo. It was obvious to me that the situation would become even worse in the future because of the increasing educational level of the average citizen: who would like to work in the monotonous assembly line after a long education? We had to find new production methods, which would provide new challenges and responsibilities.

The basic idea was that a worker does not need to stand in one given place while working. The technology must comply with the needs of human beings and not vice versa. There must be variation, different tasks, and responsibility in the work process.

The Kalmar solution has been regarded by outsiders as some sort of an ideal solution which must be accepted or rejected. This is not the case. The Kalmar solution is unique; it will not be repeated even inside Volvo. It is an important stage of development, but when faced with different contingencies we shall use other solutions. We will try, however, to preserve the basic principles. Kalmar is not the ideal solution; it fitted our purposes in a given contingency.

However, Kalmar is not an unprofitable experiment. In addition to other aspects, Kalmar is also a profitable industrial plant.

Our experiments have been wisely discussed internationally. Many opinions reflect either envy or strong prejudice. Results are viewed with maliciousness and mistakes are sought. It has been said that we had to find new solutions for our unique difficulties or that the work methods are suitable for a small plant but would not work in a larger scale.

First of all, we were not forced to the solution in any way. The conditions are much worse in many other industrial societies. Our methods can be used in a large scale by adding suitable modules. In addition, our methods can be combined with the automation of monotonous mass production. We use this technology in some other plants.

It is obvious that there are deficiencies even in our methods; this is only a first stage in an innovation process. For example, we have found out that there are people who simply do not want responsibility: they prefer security. Others may have too high expectations. Our solution requires much work from all participants, willingness to experiment and to study. All are not willing to give these inputs.

All in all, the personnel have been eager to participate in all of the phases of the renovation. We took different groups of employees to the planning process. We still use this principle. We experiment and study together.

Kalmar represents a technique more than a single manufacturing unit or its equipment. Every Kalmar will be different. It is a technique that will result in manufacturing units being:

Individualized rather than duplicated
Custom-fit for its workers
Designed and developed with the help of workers
Managed by an informal worker-management association developed and active during the design and construction period, as well as during operations

Some Research Results

Not many research results have been made available as yet about the Swedish experiments. However, the Swedish Rationalization Council (SAF-LO) conducted a study in the Volvo Kalmar plant in 1976. The sample was quite small (102 persons), but the results show at least some general opinion trends among the personnel.

First of all, most of the workers have been involved in the new teamwork—and they seem to like it, as Table A-2 shows.

More than half of the workers used the opportunity for varied work pace and worked ahead for breaks. However, this system seemed not to work as well as originally planned, mainly due to technical difficulties.

Job rotation or job switching is used systematically, and there are several different ways to do it; teams may select the system they like. The teams feel that the rotation system is fair because some jobs are good and

TABLE A-2. ATTITUDES OF VOLVO WORKERS

How many engaging in these forms of work.	Assembly workers		All workers	
	No.	%	No.	%
Practice team work	26	93	60	87
Job switching practiced in the team	25	89	52	75
Working ahead for extra breaks	16	57	36	52
Opinions of those engaging in teamwork, job switching, and working ahead.	**Assembly workers**		**All workers**	
	No.	%	No.	%
Like teamwork	24	92	55	93
Like job-switching	24	96	50	96
Like working ahead	14	88	28	78

SOURCE: Aguren, Hansson, and Karlsson (1976).

Note: Of the 102 persons interviewed, 69 were workers and 33 white-collar employees; of the 69 workers, 28 were in assembly jobs. The percentages in the lower half of the table are of workers practicing the particular form of work indicated.

others are bad and everybody should have something of "the bitter and the sweet."

The team is free to choose its own members. This is not always successful, since some persons don't seem to fit teamwork. In these cases, the company has to provide for individual jobs.

Job rotation between teams, however, is not popular, only rotation within a team. Even temporary assignment in another team is viewed negatively.

Job rotation, in general, takes place to the extent that production circumstances permit and that the workers themselves desire.

The personnel at Kalmar have more possibilities to influence their own jobs, than is the case in most industrial plants. They have longer and larger work cycles, some decisions about working methods have been delegated to them, and to a degree they can vary their own work pace. Thus, it is of special interest to see whether they feel that they can really influence their own work situation. Table A-3 shows these results.

As indicated in Table A-3, many employees feel their opportunities for influence are small. A third felt that they had considerable opportunities to

TABLE A-3. INFLUENCE OF VOLVO WORKERS

Do you have opportunities for direct influence on the work itself?	Assembly workers		All workers		White-collar employees	
	No.	%	No.	%	No.	%
Yes, considerable	7	25	25	36	21	64
Yes, though small	14	50	28	41	10	30
No, scarcely any	7	25	9	13	1	3
No, none	—	—	2	3	—	—
No reply	—	—	5	7	1	3
Total	28	100	69	100	33	100
Would like greater opportunities	23	82	48	70	16	48

Do you have opportunities for influence through discussion groups, functional council, and union?	Assembly workers		All workers		White-collar employees	
	No.	%	No.	%	No.	%
Yes, considerable	10	36	25	36	13	40
Yes, though small	14	50	32	47	10	30
No, scarcely any	2	7	7	10	3	9
No, none	—	—	2	3	2	6
No reply	2	7	3	4	5	15
Total	28	100	69	100	33	100
Would like greater opportunities	22	79	49	71	8	24

SOURCE: Aguren, Hansson, and Karlsson (1976).

influence their work situation; more than two-thirds would like to have greater opportunity.

For management, the most important question is, of course: What is the production efficiency of the new work methods? Can the Kalmar or any similar plant compete with traditional industrial establishments from the point of view of cost efficiency? The research team writes:

> We have obtained statistical information on assembly times, indirect times, control and adjustment times, capacity utilization, losses in balancing the different work stations, and so on. Our conclusion is that Kalmar is equal to or better than Volvo's conventional assembly facilities in Sweden. (Aguren, Hansson, and Karlsson, 1976)

The investment costs for the new production methods are higher than for conventional plants. On the other hand, these costs are compensated by production advantages and lower absenteeism and turnover.

As of this writing, the new production methods in Scandinavia are still a very recent development: in their present form, they started in 1973–74. This is one of the reasons why there is very little quantitative data about the results. On the other hand, some of the information is such that the companies are not willing to give too many details: profitability is usually a trade secret.

There is, however, enough evidence for some generalizations. It has been found that where the new methods have been applied, the absenteeism and turnover have decreased significantly. However, we also see a "Hawthorne effect": the new methods are interesting and nice in the beginning—absenteeism and turnover go down. In a year or two, however, the new work environment is routine, and absenteeism and turnover start to increase again. How high they will rise remains to be seen, but there is still a positive net effect. This means a decrease in the personnel budget, which compensates—in the long run—for the extra costs of new production techniques. (It costs about $2,000 to train a new worker for Volvo.)

There seems to be one net result which is not contaminated by the Hawthorne effect: quality. According to Volvo management, the greatest savings are to be found in improved quality. There are fewer faults found during production, and fewer cars are returned for repairs during the warranty period.

Are the Swedish experiments applicable elsewhere? It all depends . . .

The Swedish Experiments as Organizational Intelligence

We have summarized the results of the Scandinavian experiments in Table A-4. The Scandinavian production experiments are a good example of using the contingency principles upon which we have focused in this book.

TABLE A-4. SUMMARY OF VOLVO RESULTS AS COLLECTED BY THE SWEDISH EMPLOYERS ASSOCIATION (SEP)

Results for the individual	Results for the company
Increased job satisfaction	Better flexibility and adaptability of the organization
Improvement of work skills	Improved quality of production
Less absenteeism and change of employer	Increased costs of training, but less costs for new personnel and reserve personnel
	Increased investment costs

Conclusions concerning the Scandinavian experiments

1. Improvements in productivity and "humanization" of work methods are not necessarily conflicting goals.
2. Monotonous work steps can be improved by combining several steps to save several minutes.
3. Additions of auxiliary tasks (maintenance etc.) to the work has improved its meaningfulness.
4. More responsibility may help, but the limits to responsibility have to be well defined.
5. Job rotation does not help alone if it is not a part of the team performance. The team must decide on job rotation.
6. Production teams must be organized along the work process, not against it.
7. Internal communication in the teams is essential.
8. A separate workshop in a large plant helps the teamwork.

The automobile industry in Sweden faced specific contingencies, and management and labor worked together to develop an optimum strategy for coping with these contingencies—a strategy which resulted from the development of organizational intelligence.

References

AGUREN, S., HANSSON, R., & KARLSSON, K. G., *The Volvo Kalmar plant*. Stockholm: Rationalization Council, 1976.

ARGYRIS, C., Leadership, learning, and changing the status quo. *Organizational Dynamics*, Winter, 1976, 29–43; © 1976 by AMACOM, a div. of American Management Association, all rights reserved. Excerpted by permission of the publisher.

ASCH, S., Effects of group pressure upon the modification and distortion of judgements. In E. Maccoby et al. (Eds.), *Readings in social psychology*. New York: Holt, Rinehart and Winston, 1958.

BARNARD, C., *The functions of the executive*. Cambridge: Harvard University Press, 1938.

BAVELAS, A., & BARRETT, D., An experimental approach to organizational communication. In G. A. Yukl & K. N. Wexley (Eds.), *Readings in organizational and industrial psychology*. New York: Oxford University Press, 1971.

BENNIS, W., *The unconscious conspiracy: Why leaders can't lead*. New York: Amacom, 1976.

BENNIS, W., & SLATER, P., *The temporary society*. New York: Harper & Row, 1968.

BERGEN, G. L., & HANEY, W. V., *Organizational relations and management action*. New York: McGraw-Hill, 1966.

BERLO, D. K., Human communication: The basic proposition. Unpublished manuscript, Department of Communication, Michigan State University, 1969.

BROWNE, C., & NEITZEL, B., Communication, supervision, and morale. *J. Applied Psych.*, 1952, *36*, 86–91.

CHERRINGTON, D., The values of younger workers. *Bus. Horizons*, 1977, *20*, 18–30.

CHRISTIE, P., & GEISS, F., (Eds.). *Studies in Machiavellianism.* New York: Academic Press, 1970.

CLARY, T., Transactional analysis in organizational development. In G. Goldhaber & M. Goldhaber (Eds.), *Transactional analysis.* Boston: Allyn and Bacon, 1976.

DALY, J., & LETH, S., Communication apprehension and the personnel selection decision. ICA Meeting paper, Portland, Ore., 1976.

DALY, J., & McCROSKEY, J., Occupational choice and desirability as a function of communication apprehension. *J. Counselling Psych.*, 1975, *22*, 309–13.

DALY, J., McCROSKEY, J., & FALCIONE, R., Homophily-heterophily and the prediction of supervisory satisfaction. ICA Meeting paper, Portland, Ore., 1976.

DAVIS, K., Channels of personnel communication within the management group. Doctoral thesis, Ohio State University, 1952.

DENNIS, H. S., A theoretical and empirical study of managerial communication climate in complex organizations. Doctoral dissertation, Purdue University, 1974.

DENNIS, H. S., The construction of a managerial communication climate inventory for use in complex organizations. ICA Meeting paper, Chicago, 1975.

DENNIS, H. S., RICHETTO, G. M., & WIEMANN, J. M., Articulating the need for an effective internal communication system: New empirical evidence for the communication specialist. ICA Meeting paper, New Orleans, 1974.

DIEBOLD, J., *Beyond automation: Managerial problems of an exploding technology.* New York: McGraw-Hill, 1964.

DOWLING, W. F., Consensus Management at Graphic Controls. *Organizational Dynamics*, 1977, *5*, 22–47; © 1977 by AMACOM, a division of American Management Associations. All rights reserved. Excerpted by permission of the publisher.

DRUCKER, P. F., *The practice of management.* New York: Harper & Row, 1954.

DRUCKER, P. F., *The effective executive.* New York: Harper & Row, 1966.

DRUCKER, P. F., *Management: Tasks, responsibilities, practices.* New York: Harper & Row, 1973.

ELTON, M., & PYE, R., *Travel or telecommunicate?* Communication Studies Group paper P/73166/EL, University College, London, 1973.

ETZIONI, A., (ED.)., *Complex organizations: A sociological reader.* New York: Holt, Rinehart and Winston, 1961.

FALCIONE, R. L., The factor structure of source credibility scales for immediate superiors in the organizational context. *Central States Speech J.*, 1974, *25*, 63–66.

FALCIONE, R. L., McCROSKEY, J., & DALY, J. A., Job satisfaction as a function of employees' communication apprehension, self-esteem, and perceptions of their immediate supervisors. In B. D. Ruben, *Communication yearbook* 1. New Brunswick, NJ.: ICA, 1977.

FARACE, R., & DANOWSKI, J., Analyzing human communication networks in organizations: Applications to management problems. ICA Meeting paper, Montreal, 1973.

FARACE, R. V., MONGE, P. R. & RUSSELL, H. M., *Communicating and organizing.* Reading, Mass.: Addison-Wesley, 1977.

FESTINGER, L., Behavioral support for opinion change. *Public Opinion Quarterly* 1964, *28*, 404-17.

FLESCH, R., A new readability yardstick. *J. Applied Psychology*, June 1948, *32*, 221-33.

FLESCH, R., *The art of readable writing.* New York: Collier Books, a division of Macmillan Publishing Co., Inc., 1949.

FOLTZ, R., *Management by communication.* Radnor, Pa.: Chilton, 1973.

FORD, H., Mass production. *Encyclopedia Britannica*, 22nd ed.

FUNK, H., & BECKER, R., Measuring the effectiveness of industrial communications. *Personnel J.*, 1952, *29*, 237–40.

GALBRAITH, J., *Designing complex organizations.* Reading, Mass.: Addison-Wesley, 1973.

GIBB, J., Defensive communication. *J. Communication*, 1961, *11*, 141–48.

GIBB, J. R., TORI theory and practice. In J. W. Pfeiffer & J. E. Jones (Eds.), *The 1972 annual handbook for group facilitators.* La Jolla, Calif.: University Associates, 1972. Reprinted by permission.

GODDARD, J. B., Office communications and office location: A review of current research. *Regional Studies*, 1971, *5*, 263–80.

GODDARD, J. B., & PYE, R., Telecommunications and office location. *Regional Studies*, 1977, *11*, 19–30.

GODDARD, J. B., & MORRIS, D. M., The communication factor in office decentralization. *Progress in Planning*, 1976, *6*.

GOLDHABER, G. M., The ICA Communication Audit: Rationale and development. Communication Association of the Pacific meeting, Kobe, Japan, 1976; Philippine-American Communication Conference, Manila, 1976; and Academy of Management meeting, Kansas City, 1976.

GOLDHABER, G. M., From organizational lifeblood to society's embalming fluid: The art of organizational communication. ICA Meeting paper, Berlin, 1977.

GOLDHABER, G. M., *Improving Institutional Communication.* San Francisco: Jossey-Bass, 1979.

GOLDHABER, G. M., *Organizational communication* (2nd ed.). Dubuque, Iowa: Wm. Brown, 1979.

GOLDHABER, G. M., & KRIVONOS, P., The ICA Communication Audit: Process, status, and critique. *J. Bus. Communication*, 1977, *15*, 41–56.

GOLDHABER, G. M., PORTER, D. T., & YATES, M., ICA Communication Audit survey instrument: 1977 organizational norms. ICA Meeting paper, Berlin, 1977.

GOLDHABER, G. M., & ROGERS, D., *Auditing Organizational Communication Systems: The ICA Communication Audit.* Dubuque, Iowa: Kendall/Hunt, 1979.

HARVEY, J. B., The Abilene paradox: The management of agreement. *Organizational Dynamics*, 1974, *3*, 63–80; © 1974 by AMACOM, a div. of American

Management Associations. All rights reserved. Excerpted by permission of the publisher.

HERZBERG, F., One more time: How do you motivate employees? *Harv. Bus. Rev.*, Jan.-Feb. 1968, 53–62.

HERZBERG, F., MAUSNER, B., & SNYDERMAN, B. B., *The motivation to work* (2nd ed.). New York: Wiley & Sons, 1959.

HINRICHS, J., Communication activity of industrial research personnel. *Personnel Psych.*, 1964, *17*, 193–204.

HOMANS, G., *The human group*. New York: Harcourt, Brace, and World, 1950.

JANIS, I., Groupthink. *Psych. Today*, November 1971, 43–76.

KAST, F., & ROSENZWEIG, J. (Eds.). *Contingency views of organization and management*. Chicago: Science Research Associates, 1973.

KATZ, D., & KAHN, R., *The social psychology of organizations*. New York: Wiley & Sons, 1966.

KIRKPATRICK, D., *Supervisory inventory on communication*. Brookfield, Wisc., 1968.

LAWRENCE, P., & LORSCH, J., *Organization and environment: Managing differentiation and integration*. Boston: Division of Research, Harvard University School of Business Administration, 1967.

LESNIAK, R., YATES, M., & GOLDHABER, G. M., NETPLOT: An original computer program for interpreting NEGOPY. ICA Meeting paper, Berlin, 1977.

LIKERT, R., *New patterns of management*. New York: McGraw-Hill, 1961.

LIKERT, R., *The human organization*. New York: McGraw-Hill, 1967.

LIPPITT, G. L., *Organization renewal*. New York: Appleton-Century-Crofts, 1969.

LUTHANS, F., & REIF, W. E., Job enrichment: Long on theory, short on practice. *Organizational Dynamics*, Winter 1974, 30–38.

LUTHANS, F., & STEWART, J., A general contingency theory of management. *Academy of Management Rev.*, 1977, 2 (2), 181–95.

McCROSKEY, J., RICHMOND, V., & DALY, J., The development of a measure of perceived homophily in interpersonal communication. *Human Communication Research*, 1975, *1*, 323–32.

McGREGOR, D., *The human side of enterprise*. New York: McGraw-Hill, 1960.

McKENNEY, J., & KEEN, P., How managers' minds work. *Harv. Bus. Rev.*, May-June 1974, 79–90.

McMURRY, R., Power and the ambitious executive. *Harv. Bus. Rev.*, 1973, *51*, 140–45.

McNEMAR, Q., *Psychological statistics*. New York: Wiley & Sons, 1962.

MARCH, J., & SIMON, H., *Organizations*. New York: Wiley & Sons, 1958.

MASLOW, A. H., *Motivation and personality*. New York: Harper & Row, 1954.

MILWAUKEE JOURNAL., March 10, 1977, 3.

MONGE, P. R., & LINDSEY, G. N., The study of communication networks and communication structure in large organizations. ICA Meeting paper, New Orleans, 1974.

NEWMAN, E. S., On the viable thrust of massified dialogue. Reprinted by permission from *The Progressive*, 408 West Gorham St., Madison, WI 53703. Copyright © 1976, The Progressive Inc., p. 22–23.

ODIORNE, G., An application of the communications audit. *Personnel Psych.*, 1954, 7, 235–43.

PYE, R., Effect of telecommunications on the location of office employment. *OMEGA, 4* (3), 1976a.

PYE, R., Communication effectiveness and efficiency. *Technology assessment of telecommunications/transportation interactions* (Vol. 11). Menlo Park, Calif.: Stanford Research Institute, 1976b.

READ, W., Upward communication in industrial hierarchies. *Human Relations*, 1962, 15, 3–16.

REDDING, W. C., *Communication within the organization.* New York: Industrial Communication Council, 1972.

RICHARDS, W. D., JR., *A manual for network analysis.* Palo Alto, Calif.: Institute for Communication Research, Stanford University, 1975, 1976.

RICHETTO, G., Organizational communication theory and research: An overview. *Communication yearbook 1.* New Brunswick N.J.: ICA, 1977.

ROKEACH, M., *The open and closed mind.* New York: Basic Books, 1960.

RUDOLPH, E., An evaluation of ECCO Analysis as a communication audit methodology. ICA Meeting paper, Atlanta, 1972.

SAF, J., *Information och samråd.* Stockholm; Lagerström, 1965.

SALANCIK, G. R., & PFEIFFER, J., Who gets power and how they hold on to it: A strategic model of power. *Organizational Dynamics*, 1977, 5 (3), 2–21.

SAYLES, L. R., Matrix management: The structure with a future. *Organizational Dynamics*, 1976, 5, 2–17.

SCHEFF, T., Toward a sociological model of consensus. *American Soc. Rev.*, 1967, 32, 32–46.

SCHMIDT, W., (Ed.). *Organizational frontiers and human values.* Belmont, Calif.: Wadsworth, 1970.

SCHNEIDER, J. F., Selective dissemination and indexing of scientific information. *Science*, 1971, 173, 300–308.

SCHUTZ, W. C., *FIRO: A three-dimensional theory of interpersonal behavior.* New York: Holt, Rinehart and Winston, 1958.

SCOTT, M., MCCROSKEY, J., & SHEAHAN, M., The development of a self-report measure of communication apprehension in organizational settings. ICA Meeting paper, Portland, Ore., 1976.

SHAW, M. E. COMMUNICATION NETWORKS., In L. Berkowitz (Ed.), *Advances in experimental social psychology* (Vol. 1). New York: Academic Press, 1964.

SMITH, D. G., D-I-D:, A three-dimensional model for understanding group communication. In J. E. Jones and J. W. Pfeiffer (Eds.), *The 1977 annual handbook for group facilitators.* La Jolla, Calif.: University Associates, 1977.

TAYLOR, J. C., & BOWERS, D. G., *Survey of organizations.* Ann Arbor: Institute for Social Research, University of Michigan, 1972.

THOMPSON, V., Bureaucracy and bureaupathology. In D. Hampton, C. Summer, & R. Webber (Eds.), *Organizational behavior and the practice of management.* Glenview, Ill.: Scott, Foresman and Company, 1973.

THORNGREN, B., Regional economic interaction and flows of information. Polish-Scandinavian Regional Science Seminar, 1967.

THORNGREN, B., How do contact systems affect regional development? *Environment and Planning*, 1970, 2, 409–24.

THORNGREN, B., Silent actors: Communication network for development. In-Pool (Ed.), *Social impact of the telephone*. Cambridge, Mass.: MIT Press, 1976.

TOFFLER, A., *Future shock*. New York: Random House, 1970.

VAN FLEET, D. D., & BEDEIN, A. G., A History of span of management. *Academy of Management Rev.*, July 1977, 356–66.

WATZLAWICK, P., BEAVIN, J., & JACKSON, D., *Pragmatics of human communication*. New York: W. W. Norton, 1967.

WEICK, K. E., *The social psychology of organizing*. Reading, Mass.: Addison-Wesley, 1969.

WHYTE, E., An interaction approach to the theory of organization. In D. Hampton, C. Summer, & R. Webber (Eds.), *Organizational behavior in the practice of management*. Glenview, Ill.: Scott, Foresman and Company, 1968.

WIIO, O. A., Yrityksen viestinnän tehostamisesta. *Finnish J. Bus. Econ.*, *3*, 1969.

WIIO, O. A., *Yritysdemokratia ja muuttuva organizaatio*. Tapiola, Finland: Weilin & Göös, 1970.

WIIO, O. A., Uusimpia organisaatiokäyttäytymisen malleja. *Finnish J. Bus. Econ.*, 1971, *1*, 152–67.

WIIO, O. A., System models of information and communication. *Finnish J. Bus. Econ.*, *1*, 1974.

WIIO, O. A., Kalmarin vallankumous. *Suomen Kuvalehti*, *6*, 1975a.

WIIO, O. A., *Systems of information, communication, and organization*. Helsinki: Helsinki Research Institute for Business Economics, 1975b.

WIIO, O. A., *OCD: Organisaation kehittäminen*. Helsinki: Harkonmäki & Nissinen, 1976.

WIIO, O. A., *Organizational communication and its development*. Institute for Human Communication Research Report 2A771220, Helsinki, 1977a.

WIIO, O. A., Organizational communication: Interfacing systems. *Finnish J. Bus. Econ.*, 1977b, *2*, 259–85.

WIIO, O. A., *Viestinnän perusteet*. Tapiola, Finland: Weilin & Göös, 1977c.

WIIO, O. A., *Contingencies of organizational communication: Results of communication auditing in Finnish organizations*. Helsinki School of Economics and Institute for Human Communication Research Report 1A771218, Helsinki, 1978.

WIIO, O. A., & HELSILÄ, M., Auditing communication in organizations: A standard survey "LTT COMMUNICATION AUDIT." *Finnish J. Bus. Econ.*, 1974, *4*, 303–15.

WILENSKY, HAROLD L., *Organizational intelligence: Knowledge and policy in government and industry*. New York: Basic Books, © 1967, p. 41.

WINKLESS, N., III, & BROWNING, I., *Climate and the affairs of men*. New York: Harper's Magazine Press, 1975.

YATES, M., PORTER, T., GOLDHABER, G., DENNIS, H. S., & RICHETTO, G., The ICA communication audit system: Results of six studies. ICA Meeting paper, Portland, Ore., 1976.

ZALEZNIK, A., Power and Politics in organizational life. *Harv. Bus. Rev.*, May-June 1970, 47–57.

ZALEZNIK, A., Managers and leaders: Are they different? *Harv. Bus. Rev.*, May-June 1977, 67–78.